THE WORLD
OF THE FAMILY

THE WORLD OF THE FAMILY

■

A COMPARATIVE STUDY
OF FAMILY ORGANIZATIONS IN THEIR
SOCIAL AND CULTURAL SETTINGS

■■■

Dorothy R. Blitsten

HUNTER COLLEGE

RANDOM HOUSE • NEW YORK

■

To HELEN,

*Because she fully understands
the paradoxical character of this book.*

■

· FOREWORD ·

THE SUBJECT of this book is family life rather than *the* family. The word "family" here refers to a sphere of living that is experienced by individuals as separate from other spheres, such as economic or political ones. People seek different satisfactions within it, have different sentiments about it, contribute different services to it, recognize specific relationships that belong to it, and follow rules that are directed to its maintenance. The chapters that deal with family life in particular national and cultural settings are not descriptions of unique families of particular individuals. I have attempted to create abstract, yet descriptive, characterizations of family life in different societies which, despite variations manifested by particular families, will differentiate each way of famly life from the others.

I have done this to provide a basis for a comparative study of family institutions and organizations that is designed to reveal some of the functional consequences that different types of family organization and institutional patterning have for the range and degree of satisfactions available to individual members and for the societies in which they exist, and to reveal the influence of economic, political, religious, and educational practices on the stability of family units.

It is impossible to bring masses of empirical data together in manageable form in order that students, whose interest in the subject may be lively but is surely limited, may make comparisons of this kind. Even if an encyclopedia of information on family life existed, the disclosure of general relationships between types of families, societal settings, and individual well-being would require systematic abstraction and summaries. On the basis of a survey that is far from encyclopedic, I have presented a number of generalizations about some of the dynamic aspects of family living.

This study began in scholarly innocence. Conclusions about "the family" divorced from descriptive digests of actual family practices in various circumstances did not seem meaningful to me. Monographic studies of particular families merely whetted my desire to know more about the general range of possibilities for family life in particular settings. Therefore, I began to seek information from a variety of sources about the family life of people in many places.

Ideally, my summaries and conclusions would derive from detailed area studies made by teams of expert social investigators, participant observation, the study of history as well as current affairs, a survey of literature including ethical and religious writings, and equal familiarity with all the major spheres of each society. My presentation is drawn from much more modest resources.

My reading is inescapably limited in relation to all that might have been read, and that only partially represented in the bibliography of this book. I have read a fair sample of professional books and monographs by sociologists and other social scientists. I have drawn upon the reports of reputable travelers and journalists. Some novelists depict living experience in its great complexity far better than professional people do, and I have learned from them. Religious and ethical documents are particularly relevant to the patterning of family life and I have read the basic sacred texts. The dimension of time has been supplied by referring to histories. Letters, autobiography, and biography have supplied me with information about the impact of family custom on individuals.

My participant observation has been of several kinds. As an American I am naturally most familiar with the American scene. This kind of familiarity presents particular hazards for a social analyst. One needs exceptional experience to draw attention to what is usually taken for granted, and one also needs the opportunity to observe the experience of fellow countrymen that differs from one's own. My opportunities have come from three principal sources. First has been my professional training in the social sciences, especially in sociology. Although my training in psychiatry falls conspicuously short of professional certification in that field, it has been extensive. Of even more significance for this study is the fact that, for a dozen years, the accidents of personal history enabled me to follow the stream of cases that make up a psychiatrist's practice. My personal life has given me another special opportunity for a close, even privileged, report of the family experience of a large number of Americans. I am the daughter of an obstetrician and gynecologist who has been in practice for sixty years. My father's patients came from the array of ethnic and social groupings found in the American population. Ever since childhood, when I first went with him into a goodly sample of the heterogeneous homes of a metropolitan city, I have been witness to the family dramas that are the background of an obstetrician's cases. Thus, I have had access to a large amount of case material that includes both families who have been successful in providing for their members and those who have not. In some instances, these records cover three generations.

My direct observation of families in other societies has been much more limited. It has been made in two sets of circumstances. Hospitality in the homes of a number of American residents of foreign birth has provided one source of information. A second opportunity was made possible by my residence in Europe for several years. In addition, I visited Japan and China for six months. These opportunities have served my present purposes primarily by the illumination they provided for my reading. The meaning and significance of written reports is enhanced by direct experience.

These resources do not qualify me as an expert on the several areas I have included here. My justification for attempting these characterizations is that I know no other way to present varieties of family life for comparative analysis in a volume of reasonable size. The range of basic forms of family organization is not as great as their cultural elaborations. It is possible and useful to divide family arrangements according to their forms of organization. There are only a few basic forms of family organization in complex societies. The particular ones included in this book illustrate these basic types.

The plan of the book reflects the evolution of my inquiry. The point of departure is the general fact that family life, differentiated from other spheres of living, is found in all human societies. This suggests that there are some universal human conditions that give rise to family organization and that all families provide for some universal human needs. The first chapter deals with the aspects of family life that are common to all types of family organization. It summarizes the arrangements and practices that differentiate family life from other spheres of living—not one kind of family life from another.

The relationships identified with family membership are roughly the same in all literate societies. Patterned reciprocities between husband and wife, parent and child, sibling and sibling, aunts and uncles and nieces and nephews, and cousins and cousins, in combination with a parallel set of relations-in-law, are the principal family relationships. People so related constitute a recognized circle. However, the range of reciprocities between people in these relationships varies in societies, and so too does the number of people who customarily share a household. Comparison reveals that the unit of husband, wife, and their children, commonly called the *nuclear family*, always has some autonomy in the management of its affairs, whether it has a household to itself or is merely a part of a much larger menage. The relation of this nuclear unit to other relatives can be used to distinguish one form of family organization from another.

I have set up a theoretical continuum of forms of family organization based upon the degree of autonomy exercised by the nuclear family. The scale extends from a type of family organization in which the nuclear unit lives alone and the husband and wife assume total responsibility for themselves and their children to the corporate family, in which the nuclear unit is one among numerous others, all of which share a single household or series of households run by a hierarchy of elders. These elders in the corporate family jointly care for everyone's needs and exercise extensive powers of decision over personal matters such as marriage choice and occupation. At the middle of the scale stands family organization in which the nuclear unit is consistently oriented toward a more extended circle of relatives which includes the parents and grandparents of both spouses, but which typically manages its own household. This type is the *bilateral extended family*. Most families can be placed within these broad limits. The different forms of family organization have different effects on the personal development of their members and the kinds of satisfactions available to them. Their effectiveness is influenced by the specific societal arrangements and conditions in which they exist. This continuum is the framework for analysis in this book.

The American nuclear family is presented to illustrate the end of the continuum at which the nuclear unit is highly autonomous. The corporate Confucian Chinese family illustrates the other end of the continuum, at which the nuclear unit is a small link in a very extensive family organization. The Latin-Catholic family represents the bilaterally extended family, in which the nuclear unit has considerable autonomy but accepts some regulation by the grandparental generation of the families of both spouses. The Scandinavian family falls into the same category as the American, while the Moslem family closely resembles the Confucian Chinese in basic form. Descriptions of Scandinavian and Moslem families are included to illustrate the effect of differences in general societal and geographic conditions on the functional efficacy of similar types of families. Finally, the experiments in family living in Russia shortly after the revolution and in some of the Israeli *kibbutzim* are presented to reveal the kind of evidence that has led me to conclude that it is impossible to eliminate a clearly differentiated sphere of family living from the organization of complex societies.

Comparison requires that materials on each family organization be presented in similar order. Since all families reveal a kind of life cycle whose phases are more or less clearly differentiable, these phases are used to organize Chapters II through VII. Each family type is treated in terms of preparation for family life; conditions of life for newly married couples; periods characterized by special preoccupation with child-bearing, child-rearing, and child-launching; and, last, the fate of aging couples. The significant mutual influences between family arrangements and political, economic, religious, and educational institutions are noted. Finally, the effects of conspicuous changes in general conditions of life upon forms and functions of family life are considered.

These comparisons reveal some general connections between types of families and individual welfare; between family stability and economic, political, religious, and educational practices in societies; and between forms of family organization and some general societal conditions such as size, heterogeneity, level of technical development, and the dominant sources of social power and control. These are summarized. In conclusion, I have hazarded some predictions of general trends in family organization and practice in the light of rapid and drastic social changes that are taking place around the globe.

DOROTHY R. BLITSTEN

New York City
January, 1963

· CONTENTS ·

PART THREE

THE INFLUENCE OF DIFFERENT CULTURAL AND SOCIAL SETTINGS ON FAMILY ORGANIZATION

PART FOUR

CONCLUSIONS AND FORECASTS

PART ONE

■■■

Introduction

■

▪ I ▪

INDIVIDUAL AND SOCIAL FUNCTIONS OF FAMILIES

▪

PEOPLE LIVE together from necessity. They cannot choose to live in isolation until they are adults, and then only if they are willing to accept drastic limitations on the range of their possible satisfactions. Relatively enduring relationships with other people provide individuals with a necessary means to satisfying their needs and wants. This interdependence is the basis of social order.

Certain discernible needs and wants compel human beings to form relatively stable associations. Political, economic, religious, educational, and familial organizations are found in all societies. In preliterate or folk societies, divisions between these spheres of organization are not sharp. The religious leaders may also control the political and economic life of the society; education may go on entirely within the family sphere; and so on. Clear separation of these spheres of social organization is one of the characteristics of a complex society.

These statements are not intended to suggest that there is a fixed list of human needs, or that there is an inescapable correlation between specific needs and specific social arrangements. The social sciences have firmly established the fact that human beings are capable of great variation in development, and that the biological characteristics with which man is born can be profoundly affected by his social and cultural experience.

For human beings, except on the most elementary biological level, the means to particular satisfactions are numerous, and man's social organizations and cultural creations reflect his creativity and ingenuity. Yet they also reflect the human wants and needs which gave rise to them.

Nowhere is this more apparent than in the sphere of family living. Family arrangements, although diverse, are more closely correlated with the life cycle of human beings than are other major institutions. The extreme dependency of the human young, the effects of differences of age and sex, the effects of decreasing powers with increasing years, and, finally, death all give shape to family life. Satisfactions for the most repetitive psycho-biological needs of human beings are provided within family arrangements —sometimes exclusively, sometimes in conjunction with other sources of service and supply. In short, there are basic needs that are so overwhelmingly within the purview of family organization that the conclusion is compelling that they are the core around which family life is organized.

This chapter deals with the varieties of human needs that are the principal concern of families, whatever their form and wherever they exist. In actual experience the services that families perform are interdependent and sometimes functionally fused. For example, a family dinner supplies food, trains the young to regulate their own impulses, teaches them cultural norms, and reinforces the relationships among the family members gathered together. Child-rearing provides some family services, but not all of them; it may separate husband and wife. But despite the intricate interweaving of family functions with the functions of other spheres of life, it is possible conceptually to differentiate and classify the basic conditions for individual satisfactions provided chiefly by families.

**CONTRIBUTIONS OF FAMILY LIFE
TO BIOLOGICAL DEVELOPMENT
AND MAINTENANCE**

Families are the most biologically oriented of human social organizations. Sexual differentiation, sexual satisfaction, procreation, the long immaturity of children, aging processes, and the physical maintenance of all family members account for a great deal of family activity. These biological conditions are not sufficient explanation for the existence of human families, but families cannot be understood without them.

Sexual differentiation is one of the keystones of family life. In all societies access to sexual satisfaction is one of the important rights conferred by marriage to both men and women. While sexual satisfaction and parenthood are outcomes of shared experience, they are obviously not identical experiences for husbands and wives. The word "parent" refers to the aspects of this experience that men and women have in common, while the words "mother" and "father" represent the differences that follow basically from sexual traits. The relationships, division of activities, and cultural additions that these words represent are rooted in sexual differentiation.

Most of the activities of human life are sexually neutral. Political, economic, religious, scientific, academic, and recreational activities are equally within the capacities of men and women. Sexual differences, however, have in large measure resulted in masculine predominance in these spheres of living—not because women are destined to be less competent in these undertakings, but because the consequences of their sexual characteristics keep them busy with family affairs and make their participation in many of the neutral spheres inconvenient. This situation has been reinforced by cultural invention which has been used to prevent women from undertaking many things of which they are perfectly capable. Difference is rarely perceived by people as a neutral condition. Sexual difference is no exception, and elaborate theories of sexual superiority and inferiority have been formulated, chiefly in the interest of justifying existing social arrangements and bolstering systems of authority. Even in the family most activities are sexually neutral and many of the cultural proscriptions that rigidly assign some of them to women and some to men are unjustified by biological characteristics.

It must be stated, however, that some division of labor between men and women, both within their families and in other spheres of living, has proved highly convenient, if not "natural." Men and women need not marry and need not become parents, but if they do they discover that their sexual differences are significant determinants of their family life just as they are of the nature of their sexual union.

The sexual functions of women that specifically influence family life are pregnancy, childbirth, and post-parturient states, including nursing. Among other things, the fact that sexual intercourse may result in pregnancy obviously makes this experience different for women and men. The physical consequences of pregnancy to a woman are great and long-enduring. Pregnancy makes many activities difficult that are otherwise easy. Childbearing involves pain and sometimes even threat to life that few women can totally discount. Consequently, an increased need for protection and guarantees of maintenance are part of the experience of pregnancy for most women. To a lesser degree the biological modifications associated with the less dramatic aspects of feminine sexuality, menstruation and the menopause, also interfere with routine activities and require special consideration.

It is important to note that these conditions are not illnesses. They are not pathological changes of the order of the physical disabilities that affect men and women alike. They are merely some of the natural conditions of the life of women. In every society, a large number of cultural regulations, values, rituals, and ceremonies direct women's management of these recurrent biological conditions and men's attitudes toward them. In preliterate and folk societies they are apt to be conspicuous features in collective life. For example, women may be secluded or exceptionally privileged during these times. Men may be assigned various functions with reference to them, from ritual avoidance to the simulation of childbirth. In most western European societies, especially in those that are technologically advanced and predominantly Protestant in religion, public recognition of these functions tends to disappear. In all societies, however, the pattern of relationships between men and women includes some clear designs woven around feminine biological functions. They influence the core of family life everywhere.

Strictly speaking, it is parenthood, not marriage, that establishes a new family unit. Women, by virtue of the fact that they carry children as well as contribute to their conception, are more vital than men to the initiation of a family and its continuance. A mother and child can insure the survival of a family even if the husband and father dies before the child's birth. Women, moreover, are responsible for children in ways that men can never be. The utter dependency of children on women in prenatal life and in infancy, including nursing, which has been the usual source of nourishment for infants until recent years and remains so in many parts of the world, predisposes most mothers to care for their children. Their attachment to children is not evidence of a "maternal" instinct that would guarantee that all women "naturally" care for their children to the best of their abilities. The special concern of women for children is probably a matter of their great biological investment and deep psychological involvement in the process of bringing them to life.

Regardless of cultural connotations, this biological commitment makes the significance of parenthood different for men and women from the beginning. Fatherhood is not achieved at the cost of organic change. A man's concerns regarding pregnancy are focused on the woman, not on the child. The pregnancy of the woman and the arrival of the child have significance for men as manifestations of their potency and the completion of their biological maturity, among other possible satisfactions. But the relationship between women and their children before birth colors their relationship after it, and this earlier experience is missing in the relations of fathers to their children.

The early phases of family life are shaped more by the needs of women and children than by those of men. Within the family, the relation of husband and wife is usually subordinated to their parental relations to their children. The differences inherent in the experience of parenthood for men and women tend to bring about a division of labor between them. Division is not inescapable, of course, and is modified by differences in values, in the organization of the society, in technology, and by differences between individuals. But the biological needs of young children for the first five or six years are repetitive and compelling; mothers are more or less bound by them according to the amount of help available and, to a lesser degree, the availability of technical aids. Whether they are in full or part-time charge of their offspring, their lives for a good many years are likely to be dominated by the welfare of their children. The biological contributions of men to their children, on the other hand, do not restrict their mobility or physically bind them to their offspring. They are free to work outside their family circles to provide maintenance and protection for their wives and children. These services are almost universally the contribution of men to family life. The authority of men in their families stems largely from the dependence of women and children upon them in this respect. Whatever the cultural definitions that determine some aspects of the relations between men and women, their sexual differentiation disposes them to a division of labor according to which women dominate in the sphere of family life while men are in charge of other major areas of living in societies.

Families provide for the needs that arise as people grow old. Traditionally, established reciprocities between parents and children have included the right of parents to support from children whenever illness or age has incapacitated them. The appearance of grandchildren has been viewed as an important event that brings psychological fulfillment to the aging by insuring their own support and the continuity of their families and by easing their anxieties about death. Although some responsibility for the care of the aged is being shifted to non-family organizations in some societies, many of the characteristics of the later phases of family life are determined by the needs of grandparents, and in many societies households include them as functionally significant members.

CONTRIBUTIONS OF FAMILY LIFE
TO PSYCHOLOGICAL DEVELOPMENT
AND MAINTENANCE

The most striking characteristics of human beings that distinguish them from other living creatures are their highly developed psychological potentialities. Man's central nervous system enables him to organize experience by the use of symbols and meanings. Human beings can transcend immediate experience and sense impressions, view themselves as objects as well as subjects and others as subjects as well as objects, evolve the whole realm of culture, and by virtue of all these abilities, establish with each other relatively stable relationships of great complexity. In short, all forms of social life depend upon the development of complex processes called "mind" in every individual human being.

Although mental abilities rest on biologically given capacities, mere biological growth does not guarantee their development to maturity. The central nervous system, the organic apparatus that enables people to create and learn symbols and understand meanings, does not itself provide those symbols or meanings. They are products of collective life, of communication between people, and of agreement. Without an adequate repertoire of meanings and symbols, an individual is not equipped to think competently, and his self-development suffers.

Families are of vital importance to the psychological development and integration of children and their elders, as well as to their physical maintenance. For most people, selfhood is initiated in families, where its early stages are also achieved.

The utter dependence of human infants on adults for biological satisfactions makes their psychological cultivation possible; it is the basis of power of parents, and other guardians, over infants and young children. In the course of keeping them alive, the people who care for children do two important things simultaneously. They impose limits on the biological impulses of their children for absolute and immediate satisfactions, and they add cultural conditions to biologically required ones as means to satisfactions and as part of the satisfactions themselves.

Whatever the routine patterns of feeding, cleaning, handling, and sleep that parents follow, within a short time after birth infants begin to whimper for food or attention, to sleep and to wake, according to the schedule imposed. As time goes on and biological growth decreases the helplessness of children, parents impose increasingly complex conditions for achieving satisfactions. In addition to the crude manipulation of biological need (as applicable to the training of a puppy as it is to an infant) parents deliberately increase and decrease tenderness as a sign of approval and disapproval. Tenderness is an expression of willingness to attend, and the continuing dependence of children makes any threat of its withdrawal a powerful coercion. As infants move into childhood, relatively systematic rewards and punishments are used to reinforce these means of control. They are all part of the experience of eating and sleeping, of being dressed and undressed, of being kept clean, of playing, and of exploring the physical world and the nature of other people. They are all pre-eminently family techniques.

It is not necessary to teach children to eat, sleep, eliminate, crawl, cry, or explore their environment. Parents employ coercions to *direct* these biologically motivated activities into particular patterns of behavior associated with particular times, people, implements, and sentiments. Eating, for example, is not culturally determined, but what to eat, when, and how are. The meanings, skills, and values that have come to regulate the behavior of parents and which are probably shared by a good many people among whom they live and among whom the children will be expected to live, are implicit in this early training. As a result, children come to associate them with their originally simple biological satisfactions.

Of even more significance for their psychological development, children learn to want some of the cultural additions independent of biological satisfactions—even, sometimes, at the expense of their biological needs. Thus the selection and preparation of foods originally imposed by parents according to cultural prescriptions may come to be requirements for eating itself. Food that was not included in family diets, or that is not prepared in prescribed ways, may evoke disgust even in a person who is extremely hungry. This is true for many people who have been raised in homes where religious food restrictions are practiced. The wearing of clothing becomes a matter of elaborate meanings that have little to do with warmth or the protection of the body. People will not show themselves to others in social situations unless they are "properly" dressed. After the revolution in Turkey, many women chose to remain in their homes rather than appear on the streets without their face veils when the practice of wearing veils was discouraged by the new political regime.

These complex transformations depend on the psychological potentialities of human organisms. They are necessary for both individual maturity and collective human life. Among the most important of them is the transformation of the biologically given capacity for making sounds into the ability for speech, and of speech into the relatively precise tool for communication called language. This skill is usually achieved in families. The language individuals learn first is almost universally called their "mother tongue." The speech of the people around them patterns the hearing and noisemaking abilities of children from their earliest years. As soon as children become able to differentiate sounds and their own babbling noises, parents begin to encourage some kinds of sound-making and to discourage others. They do this by countless repetitions of the sounds in word order, like "mama," "dada," "doggie," and so forth. The day an infant succeeds in combining these sounds into a word and can repeat it on demand is usually a landmark in family history. His capacity for speech so modifies the responses to him of the people around him that it can be taken as a sign of his transition from infancy to childhood. Once it begins, the acquisition of vocabulary proceeds rapidly. Within a few years the sound patterning of individuals becomes so precise and so limited to the phonemes of their mother tongue that they find it extremely difficult to utter sounds not included in it. Fluency in another language learned after childhood rarely eliminates the accent that reflects the success of early training. For most adults, use of their own language seems so "natural" that they can hardly recall that they had to learn it.

The modification of the biological structure and function of individual organisms by the selective training of people and the resulting fusion of biological and cultural phenomena that are exemplified by the learning of language occurs to all the physiological systems of human beings. This "acculturation" [1] is a manifestation of psychological development. So is "socialization" [2]—the self-regulation of biological impulses by individuals that is an outcome of the restraints regularly imposed by others. By providing a stable association of old and young, of the personally mature and immature, of the knowledgeable and ignorant, families supply the basic conditions for socializing and acculturating children. These are essentially psychological processes, but they depend upon access to social relationships and a cultural repertory and they evolve the ability of individuals for membership as well as developing their personal traits.

Social maturity requires more cultivation and training than the family arrangements in most societies can provide. Associations with peers and friends and potential mates and strangers are also essential for the realization of many human potentialities. Once the development of language and mental processes is well begun and the basic cultural patterns have been transmitted, further acculturation can be more effectively achieved by social arrangements other than families. In modern societies schools supplement family training for an increasing number of years. Churches, political organizations, and economic agencies take over a larger share of cultural development. Books, pictures, and mass media of communication are sources from which individuals add to their own cultural repertoire. But no one reaches social maturity who is deprived of the kind of experience that is universally made available to most people by families. To date, no other arrangement has been found to work as well.

Adults, as well as children, depend upon family arrangements for essential psychological satisfactions. The maintenance and development of effective personal integration of adults require regu-

[1] The "technical" word *acculturation* has several meanings in social science literature. Its use is sometimes limited to the assimilation of a new culture by adults, for example, by immigrants. It is used here to refer to the modification of organic structures and processes due to the acquisition of cultural traits under any and all circumstances.

[2] The word *socialization* as it is usually used includes what is here called acculturation, but it refers to other changes as well.

lar access to other people. Self-esteem is a necessary ingredient of mental health and it depends on the individual's receiving respect and sympathetic attention from particular other people to whom he is of intrinsic as well as instrumental significance. He must be acceptable in sickness as well as in health, in failure as well as in success, in sorrow as well as in joy. Family circles are the only groups that universally offer this unconditional welcome.

Families provide another psychological asset. Whatever is unknown, uncertain, or unusual is likely to evoke uncomfortable tensions in human beings. Despite the fact that human beings apparently need some measure of new experience, surprise, and improvisation in their relationships, they need stability and predictability of response from others even more. Again, family relationships meet these requirements more frequently than other associations do. The word "familiar" derives its meaning from this fact.

For most people there are many more risks involved in their relationships with people in political, economic, educational, and recreational activities than there are in their family circles. Furthermore, most of their relations with people in other spheres are primarily instrumental. They are based on specific and immediate mutual services and include standards of performance as requisites for acceptance. In cities, especially, the number of these restrictive relationships and of demands to meet new conditions and new people increases. The family can provide intimacy and communication beyond the system of approvals and disapprovals, rewards and punishments, that operates in associations outside family circles. The value of such intimacy is dramatically disclosed in the consequences for people whose family members provoke, rather than reduce, their anxiety. Psychiatric evidence provides ample testimony of the destructive effects of inadequate psychological maintenance in families for both their young and adult members.

Two other major sources of psychological security are provided primarily by the family. First, within his family the individual derives security from the assurance of biological care and maintenance. Second, in family life his widest range for the expression of emotion and sentiment is usually permitted. Intimacy implies freedom from many conventional constraints on manifestations of feeling, and everywhere families are the most intimate of all social organizations. Uncontrolled expression of feeling is not permitted the young indefinitely anywhere, and emotional exchanges are influenced by cultural modification even within the family. Nonetheless, more spontaneity in the expression of affect and thought is allowed in families than in other relationships.

The psycho-biological requirements of human beings are so extensively the concern of families that family life itself falls into discernible phases of development that correspond roughly to the stages of development of their members. In modern, industrial societies, *marriage*, by supplying the conditions for the establishment of a stable relationship with a member of the opposite sex and the experience of parenthood, brings a young couple into the category of the socially mature. At the same time, this is the first phase of a nuclear family unit.

The second stage, *child-bearing*, is characterized by the pursuit of satisfactions associated with young adulthood, such as acquiring children, establishing a household, and achieving occupational competence. This stage is conspicuously organized around the needs of human infancy and early childhood.

When adults approach middle age their concerns shift from the acquisition of many things to their conservation. Their children at this time require the means for the development of the resources of the juvenile era and pre-adolescence. To this end, parents direct their children to schools or apprenticeships that are necessary for their competent acculturation and encourage them to establish relationships with peers that they need for their adequate socialization.

When children reach adolescence and move toward their own marriage and occupations, their parents usually make new adaptations in order to assist them and to reorganize their own lives for the time when their children will no longer be dependent upon them. This is the *launching period* in families.

The final phase of a nuclear family unit is plainly occupied with the effects of *aging* on family members and of the awareness of approaching death. Whatever the cultural variations of the means by which different populations meet the psychobiological needs associated with these universal human conditions, family life is patterned by them in all societies.

CONTRIBUTIONS OF FAMILY LIFE
TO SOCIAL ORDER

Family organizations and practices are influenced not only by universal human traits, but also by the nature of, and their relation to, other institutional arrangements. All the major spheres of life in a society, including the familial, are affected by such general factors as the size of the territory and populations of a society, the extent and development of its material resources, the level of its technology, and the richness and distribution of its culture. Conversely, some of the routine activities of all specialized organizations, including the familial, are more important to the maintenance of the society of which they are a part than to the maintenance of their members as individuals.

The extent of control by families over the resources of a society and lives of individuals tends to be less with the decrease in the size of the basic family unit. In societies in which the nuclear unit—father, mother, and children—is functionally isolated from a larger circle of relatives, family influence is almost certainly focused chiefly upon the activities that deal with the welfare of the individual members. This is the case in the United States, for example. In societies such as the traditional Chinese, in which very extended family organizations are dominant, families are generally vital units in all spheres of life. However, all forms of family organization contribute to the general social order in their societies as a consequence of the very functions which provide for their own members.

The *rate of* procreation is always an important factor in the determination of the numerical level of populations and may become politically and economically significant. Such circumstances as a general need for increasing the labor force, or need for military personnel, or the amount of food that a society can produce, lead to social evaluations of the number of people included in a society. When birth rates are considered too high or too low, the procreative function of families becomes the concern of social agencies outside the family. Excessive population is sometimes countered by political campaigns for late marriages and the use of contraceptives. The governments of Japan and India have instituted programs of this sort to influence prospective parents. When increase in population is desired, young couples are frequently encouraged to marry by being given government subsidies, parenthood is rewarded by tax benefits and special privileges, bachelors and childless couples are penalized by higher taxes, and strong arguments against methods of birth control are broadcast. The Fascist government of Italy, the Nazi government of Germany, and the Communist regime of Russia have used these devices extensively. All efforts to influence population levels, whatever their source, are chiefly directed toward influencing family practices.

Health is always a major family concern, and so is care for family members when they are ill or suffer from the effects of aging. This interest makes family units important agents for the maintenance of public health and hygiene. Sanitary storage and preparation of food, nutritionally balanced diet, safe disposal of wastes, protection of water supply, elimination of disease-carrying pests, teaching of personal hygiene to the young, and supervision of inoculation against contagious diseases are all routine family activities in modern societies. In societies for which scientific medicine is new, especially those in which endemic and epidemic diseases have seriously handicapped the development of their people and resources, the dissemination of information to improve the health of whole populations is largely directed to housewives and family elders. The reduction of maternal and infant mortality has been achieved mostly by changing the attitudes of women during their prenatal and postnatal care. Families are the most important units to which public and private programs for the reduction of mental illness and other forms of personal failure that disturb collective life are directed.

The contributions of families to the *socialization and acculturation* of children do more than provide for their individual welfare. Through this training children are transformed into members of their societies. They become capable of relating to their fellows in the various and complex ways that make social organizations possible. By cultivating the individual traits of children in accordance with accepted, culturally defined patterns for living, families insure the continuation of the institutions of their societies. By transmitting the folkways and mores that are the basis for the level of consensus necessary for collective activity, families provide the foundation for social control without which no society can exist.

Families make important *contributions to the economic life* of their societies. Wherever agriculture, craft production, and local trading prevail as the basis of economic life, families are important units of economic production. One of the conspicuous changes associated with the development of modern industrial techniques has been the gradual elimination of families from this economic function. However, they remain important units of consumption, and in this capacity they serve in their societies as a kind of unplanned, decentralized system for the distribution of goods and economic services. In autonomous nuclear families, moreover, the economic dependence of wives and children on husbands and fathers exclusively has greatly increased the latter's significance as providers at the expense of their other functions —the exercise of authority in their households, for example. Consequently, these families tend to reinforce the occupational absorption of men that modern economic organizations demand.

In some measure, all families are communal. In return for the combined efforts of all family members, each member has many things that he could not have if he acted alone. The range of family-provided economic goods and services varies greatly in different societies; however, most people depend upon their families for food, a place to sleep, facilities for cleanliness, and clothing. It is possible for other agencies to provide these things. Small, cooperative communities and, to some extent, contemporary socialist governments have done so, as have large military forces. But wherever provisioning is achieved by large centralized organizations, the number and variety of items and services are rigidly limited. They may be better than many individual families can provide, but not as ample as families can potentially provide in societies with a substantial standard of living. The success of centralized organizations for this kind of distribution is related to the goods available. When these goods are plentiful, families provide more and better for more people in what is, economically, an informal way.

All populations are divided into fairly stable social strata. The place of individuals in them is only relatively fixed, however. The movement of people from one to another is called "social mobility," and their position with reference to social strata is called their "status." In all societies, the status of individuals is initially determined by their families. Whether or not their family-determined status remains their last, as well as their first, depends on many factors. But even in societies characterized by a high degree of social mobility, original family status greatly influences the final status an individual achieves by *setting the distance* that he has to move socially to obtain a larger share of the goods and services that his society potentially offers. His *means* for social mobility, such as the schools he will attend and whether or not he will have access to professional training, are also determined to a great extent by his family membership.

Families serve as *bridges to organizations and relationships* in all spheres of life in a society. Most people's choice of religious and political memberships, educational goals, occupations, types of recreation, marital partners, and friends are greatly influenced by their families. These associations constitute their "ingroup" and "primary" relationships, for the most part, and evolve strong affectional ties and ideological commitments. These are usually experienced as sharply differentiated from those of people outside them, and therefore are frequently judged to be superior and more desirable as well. Thus, family experience and the associations it engenders lay the groundwork for the perpetuation of the status quo. They predispose individuals to remain attached to the social arrangements and beliefs to which they were introduced when young.

CONCLUSION

The services rendered by family organizations for their individual members and for the society of which they are a part are numerous and essential. They provide for the physical care of each individual member. They provide for his mental and emotional development. By training the young they pass on the social and cultural values that prevail in the larger society and prepare their members to enter into relationships within it. But major spheres of life in societies are not mutually exclusive and these functions are not solely in the purview of family organizations. Educational and religious organizations are often important socializing and acculturating agents. Economic organizations are clearly essential for the maintenance of families as well as of societies. Political organizations frequently guarantee the fulfillment of family functions and assist in providing the means for so doing; so-called "welfare states" are characterized by the assumption of a number of family functions by political organizations.

Whatever the pattern of distribution of major services in societies, those that have been discussed in this chapter are chiefly provided by family organizations in almost all of them. There have been experiments with social arrangements designed to eliminate families from the social order. (Some of these will be discussed in Chapter 10.) The conclusion drawn from these experiments is that, despite the fact that some family functions can always be performed by other organizations, no other organization yet devised can perform them so effectively as families.

The range of functions that families can perform, and the ease or difficulty with which they perform them, vary with each particular family organization and with differences in the position of families with respect to the other kinds of organizations in their societies. Every modern society includes several types of family organization. Increase in the number and variety of organizations in all spheres of life is one of the chief characteristics of modern societies. Such factors as increase in the size of a population, increase in opportunities for geographic mobility due to new forms of transportation, changes in economic techniques, and increased division of labor, change the conditions in which people associate with each other and, therefore, modify the nature of their relationships as well.

New forms of organizations do not completely eliminate other arrangements, however, not only because of inertia or "cultural lag" or the inability of some individuals to adapt to new conditions, but also because the changed conditions are not equally significant for all aspects of living or for all members of a society. Old and new organizations, and combinations of the two, exist simultaneously. For example, monarchy, representative parliaments, socialist controls, and extensive democratic participation by individual citizens make up the political life of the Scandinavian countries and Great Britain. Vast corporations and small businesses, large mechanized farms and small farms, nation-wide chain stores and neighborhood shops are all part of the economic life of the United States. In all the countries of Europe, the Americas, and the modern countries of the Orient, corporate families, extended families, and autonomous nuclear families are found.

The selection of one form of family rather than another as representative of a society depends on several factors. It may be conspicuous because it is statistically the most numerous. It may be characteristic because it exercises significant and pervasive power and influence. It may be typical by virtue of being the normative ideal for a large proportion of a population. The form selected may be representative because it combines these traits. As individual units, autonomous, nuclear families do not exercise power in the political spheres of American life, whereas some extended American families do. Nonetheless, when one thinks of American family life in general, one does not think of extended families like the Du Ponts or the Kennedys, but rather of autonomous, nuclear families, which are probably both the most numerous and the ideal family form in the United States. Consideration of the family life of prerevolutionary China, on the other hand, does not focus on independent, nuclear family households, even though they were more numerous than Chinese clans and extended families. It was the corporate family organization of Confucian China which was overwhelmingly significant because of its power in all spheres of the society, its control over natural resources, and because it was the ideal family of Confucian doctrine and therefore the ideal for most Chinese. Although Latin-Catholic countries, especially European ones, have distinguished corporate families and many independent nuclear ones, it is the bilateral extended family —grandparents, parents, children, aunts, uncles, and cousins—that is typical by virtue of its numbers, influence, and monopoly of popular sentiment.

Three forms of family organization will be described in Part II of this book as they exist in particular social settings. Chapters II and III examine the small *autonomous nuclear family*, as it is found in American society. Chapters IV and V describe the largest and most complex form of family organization, the *corporate family* as it was manifested in the clans of Confucian Chinese society. Chapters VI and VII describe the European Latin-Catholic *bilateral extended family* which falls between the other two with regard to size and autonomy of its nuclear units. These presentations are not empirical descriptions. They are meant to be descriptive abstractions, however. The experience of many families of each type has been somewhat arbitrarily ordered to reveal the general characteristics of the particular form and the range of assets and liabilities for individuals, for families, and for societies that each form of family organization potentially provides.

Abstractions impoverish reality. Their justification is that conceptual organization exposes patterns and connections that the complexity of life itself conceals. Understanding of reality by human minds is achieved by the imposition of arbitrary order and fixity on the always somewhat accidental and fluid events of experience. No man is identical with another, and yet we may generalize about "the nature of man." Each family is a unique social unit and yet, as the preceding discussion has revealed, familial life may be distinguished from other spheres of living by certain general and universal functions.

SUGGESTED READINGS

COOLEY, CHARLES H. *Human Nature and the Social Order*. New York: Scribner's, 1902.

A classical work of lasting influence that deals with the dependence of individuals on other people for the development of their personal traits.

————. *Social Organization*. New York: Scribner's, 1909.

Cooley's discussion of the nature and function of primary groups laid the foundation for sociological study of small groups.

DURKHEIM, EMILE. *Division of Labor in Society*. Translated by George Simpson. Glencoe, Ill.: The Free Press, 1949.

Book I is a classical statement of the functions of social differentiation as well as of the sources of cohesion in societies.

————. *Suicide*. Translated by John A. Spaulding and George Simpson. Glencoe, Ill.: The Free Press, 1951.

A book that has had profound influence on sociological methods and theory. The concept of "anomie" is discussed in Book II.

MANDELBAUM, DAVID (ed.). *Selected Writings of Edward Sapir*. Berkeley: University of California Press, 1949.

"Language," "Culture," "Custom," and in Part Three all of the essays entitled "The Interplay of Culture and Personality" are especially relevant for sociologists. Sapir was one of the first truly "inter-disciplinary" social scientists and a pioneer in the study of the relationship between the personal traits of individuals and their cultures.

MEAD, GEORGE H. *Mind, Self and Society*. Chicago: University of Chicago Press, 1916.

One of the early formulations of the developmental nature of "self" and personal traits that is still a principal source of theoretical statements on these subjects.

SPYKMAN, NICHOLAS. *The Social Theory of Georg Simmel.* Chicago: University of Chicago Press, 1925.

Chapter I, "The Concept of Society," Chapter III, "The Numerical Relations of Social Forms," Chapter VI, "Social Differentiation," and Chapter VII, "The Individual and the Group" are especially relevant. Simmel's theoretical formulations are more closely oriented to human relationships than to cultural phenomena and for this reason are especially fruitful for sociological study.

SULLIVAN, HARRY STACK. *The Interpersonal Theory of Psychiatry.* New York: Norton, 1953.

Although Sullivan was a psychiatrist by profession, he was well versed in the main branches of social science. His general conceptions of the development of "self" and personal traits deal with the phenomena that underlie what sociologists call "socialization."

SUMNER, WILLIAM GRAHAM. *Folkways.* New York: Ginn, 1906.

Current use of the terms "folkways" and "mores" and much theory concerning their relation to social control are based on Chapters I and II of this book.

THOMPSON, CLARA. *Psychoanalysis: Evolution and Development.* New York: Hermitage Press, 1950.

This is a useful survey and summary of psychoanalytically oriented theories of personal development by a distinguished psychiatrist and psychoanalyst.

WALLER, WILLARD AND HILL, REUBEN. *The Family: A Dynamic Interpretation.* New York: Dryden Press, 1951.

Waller's analysis of American family life in terms of a family life-cycle is the basis for the analysis used in this book.

WEBER, MAX. *The Theory of Social and Economic Organization.* Translated by A. M. Henderson and Talcott Parsons. New York: Oxford, 1947.

Pages 109-12 present a succinct statement of the problem of formulating general concepts from empirical data in the social sciences. The distinction is made between "ideal" and "average" types.

——. *The Protestant Ethic and the Spirit of Capitalism.* Translated by Talcott Parsons. New York: Scribner's, 1952.

A classical study of the ways in which the organizations and institutions in one sphere of a society can determine aspects of organizations and institutions in another.

PART TWO

■ ■ ■

Forms of
Family Organization

■

· II ·

THE AUTONOMOUS
NUCLEAR FAMILY IN
THE UNITED STATES

■

Its Roots in American Society

THE EXTENT and endowment of the land on which a society lives, the number and variety of its people, the level and distribution of its culture, and the nature and degree of differentiation of its organizations all influence the family life of its people, directly and indirectly. The relatively recent origin of the United States, its brief history in comparison with that of most other societies, the establishment of its basic institutions by deliberate enactment rather than more or less unwitting accretion, and the fact that its territory imposed few limits on the expansion and development of the American people have all been significant determining factors for some of the outstanding characteristics of American society. To understand the development of family life in the United States, it is necessary to examine some general characteristics of American society.

AMERICAN POPULATION AND CULTURE

One of the most remarkable achievements in the United States is the degree to which its population, drawn from a great variety of other societies in large part, has emerged as a clearly recognizable American people. This transformation has been so successful that Americans themselves overlook the fact that the United States is not purely an English-speaking country with the common heritage that term implies. Thousands of Americans speak a language other than English in their homes, and thousands more at least understand one other language. The fact that a fairly large proportion of the population of the United States is multilingual reflects the ethnic diversity that has been, and still is, a conspicuous feature of the population of the United States, particularly its urban population. Many aspects of American life cannot be understood without due regard to the fact that its population was, until recently, regularly enhanced by large numbers of immigrants.

The assimilation of immigrants in the United States has not meant simply their acquisition of the cultural traits of the founding settlers. It has meant a kind of reciprocal exchange of diverse traits by each ethnic category. Clusters of people, living in relative isolation and preserving the ways of the societies from which they came, soon found themselves surrounded by circles of new immigrants. In time associations between them, sometimes including marriage, resulted in the diffusion of custom and usage. In every generation some members of ethnic enclaves developed traits that were markedly different from their old-countrymen and emerged as clearly identifiable "Americans." This has been the experience of so large a proportion of the American population that the descendants of the original settlers, insofar as they maintain their distinctive cultural traits, are themselves a "minority" today.

Assimilation has been facilitated by a number of conditions of life in the United States. The mere fact of a new physical environment tends to break up old habits and associations. People coming from rural areas and small communities abroad could scarcely maintain in large urban centers the kind of relationships and ways of life they had left behind. Distance itself diminished the significance of many of the old ways of life as memories faded and no direct associations reinforced them. The size of America, the urge to be "moving on," loosened old ties still further. In the frontier lands, geographic isolation and the rigors of breaking new ground required new adaptive techniques. In many instances, the hazards of frontier life impelled people of different backgrounds to band closely together, intensifying the processes of integration.

New means for earning a living introduced great changes. Industrial techniques required individual skills rather than the cooperation of families. Jobs took men and women away from their homes and away from each other. The increase of mass-production techniques in the manufacture and distribution of goods rendered many individually developed skills and crafts obsolete.

American public schools—and the laws that made school attendance compulsory—were extremely influential in producing a distinctly American population. These schools provided Americans with a common culture which augmented the family culture of many of them and provided a basis for new relationships. They taught the language that all came to speak, whatever their mother tongue, as well as the tastes and manners, the customs of dress, and the forms of recreation that all came to share. American history, American institutions, and American values were taught so successfully that foreign-born Americans, or those of foreign-born parents, assumed quite naturally that the American Revolution, George Washington, the Founding Fathers, and the American Saga applied to them as fully as to the descendants of the original colonists. For most Americans, the Mayflower was merely the first among the many ships that came bearing immigrants.

AMERICAN INSTITUTIONS AND ORGANIZATIONS

American society is strongly egalitarian. Social mobility and the freedom to pursue individual interests and espouse different beliefs are basic political tenets in the United States. As a nation, Americans have always had representational government. Although the conditions of contemporary life and the growth of the population make it increasingly difficult for most Americans to participate directly in political life, they strongly believe in the principle of government by and for the people. They are traditionally suspicious of centralized political organization and hold to the separation of powers built into American government.

The separation of church from state and the establishment of equal rights for all religious organizations is a basic tenet of American political belief. Perhaps no other society has such a variety of churches and religious sects. Although all are given political protection, none is given political support. Both public sentiment and the law forbid the attempt of one religious organization to suppress another. Thus religious membership is relegated to the domain of private affairs. Many spheres of life—particularly education and the family—that in other societies are closely related to religious institutions are not generally under religious authority in the United States.

Yet the majority of Americans have had some religious training. Church membership is large, although nominal for a significant proportion of the people listed on church registers. Although religious instruction is excluded from public schools, religious schools abound. Religious groups, individually and collectively, exert considerable power over national life. They influence legislation and access to public office; they define public morality, and they directly or indirectly censor art and literature. The right to observe the holy days of one's church is respected by the entire population.

The vast natural resources in the United States, its early industrialization, and rapid economic growth have enabled Americans to eliminate many of the differences in dress, household equipment, means of transportation, and personal manners which tend to separate the various social categories in other societies. Whatever the aesthetic result of this standardization, socially it has been an asset to Americans. Class lines can be rigidly maintained only when they are supported by marked differences in styles of life. If workers wear workingmen's clothes, ride bicycles, and drink ordinary local wines; if farmers wear regional costumes, drive horses or donkeys, and drink beer; and if upper-class people wear business suits, drink vintage wines, and drive cars, members of one

class will be most unlikely to associate with those of another except under limited and special circumstances. In the United
States, standardization of goods, a highly developed money economy, an expanding economic base, and long-term buying practices
have combined to blur visible signs of class difference. In schools,
at work, and in public places of recreation and amusement, the
protective coloration of standardized possessions has facilitated
the establishment of personal relationships across class lines and
the movement of Americans from one class to another.

The external uniformities of Americans and the relative ease
with which they mingle with people of different religions, education, and classes might tempt a casual observer to overestimate
their homogeneity. There are some sharp divisions in the American population. Tensions based on conflicts of value, sentiment,
and interest sometimes threaten to disrupt American society itself.
The country is large, and regional differences are conspicuous,
especially those between the North and the South and between
the East Coast, the Middle West, the West, and the West Coast.
Settlement of the land in successive stages by people who differed
in race and culture has left its mark on the present populations of
these areas. Variation in natural resources and degrees of urbanization augment these differences. Nevertheless, only a few issues,
such as the relations between races, evoke great bitterness in the
American population. National unity usually takes precedence
over local interest. The solidarity of the population is great
enough to lead some observers to refer to it as a homogeneous
mass society.

The increasing number of large organizations and the shift
from rural to urban patterns of life have also contributed to the
fusion of the American population. Bigness and impersonality go
hand in hand. Americans today pursue their individual ends in the
company of a great many people whom they know in varying
degrees, but few of whom are friends or relatives. While this condition has some personal disadvantages, its contribution to national unity and social mobility is great. The reduction of extensive dependence on a few people augments the range of available
satisfactions as well as the freedom of the individual to seek them
in a variety of ways and places.

Since goods and services are exceptionally uniform throughout the United States, and means of transportation are widely available, Americans have become a geographically mobile population. Their movement has broken up local and family solidarity in many places and moderated the cultural differentiation that regional isolation once fostered. Modern techniques of communication, by making it possible for millions of Americans to read, see, and hear the same things, have hastened the advance toward a homogeneous American culture—one that is shared by the majority of American citizens, whatever ethnic, class, occupational, or regional differences they still cherish.

Since the beginning of the twentieth century the lives of most Americans have been changed by the shift from an economy of small, relatively personal and autonomous organizations to one dominated by large, impersonal, semipublic corporations. Increased wage levels; employee benefits in the form of pensions, health insurance, paid vacations, and training programs; and government-administered social security payments have raised the national standard of living. Taxation has reduced the opportunities to amass vast fortunes, while installment buying has made a great range of goods and services available to millions of Americans. Certainly, many Americans who did very poorly in maintaining themselves and their families in the past do less poorly today by virtue of the economic floor provided by new collective arrangements. The majority of Americans have become middle-class citizens.

Not only their economic situation, but the habits and values of Americans have been changed in many ways by the fact that they now depend upon a growing number of collective organizations, public and private, for the services, protection, and income that they were formerly expected to provide for themselves. In part, new organizations have taken over functions that other organizations—such as the family, or civic and philanthropic agencies—can no longer perform. Many Americans now acquire their education, earn their living, buy their possessions, obtain their medical services, and provide for their old age by participation in large organizations. The current preoccupation with security in America—especially among young people—and the assumption that the government, or corporations, or unions should provide that security, may well reflect the fact that changing life conditions in the United States have made the shift of responsibility to these organizations necessary.

It would be difficult to say whether or not the total store of individual ingenuity and talent in the American population has been significantly stunted by the expansion of large organizations of all kinds. Life in small communities, extended families, small shops and companies, small schools and frontier villages did not necessarily encourage remarkable individual achievement. Although the *means* to individual achievement have changed, it seems probable that the *opportunities* for individual accomplishment are sufficient for at least as many of the ambitious and clever as they were in the past.

However, the present over-all conditions of economic life in the United States do not fit the traditional formulations about *laissez-faire*, individual enterprise, and free competition which many Americans seem to consider accurate descriptions of their economic principles. Competition can go on only in situations of relative equality, and there would be little economic competition today without government interference, which serves much the same function that handicapping does in golf tournaments and horse races. Technical development, a growing population, and increasing inroads upon our natural resources have also given rise to regulations for conservation and control. Centralized organization has increased to meet new needs. Management and control of economic resources have replaced individual ownership. "New Deal," "Fair Deal," and "Welfare Programs" are the terms used to refer to this relatively new relationship of economic and political agencies in the United States. While Americans may be divided in sentiment and belief about their economic affairs, they are far less divided in their actual economic behavior. Federal subsidies for schools, industries, agricultural development, public utilities, transportation, and many other things are being demanded of the American government by people who oppose any political candidate who frankly espouses government participation in economic activities and local administrations.

GENERAL CHARACTERISTICS OF FAMILY LIFE
IN AMERICA

The general social and material conditions of life in the United States have discouraged the rise or continuation of extended families. They do exist; a few of the old families associated with the early settlement of the country and some that have been connected with large industrial ventures exert considerable influence in American society. But the extended family is not the ideal among Americans. When immigrants from lands in which this form of family is representative are assimilated into the main currents of American life, the break-up of their large family circles is often a sign of their Americanization.

The prevailing form of family organization in the United States has been, and still is, the highly autonomous nuclear family. Parents and their children are "a family"; recognized familial relationships beyond this small group are "relatives." The number of relatives that individual Americans acknowledge varies greatly. It usually includes grandparents; some, but not all, of the grandparents' brothers and sisters and their children; some, but not all, of the siblings of the husband and wife and their children. Not all of this larger circle are likely to be known to one another. In most cases they gather together, if at all, only for exceptional occasions such as weddings and funerals.

When Americans marry they usually expect to set up a household that is functionally independent of the parents of each spouse in all respects. The couple expects to support itself and its children by its own efforts and to provide for all the needs and contingencies that each member of the nuclear unit will encounter until the children have married or support themselves. A husband and wife may acknowledge a limited responsibility toward their own parents in case of need, but generally this sense of obligation does not extend to other relatives outside the nuclear unit.

Many Americans make certain general assumptions about their family life. Above all, they take it for granted that marriage and parenthood are part of every "normal" person's life cycle and that personal happiness and fulfillment are to be found only in establishing a nuclear family. They measure the success of marriage and family living in terms of the contentment, if not "happiness," of individual family members—a vague and relative standard. The choice of marriage partners is considered to be an entirely personal matter. Americans assume that every individual has the right to find a spouse without regard to the opinions, preferences, or needs of other people. Others may, and usually do, influence the choice of partners, but they cannot make the final decisions. "Romantic love" is considered the best criterion for the selection of a marriage partner. The romantic ideal is certainly not limited to Americans, nor are all their marriage choices based upon it, but more than many other people Americans associate marriage with the phenomenon of falling in love and they consider romantic love to be close to one of the most exalted of human conditions.

Although today more North Americans than before frankly recognize that sex is a constant and important ingredient in social life, the "puritanical" attitude of many of them toward sex continues to affect their family life. Most societies make the family the proper sphere for parenthood and the principal accepted arrangement for sexual satisfaction. Americans differ from many other people in their moral emphasis on marriage as the *only* proper channel to sexual gratification. This contributes both to many young people in the United States marrying before they are capable of meeting the demands of family life and to marital relationships being seriously threatened when sexual satisfaction is sought outside the family—as it is to some extent in all societies.

The rigid mores that remain the foundation for sexual morality for most Americans make sex a subject of furtive preoccupation and guilt for many of them—to the extent that it sometimes interferes with their sexual functions and, hence, with their marriages and competence as parents. A double standard for sexual freedom tacitly persists, and men are its beneficiaries. However, in a society in which sexual equality is a normative ideal and sexual chastity outside of monogamous marriage is supposed to be maintained by males as well as females, many men cannot enjoy their privilege without emotional conflict. The ambiguous attitudes of many Americans toward sexual matters is reflected in the widespread ambivalence and uncertainty in the relationships between men and women in the United States, including the relations between husbands and wives and between parents and children of the opposite sex.

American attitudes toward youth and old age have also contributed to characteristics of the nuclear family in this country. American emphasis on activity, on independence, on individual achievement, and on geographic and social mobility has led to the assumption that childhood, youth, and early adulthood are by far the best years of life. Conspicuous, if unintended, consequences of this assumption have been neglect of the resources of the second half of the life span and indifference to, if not deprecation of, the aging and the old. The relative insignificance of the aging has been one factor that has contributed to increase of the autonomy and isolation of nuclear families in the United States. Few obligations toward aging parents or other relatives restrain the pursuit of advantages for the nuclear unit. Meanwhile, the plight of the old has become a national scandal.

The correlate of this lack of respect for age is an unusual emphasis on youth in the United States. This has always been the case. For pioneers and immigrants, children were often the means to the fulfillment of their visions. Indulgence of children became a sign of parental achievement. Americans who had succeeded in improving their lot did not wish their children to live as they had lived. Rather, they tended to shield their young from adult responsibilities, which to this day American parents rarely expect their children to share. Even in lower-class families, children are permitted to work for their own satisfactions—for education, clothing, and recreation—rather than for the maintenance of the family.

Parental authority has greatly diminished in the United States. Emphasis on equality and democratic procedures for making decisions are broadly assumed to be applicable to family life as well. The traditional division of labor between husbands and wives is generally in effect even though many married women have jobs outside the home. But husbands and wives are assumed to be equal before the law with respect to property, right of divorce, and custody of their children; equal in the exercise of authority in their homes; and equal in terms of personal dignity. A more exceptional equality within the American family is that between parents and children. The American child is treated as an equal by his parents not merely upon his attainment of maturity and self-reliance, but during the long period of training and cultivation.

Emphasis on individual personal satisfaction in family life, complicated attitudes toward sex, a romantic view of marriage, deprecation of the assets of age and exaggeration of the assets of youth, curtailment of parental authority, and extreme notions about equality in family relationships—these factors in combination account for much that is unique in American family life. American families include all the variations that flow from religious, ethnic, class, and racial differences as well as differences in place of residence. But these differences have not prevented the emergence of patterns of family relationships and family behavior that are readily identifiable as American.

THE CHANGING PATTERN OF INSTITUTIONS IN AMERICA

Divisions and separation of powers between church, state, educational facilities, economic organizations, and families have been clear in the United States. This is not to say that organizations and relationships have not been established across these lines. Rather, the degree of autonomy exercised by organizations within each of these spheres has been greater than it is in many other societies.

In recent time, however, interpenetration between some of these spheres of organization has been increasing. The multiplicity of churches tends to keep the religious sphere to itself, and religious influence on political and other organizations is exerted only indirectly for the most part. But the activities of political and economic organizations are now overlapping in many areas. Also, schools of all kinds are becoming increasingly dependent upon the assistance of the federal government for their maintenance. This has not so far greatly influenced policies concerning who will teach or what is taught; in any case, local school boards have always been influential in these matters. But many Americans who once believed that the decentralized nature of their educational system kept it safe from political domination have come to view the trend toward federal participation in educational activities as a threat to the autonomy of education in this country.

Among the major organizations and activities in the United States, family units have been, at one and the same time, the most isolated and the most dependent. Legal requirements for marriage, divorce, the care of minor children, school attendance, and inheritance have been almost the only political controls on families. The influence of religious regulation has been a matter of individual choice. In other respects, however, nuclear family units are quite dependent upon non-family organizations. American families are all-providing only for the very young. They are not themselves important as political, economic, educational, or religious units, and individual family members have to seek many of their satisfactions in relationships outside the family unit.

The prominence of the autonomous nuclear family is not new in American family life, but the conditions in which such a family must be maintained have changed. As long as residential communities were small, means of transportation limited, and the alternatives for earning a living relatively few for most people, the dependence of the family on outside facilities was not exposed as a potential threat to its maintenance and functions. But as these aspects of American life have become increasingly large and complex, the nuclear family without compensating powers of its own is strained by its dependence on non-family organizations and by its isolation from relatives. The effects of modern social conditions on family experience and on individuals as family members will be explored in Chapter III.

SUGGESTED READINGS

BARZUN, JACQUES. *Teacher in America*. Garden City: Doubleday, 1954.

An informed, witty, and readable discussion of contemporary education in the United States.

BERLE, ADOLPH A., JR., AND MEANS, GARDNER. *The Modern Corporation and Private Property*. New York: Macmillan, 1951.

The first detailed analysis of the growth of corporate organizations in the United States and some of its effects on American life.

BLACK, HILLEL. *Buy Now, Pay Later*. New York: Morrow, 1961.

A well documented report on the revolution in the buying habits of Americans which gives an intelligent and illuminating analysis of the effects of current credit practices on various aspects of American life.

GALBRAITH, J. K. *The Affluent Society*. Boston: Houghton, Mifflin, 1958.

Galbraith views the economy of the United States as one of abundance and discusses the effects of this new and unusual condition on a society. He presents controversial but interesting thesis.

GLAZER, NATHAN. *American Judaism*. Chicago: University of Chicago Press, 1957.

A good sociological analysis of Jewish communities, both religious and nonreligious, in the United States.

HERBERG, WILL. *Protestant, Catholic, Jew*. New York: Doubleday, 1955.

A comprehensive and objective discussion of the current nature of religious life in the United States.

LERNER, MAX. *America as a Civilization.* Vol. I. New York: Simon and Schuster, 1957.

An ambitious and largely successful effort to describe American society in all its aspects. Mr. Lerner's interpretations are provocative.

MYRDAL, GUNNAR. *The American Dilemma.* New York: Harper, 1944.

A scholarly study of American Negroes and Negro-white relations in the United States. Although much has happened since it was completed, this work goes far toward explaining current trends in race relations.

TOCQUEVILLE, ALEXIS DE. *Democracy in America.* New York: Knopf, 1944.

A classical study of American society written in 1830. Tocqueville's analysis was so penetrating that it has been unnecessary to modify many of his generalizations concerning the emphasis on equality and voluntary associations as it affects the life of a society.

WHYTE, WILLIAM H., JR. *The Organization Man.* Garden City: Doubleday, 1956.

A journalist's interpretation of how an economy dominated by large corporations affects the lives and characteristics of an increasingly large segment of the American population.

THE AUTONOMOUS NUCLEAR FAMILY IN THE UNITED STATES

■

Its Phases and Effects

PREPARATION FOR MATE SELECTION AND MARRIAGE

EXPLICIT TRAINING for family life is not characteristically a part of the rearing of young people in the United States. Indeed, specific training of children for adult life in general is exceptionally delayed in this country as compared with training in Western European societies. The widespread American conviction that childhood and youth are the best years of life predisposes Americans to protect their children from adult responsibilities and concerns. "Children will be children" and "They are only young once" are typical statements of modern American parents. American children are encouraged to grow in a juvenile world. Their immediate needs and wants are indulged. They frequently decide what they eat, what they wear, what they play and with whom. They not infrequently determine what their elders do as well. American children are likely to assume that parents exist for their benefit and that their own obligations are negligible.

Cleavage between generations is universal, but the degree to which young Americans are left to themselves is unusual. Their lives are dominated by household and school routines, as are the lives of young people in most societies, but neither parents nor teachers supervise or regulate their intervening hours, and American children have a great deal of free time. The peer-group life of children and young people in the United States has been noted by many observers. Delinquent youth groups have attracted too much attention, perhaps, since the majority of young Americans is not delinquent. But the majority, to a much greater degree than children in Western European societies, does evolve its own standards and values and avoids scrutiny and correction by adults.

It is relatively easy for American young people to believe that their very partial formulations adequately represent the world they live in and to be convinced that they are competent to make significant decisions without advice or counsel. American adults do not consistently present their ways of life as potentially richer in personal satisfactions than those of the young. American children are often left with the impression that youth is an end in itself. The advantage of adult life is seen primarily as freedom from restraints, such as having to go to school and economic dependence on parents.

In the United States, the training of children does not clearly presage the complementary nature of the relationships between adult men and women. The majority of schools are coeducational and courses of instructions are the same for both sexes. So are most recreational activities. There is little differential treatment of sons and daughters in American homes during their early life. Codes of deportment that do define appropriate behavior for members of each sex toward the other are more concerned with manners than with the essential nature of the relationship between the sexes.

By the time American children reach adolescence, a good many of them have been taught the physiology of sex, but fewer have been provided by their parents with useful information and guidance on sexual matters or taught that sex is an integral part of human relationships. Most American parents are satisfied to impress their children with the moral conviction that sexual satisfaction is to be sought only in marriage. Side by side with this somewhat puritanical sex education is the informal teaching of the mass media. Advertisements and movies make a fetish of a particular type of female with allegedly potent "sex appeal." In terms of adult sexual experience, these displays are more representative of physical culture than sexual union, and lead to confusion and misconceptions in the minds of the young.

All in all, American young people receive relatively little guidance in their efforts to stabilize their sexual impulses and establish satisfactory relationships with the opposite sex. Many of them have been imbued with the conviction that sex is immoral except between husbands and wives, and they have been made well aware of the dangers of pregnancy and disease that may result from sexual indulgence. Consequently, their sexual curiosity tends to be furtive, and experimentation is full of tension and frustration. Dating among adolescents in the United States is more often associated with sex play than sexual satisfaction. A good many young Americans are driven to "going steady" and early marriages in order to escape the anxiety that their dating practices engender.

By late adolescence, young Americans are impelled toward marriage—as are young people in all societies—by the social expectations of parents and peers and by their own biological impulses. In many societies, the young have been oriented to adult tasks, especially family responsibilities, by this time. American young people are not entirely undirected in family matters or marriage choice; their training in this respect is informal and unwitting in large part, but it also includes some formulations of the general expectations of their parents. American parents define a "good" marriage in much the same terms that professional matchmakers have used in many places for many centuries. Aside from personal attributes, such as health, beauty, and fertility in women, and good character, intelligence, and the promise of occupational success in men, they look for similarities in social background. They hope that upbringing, education, religion, race, and ethnic derivation will be matched. Like parents elsewhere, American parents are not averse to their children's achievement of higher class position and social opportunities through marriage. And, like other parents, they are usually distressed when their children marry "beneath" them. American young people are more or less aware of these expectations and generally share some of them.

But the widespread "romantic" approach to marriage in the United States tends to suppress forthright appraisals of marriage candidates in these terms when young people reach the point of actually selecting their mates. They consider their marriage to be an individual and personal matter. They envisage the goals of marriage in terms of personal happiness, and consider the choice of mates to be their own affair. American parents may exhort their children to marry, may encourage or inveigh against particular choices, but they have no direct means for enforcing their views if their children are of age and choose to go their own ways.

Various courses are open to Americans for finding their marriage partners. Many of them marry following long association with each other in neighborhood, school, or church. This permits the families to influence marriage choice considerably. Since it is usually the family that provides residence, school, and church membership, this results in a fairly homogeneous circle of acquaintance.

However, many Americans do not grow up in one place, attend one set of schools, or go to one church.

Since 1950 annual reports indicate that approximately one-fifth of the population changes residence each year, about 1 out of 15 move outside of the county each year, and in excess of 3 per cent cross a state line in their move. In 1950, one-quarter (25.6 per cent) of the native-born population was living in a state other than the one in which they were born.[1]

[1] Bossard, James H. S., and Boll, Eleanor Stoker: *The Sociology of Child Development* (New York: Harper & Brothers, Publishers; 1960), p. 434.

The children of families that have changed their place of residence several times have no ready-made circles from which to choose their mates. A common route to marriage for these young people is membership in a variety of groups initiated by the young themselves. Within their colleges, for example, young men and women seek admission to fraternities and sororities and other clubs which perform the important function, among others, of supplying dates and promoting marriages.

Young people who cannot go to college join church or recreational groups. Sometimes young women take jobs in the hope of meeting a suitable man. The young help one another. The more successful find dates for their friends or facilitate their admission into clubs. The prerequisites for membership in these organizations serve as a kind of selecting device that brings people of somewhat similar backgrounds and tastes together, although homogeneity in such groups does not equal that of the partially family-provided circles.

There is another path to marriage used by Americans. Sometimes it is merely an accessory to the two courses noted above. Sometimes it is the only way for young people who have no "connections," or for not-quite-so-young Americans who have not succeeded in finding a mate. If they can afford it, some of these people try resort hotels, cruises, and touring parties in search of marriage partners. Selection in these circumstances is far more hazardous than it is by other means. These people meet without recommendations. The pairing must be achieved quickly. And while it may be, the circumstances that bring it about are so exceptional (the "shipboard" or "summer" romance of popular story and song) that they provide almost no indication of what the individuals are like in more commonplace situations. These forays allow for a great deal of deception and exploitation, and young people who embark on them take considerable risk.

Young men and women who do not find the kind of mate they want in any of these ways are very much on their own. Their matings are largely a matter of chance. They "just happen" to meet at work, or at the home of a friend, or in a theater, or walking their dogs—anywhere, in fact. These pairings depend largely on factors of mutual personal attraction that are not related to membership in any particular group or category. In some respects these matings are less risky than they seem. There is no time limit on the premarital association of people who meet in this way. They may see each other often enough to explore their personal histories and their personal traits.

Since access to marriage in the United States is relatively detached from regulation and assistance from family elders, the achievement of this important relationship is more hazardous for American youth than it is for young men and women in many other societies. The fact that young people of different religious, ethnic, and class backgrounds mingle at school, work, and play increases the number of couples who are not "well-matched" in these respects. Yet Americans are not generally aware that their facilities for achieving marriage are unusually risky. For the most part, they become aware only after they have married that their preparations for family life are not extensive, and may be inadequate. The majority of Americans do achieve a reasonably satisfactory family life and some do better than that. But the American divorce rate is notoriously high and so is the rate of desertions. This suggests that the confidence of a number of Americans in their personal judgment was unfounded and that their training for family living was inadequate. Poor preparation is not the only factor that make Americans more prone to divorce than other people, but it cannot be discounted. The incidence of divorce in the United States is especially high during the first few years after marriage.

Whatever the means, most American young men and women do marry. Marriage is greatly valued as an end in itself by parents and children, and weddings are usually as elaborate as the parents of the bride can afford—and often more so. They are family affairs. The prestige of the families of both the bride and groom is enhanced by a successful wedding. But the marriage itself is a personal commitment between the young man and woman, not a contract between their families. Exchange of goods or property takes the form of free gifts, not of dowries or bride prices. The wishes of the wedding guests are for the personal happiness of the couple, not for the prosperity of their families or their continuity through sons whose special significance would derive chiefly from the fact that they would be bearers of the family name.

THE NEWLY MARRIED COUPLE

In the United States, young men and women expect their marriages to mark their emancipation. The autonomy of the nuclear family begins with the autonomy of the young couple. Anything that interferes with it, such as continued economic dependence on parents or continued residence in a parental home, tends to cause tension. There are no traditional rules to promote harmony in households that include more than one nuclear family.

To approximate the American family ideal requires a considerable range of personal resources, a high level of self-regulation, and access to adequate means for maintenance. With these assets, newly wedded couples in the United States can be expected to enjoy their emancipation from parental control and to be compensated for the increasing complexity of their lives by new satisfactions.

But many young American couples are not well prepared for exercising the new freedoms marriage brings. The right to sexual satisfaction is one of them. As in most societies, it is possible for young men in the United States to become socially mature with regard to sex before they marry and to become competent to cultivate the sexual impulses of their inexperienced wives. Also, it seems likely that more well-brought-up young women have indulged in sexual play than have their counterparts in many other societies. But in the United States, as in most societies except preliterate ones, marriage is the only sanctioned means for establishing a fully heterosexual relationship for women. For many Americans, sex is still so furtive a subject that young men are often as sexually insecure when they marry as their wives. A good many American marriages flounder on the sexual immaturity of both spouses.

As a consequence of their long freedom from responsibility for anyone but themselves, and of their orientation toward their peers rather than their elders, many young newlyweds are confronted with a large number of lessons to learn in a short period of time. If their early experience has left them merely ignorant but not seriously handicapped for continued personal development, and if they have been fortunate in their personal choice of a spouse, the early years of marriage can be immensely stimulating. But the conditions needed for marital stability and satisfaction are not easy to achieve in the United States. There are some general aspects of American life that mitigate against the likelihood of marital success.

The extensive participation in relatively autonomous peer groups that is so large a part of the experience of young people in the United States provides useful training for the companionate aspects of marriage, which are greatly emphasized in this country. A capacity for cooperation and friendly competition, pleasure in working with others for collective goals, ability to exercise authority among equals and to submit to it, talent for improvisation, and willingness to learn are in the United States excellent traits to bring to marriage, and many Americans have them.

The ideal of the isolated nuclear family requires Americans to modify their family relationships in important ways when they marry. In societies in which elders in general, and parents in particular, are in a position of superiority over the young, some deference and attention is paid them after the marriage of their children as well as before it. In the United States, however, a tacit assumption that children will become the equals if not the superiors of their parents has greatly changed traditional parent-child relationships. Parenthood has ceased to be a lifetime activity. In theory at least, Americans do not expect to be treated as children by their parents once they have married, while their parents, once their children have left home, look forward to a release from all parental responsibilities. In practice, emancipation is often difficult for both parents and children. With the increase in early marriages and the lengthening of time required for occupational training, children have become less frequently able to fend for themselves without help when they marry. The conflict between their desire to be free of parental interference after marriage and their need for it can sometimes confuse the young wife or husband seriously enough to prevent the integration of the marital relationship. Some parents, especially mothers, who have devoted so much of their time and thought to their children that they have failed to cultivate their own resources, find that they have little to sustain them after their children have left home. If the loss of their significance as parents seriously threatens their self-esteem, they not infrequently exploit their children's needs and interfere with their marriages.

The lack of fixed obligations to relatives makes the adaptation of brides and grooms to each others' families more problematic than it is for people whose family ties are less dependent upon accident and personal inclination. The families of both spouses are generally considered to be of equal significance—or insignificance—in the United States. Preferential treatment of the family of either spouse is apt to be resented. Like so many aspects of American family life, the establishment of harmonious relationships with relatives-in-law is a highly personal matter. It is often complexly involved in the relation between husbands and wives. Harmony between them often depends, in part, upon the ingenuity with which each one determines the parent, or sibling, or uncle, or cousin from among the whole family circle who is important to his or her spouse. To a degree, the American situation makes the relation between couples more vulnerable to conflict over in-laws than it is in more family-oriented societies. The potential advantage of the American arrangement is the freedom of young married people from obligations that in very extended families can be burdensome and restrictive.

Recent changes in economic conditions in the United States influence marital success or failure for an increasing number of Americans. In the not very distant past, Americans assumed that they would be able to support their wives and children when they married. Today, however, occupational opportunities have come to depend more and more on technical skills. Special career training for young men cannot be completed before they are twenty-five, or even in their early thirties. Since neither the young men nor women are willing to postpone marriage until that time, an increasing number of American men are marrying not only before they are established in occupations, but before they have even begun their training for future economic pursuits. Some Americans marry while they are still in high school. Most of these young people leave school, take relatively unskilled jobs that are open to them, and live by their own efforts. With few exceptions, they limit their future opportunities and those of their children by so doing. In the United States, the earning capacity of people without technical skills or higher education is greatly restricted.

Young couples who are not content to limit their prospects in this way and who do pursue their education are, as a result, not in a position to set up independent households and to enjoy the freedom from restraints which they associate with marriage. This intermediate state between adolescence and maturity, between school years and adult autonomy, is not so clearly differentiated in the United States that it is anticipated as a regular stage of growing up; nonetheless, it is becoming conspicuous enough to warrant the prediction that it may become institutionalized in the relatively near future. The consequences of this increasingly widespread situation for individual Americans and for their marriages are problematic, but there are beginning to be some discernible patterns of adaptation by young people and their parents who are supporting them while they are finishing their education.

If both the young man and the young woman marrying at an early age come from upper-class or upper-middle-class homes, the potential strain on their marriage is greatly reduced. Parental approval may not be wholehearted, but it will not usually be withheld or grudging. Both sets of parents will probably arrange a unified plan for the support of the couple. With both sets of parents providing support, neither bride nor groom is placed in a subordinate position to the other. With characteristic American indulgence, the parents attach few strings to their contribution and the young people are left free to run their own affairs. Parental support enables them to set up their households and continue their pursuits. They feel that they are independent.

If their progress toward genuine independence of their parents is unimpeded, the young couple's temporary dependence imposes no special hardships on their marital relationship. It often has the added assets of creating ties between the two sets of parents and strengthening the bond between them and their children. This pattern of adaptation to somewhat new conditions of marriage in the United States seems to unite isolated nuclear families into a partially extended one. When extended families are substantially supported, they easily make room for economically nonproductive couples.

When only one spouse belongs to an upper-class or upper-middle-class family, their marital relationship is frequently less felicitous. The lower-class parents are apt to favor the marriage since it assures social advancement for their child. On the other hand, the higher-class parents are likely to be less sanguine about the marriage and, in many instances, to oppose it. Even when they publicly acknowledge the marriage and agree, with some reluctance, to support the couple, problems still ensue. One-sided support for the couple subordinates the lower-class parents and spouse. Care may be exercised to keep this fact out of the awareness of everyone concerned, but it is there to be exposed in the event of personal strife. Differences in styles of life make it difficult for the two sets of parents to establish comfortable relationships with each other. This situation is sometimes resolved by practicing as much social avoidance as can be managed respectably. Because of its dependence, the couple tends to be drawn into the circle of the upper-class family. As a result, the higher-class spouse fails to develop strong ties to the lower-class in-laws, and the lower-class spouse begins to withdraw from his or her own family relationships. This withdrawal can only result in a personally destructive ambivalence for the lower-class spouse. His or her affectional ties to the mate, in conjunction with the advantages that the upper-class parents provide, pull this spouse in their direction. But the emotional bonds of youth are not easily broken; the withdrawal from family ties when it is so clearly motivated by individual advantage is felt to be morally tawdry; and disregard of past benefits evokes guilt. This personal burden is a great hazard to the marital relationship and so are the differences in personal tastes and expectations that the two spouses bring with them to their marriage.

Tensions such as these are not inevitable in marriages of this kind. The economic advantage of one side may be matched in the other by other forms of social distinction, such as political or artistic or intellectual achievement, in which case the problems that stem from personal feelings of inequality may not arise. The young man or woman of the lower class may be exceptional enough to transcend the difficulties that financial inequality presents. But these couples start their marriages with some conspicuous odds against them. Some might more readily achieve a satisfactory life together if they were free from dependence on either set of parents.

This possibility is the third course taken by a good many young people who marry before they have dependable means to support themselves. The demands upon their limited resources are very great. The fact that a considerable proportion of them fail to reach their occupational goals, or to remain married to each other, is not as noteworthy as the fact that so many of them succeed in doing both. They are usually faced with two major problems—maintaining themselves and continuing the occupational training of the young husband. The attempted solution is relatively uniform. The wife takes a full-time job and the husband takes as many part-time jobs as he can manage while in his training program. The couple is fortunate if the young woman has competent secretarial skills or is certified for a special occupation, such as teaching or nursing or social service. If so, her income will be sufficient for basic maintenance and it will be steady. If the husband has a special ability which can be profitably employed on a part-time basis, the couple will manage to support itself quite well. If both of them are only capable of filling odd jobs, their economic position will be precarious.

The business of supporting themselves is but one problem these couples face. Their means of solving it often strain the marriage in other ways. The commitments of the young wife to her job, to looking after her husband's needs, to the preparation of food, and to housekeeping take most of her time and energy. The commitments of the young husband to his training, his jobs, and often to part-time housekeeping leave him with little reserve capacity for other activities. Frequently, his jobs and obligations to his wife seriously interfere with his occupational training. Both husband and wife must sacrifice a good many of the companionate activities of their marriage. At the same time, both are cut off from friends and relatives by their crowded schedules.

Considering the very drastic changes that their marriages entail, and their rather meager preparation for them, it is remarkable how many young men and women succeed in meeting the demands of marriage and in consolidating their personal relationships as well. This suggests that a lack of training for specific tasks is not as hazardous in this country as it would be in some other societies. The training of youth in the United States seems to foster the ability to improvise, and more of family life is improvised in the United States than it is in tradition-bound societies regulated by an authoritarian elite. For those American couples who do succeed in achieving adult competence, with or without parental assistance, the fact that they have "grown up" together provides a dimension to their marriage that is probably not obtainable by people whose induction into family life is extensively regulated by their elders. This kind of experience is also an excellent foundation for the establishment of equality between husbands and wives—a cherished part of the American family ideal.

The heterogeneity of the American population is another factor that creates special marital problems in the United States. Ethnic, religious, racial, and even regional differences are present to a significant degree, and marriages between people who belong to different categories of the population are common.[2]

In general, American parents are extremely tolerant of their children's associating during childhood and youth with people

[2] "Among married couples in which the husband or wife were reported as Roman Catholic, 22 per cent of the husbands or wives reported that they were Protestants or Jews. For couples in which one spouse was reported as Protestant, 9 per cent of the husbands or wives were reported as Roman Catholic or Jewish, 7 per cent of the husbands or wives were reported as Protestant or Roman Catholic.

"About 4,148,000 children under 14 years old were in families in which the family head and his wife were not both reported as in the same major religious group." (U. S. Bureau of the Census: *Current Population Reports, Series P-20,* No. 79, 1958, p. 2.)

Different ethnic membership is significantly correlated with difference in religious affiliation.

who differ from them in race, religion, or class. It is not surprising, therefore, that a significant number of them wish to marry. Many are startled when their parents, who have been most tolerant of mixed companionship during their school years, strongly oppose these marriages. The opposition appears irrational to the young people—which indeed it is, unless they have been trained in religious orthodoxy or unless the choice involves racial differences, which are still widely accepted as a bar to marriage in the United States. To children who have grown up with friends whose backgrounds differ from their own, ethnic, class, and educational differences are not easily advanced as barriers to a happy marriage.

The knowledge that these social differences do make for difficulties in the integration of intimate personal relationships has for centuries been the reason for matchmaking in other societies, where parents make clear to their children from their earliest years the boundaries for a suitable choice of mate. American parents also understand that socially ill-matched couples will have difficulties in consolidating their marriages, but their failure to educate their children in ways that will convince them of this fact, coupled with the attenuation of parental authority, makes it difficult for most parents in the United States to prevent "mixed" marriages. However, they are often quick to take advantage of every friction between the new husband and wife to reassert their claims. "If you had only married (a nice Jewish or Catholic or Protestant boy or girl)" or "What can you expect from (the pertinent ethnic category)" are the kind of remarks and insinuations with which they reinforce their children's discontents. If the young married couple is dependent on parental assistance, this kind of sabotage can be very effective.

When people marry whose self-development has included markedly different, sometimes mutually exclusive, manners, tastes, expectations of achievement, and other outcomes of home training, these differences are enough to drive them apart even without external pressures. This is especially true of those habits and practices that pertain to early religious training, or to the deeply entrenched mores of an ethnic enclave, or to restrictive racial attitudes. These differences evoke anxiety and its derivatives such as shame, embarrassment, and anger—all serious impediments to intimacy. The self-organization of these couples resists compromise with the conflicting social needs of their mates. Their parents and other people are inclined to urge the priority of their convictions. Thus from within and without, socially ill-mated couples are handicapped by persistent claims stemming from their past. These are powerful pressures on a new, uncertain, and untried personal relationship; they are heavy odds against the success of a marriage.

Although the prognosis for the stability of mixed marriages is not as good as it is for homogeneous ones, some factors in the United States are favorable to them. A good many Americans are genuinely tolerant of relationships that include differences of religion, ethnic background, education, and class position. Interracial relationships are an outstanding exception; very few Americans are prepared to accept interracial marriages. In the course of the history of the United States there have been many mixed marriages and many of the children of these couples have no special allegiances to the particular categories of the population to which their parents and grandparents belonged. In the United States, young people who marry outside the social boundaries that their parents wish to maintain are not condemned to being outcasts. If they are cut off from the associations of their childhood and youth by their marriages, there are usually other people who are willing to accept them.

The conditions in which young Americans begin their married life are as various as their routes to marriage itself. The emphasis placed on the autonomy of each married couple puts the responsibility for their marital success largely on the personal resources of young husbands and wives. Nevertheless, the nature of their relationship to their parents, the degree to which their personal traits and expectations coincide, and the extent of their mastery over the means of access to what they need and want, influence the outcome of their individual efforts in important ways. But whether they succeed or not, by accident or design, the period in which American couples are almost completely absorbed in themselves is usually brought to a close after a relatively short time. The wife's pregnancy foreshadows its end. The birth of their first child marks the beginning of a new phase of family life.

THE CHILD-BEARING PHASE OF FAMILY LIFE

The advent of the first child brings a new nuclear family into being. In the United States, the autonomy that is usually enjoyed by young married couples, and their absorption in their personal satisfactions, leave many young Americans unprepared for the extensive changes in their ways of life that parenthood engenders. In societies in which young men and women are oriented to a large family circle and children are considered the chief justification for marriage, the birth of the first child increases the autonomy of its parents. In the United States, on the other hand, parenthood greatly curtails the new freedoms that marriage has provided; nor does it conspicuously enhance the social position of the new parents. Motherhood does not ensure security in marriage in the United States as it does in societies where family continuity is highly valued, and the social significance of fatherhood has become almost negligible. In principle, Americans consider the birth of their first child—or any other—a welcome and happy event, but whether it actually is or not depends upon a variety of individual circumstances.

The effect of the birth of their first child on a young American couple varies with the time that has elapsed between their marriage and this event. The fact that many Americans learn the rudiments of housekeeping, adult maintenance, and occupational skills only after they marry makes it desirable for newly married couples to enjoy a reasonable period of time together unencumbered by the flood of responsibilities that parenthood entails. This is especially the case when the young husband is either still in training for his future occupation or just beginning to practice it, and the young wife is the chief breadwinner. Most young women cannot continue to work after their child is born. The young men are compelled to assume responsibility for the maintenance of their wives and children. If this necessitates the abandonment of an occupational choice, it may be a potential source of bitterness for both husband and wife.

For young couples who are not prepared to support them·

selves and who have no help from parents, the economic and personal demands associated with an early pregnancy can be devastating. The increasing isolation of nuclear families from a circle of relatives has greatly augmented the responsibilities undertaken by parents. Current standards of child-rearing have increased the investment of time, energy, and material resources that American parents feel they must make on behalf of their children. These circumstances have encouraged the practice of planned parenthood in the United States. This practice conflicts with the mores of some segments of the American population, but the welfare of many young men and women and the future stability of their family units have come to make it more and more desirable to young married people.

The initial impact of parenthood is greater for the wife than it is for the husband. Pregnancy itself evokes great personal, as well as physical, changes and the care of her infant and household almost completely absorbs the mother's time and energy. Potentially, there is great satisfaction for her in the performance of these functions, but she is cut off from many activities and associations that were important to her before her baby was born. The effect of this drastic shift in the lives of the increasing number of young women who are college graduates is especially significant. Many of them are extremely ambivalent toward their children when they are forced to interrupt a professional career.

Much has been made of the technological aids to housekeeping available in the United States that are said to reduce the cares of American housewives to negligible proportions. However, in one report the Department of Agriculture concluded that the modern housewife may have a heavier load than her grandmother did, because mechanical devices have returned to her some of the chores—laundry, for example—that her grandmother had had done by others. Without their gadgets, of course, young American women with small children could hardly manage their household chores, but mechanical aids are no help in child-tending. The needs of infants and young children are impelling and imperative. Babies and toddlers cannot safely be left long without supervision. Unless her own mother is living nearby or other human help is available, young mothers are tied to the routines of child care, and in the United States assistance from reliable domestic help or from relatives is increasingly scarce.[3]

The fact that American men, more than men in other societies or in the United States in the past, perform household tasks and help with infant care is also often presented as evidence that the life of American mothers is easier than it once was, or than it is elsewhere. Like mechanical aids, occasional assistance from husbands has become almost a necessity for many American mothers who are without other help. Many American men do wash dishes, market on Saturdays, mind the children on Sundays, and perform other chores, but their own occupations make these activities sporadic; they do not constitute a substantial release from responsibilities for women.

American mothers of young children are usually on call twenty-four hours a day. If they have two or three children it is entirely possible that they do not have an uninterrupted night's sleep for periods as long as ten years. In these conditions, only very exceptional women can manage to maintain their circles of friends and keep up with earlier interests. A frequent complaint made by American women who have had several children before they reach the ages of thirty or thirty-five is that their absorption in the world of juveniles and household chores leaves them feeling stupid and dull. American women, and especially the increasingly large number who are college-educated, are not trained to expect personal fulfillment primarily in the execution of their family functions. Housekeeping and child tending do not evoke special commendation from others; therefore, for American women, they are not always sources of self-respect.

A serious result of the circumstances in which American women frequently spend their child-bearing years is the subordination of the husband-wife relationship to the demands of parent-

---

[3] "A study by Dr. Elizabeth Wiegand, at the New York State College of Home Economics at Cornell University, found that the typical homemaker works 9 hours daily. In a nationwide poll conducted for the General Electric Company, the figure was 58 per week.

"But these totals do not include child supervision. . . . A survey discloses 97 per cent of the country's housewives have no full-time paid help." (*This Week*, Oct. 9, 1954, pp. 7, 20.)

hood. The Family Service Association of America recently reported in a nationwide survey that "As the age of the first child increases from under 6, to 6 to 11, and finally to 12 to 17, the proportion of families reporting a marital problem declines rapidly while the proportion reporting a parent-child problem increases. When the oldest child is under six, surprisingly few young parents even report a parent-child problem, while about two in three request help on a marital problem. This contrast suggests that young children put a heavy strain on the marital relationship possibly because the wife has little time left for her husband when the babies are young. . . .

"Among couples married six years or less, about two-thirds mention a marital problem. The peak period apparently comes between the fifth and sixth year, when almost 80 per cent reported a marital problem." [4]

This strain on marital ties is particularly unfortunate in the United States because Americans place so much value on the companionate aspects of marriage. American women are chiefly valued *as women* for being physically attractive, good company, and successful at all kinds of things that have nothing to do with homes and children. The ideal wife in the United States is often described as one who is simultaneously a competent and attractive wife, mother, housekeeper, mistress, and friend. She is also expected to participate in community affairs. This is a very large order, yet a great many American women expect to fill it and strive to do so. Considering the demands upon their resources, it is surprising to note the degree to which many of them succeed.

But a great many women cannot cope with the variety of demands made upon them. Some expectations have to be abandoned and frequently it is the companionate aspects of their relation to their husbands that are sacrificed. As time passes, the only interests shared by many American husbands and wives are those that center around their children and the needs of the household and its members. This is not an unusual outcome between husbands and wives anywhere, but Americans expect more from their mates to begin with. Since there is no explicit double standard of

[4] Beck, Dorothy F.: *Patterns in Use of Family Agency Service* (New York: Family Service Association of America; 1962), pp. 16-17.

sexual behavior in the United States, American men are not morally free to seek sexual gratification and feminine companionship from women other than their wives. Yet in many instances their wives, once they are mothers, cannot continue to provide these stimulations. Husbands feel neglected and wives feel inadequate as well as deprived of personal satisfactions that they also had anticipated.

These are serious strains on marital relationships. Moral convictions about fidelity to spouses and responsibilities toward children conflict with equally widespread assumptions that personal satisfactions are the chief justification for the continuation of a relationship. This is why the effect of the birth of children is so contingent upon the integration of the relation between husbands and wives before this event. If an early pregnancy has interfered with the development of strong bonds between husbands and wives, the child-bearing years may prevent it altogether.

The birth of the first child presents the father with problems almost as great as those of the new mother. Advancement to substantial income is relatively slow, and economic demands during the child-rearing years tend to multiply faster than economic gains. This situation is complicated by the American ideal of a high material standard of living. Americans consider many luxuries to be necessities without which daily living would be impossible. Despite high wages and salaries in the United States, it is not easy for young Americans to meet current expenses. Many American families carry a substantial debt load incurred principally through long-term buying of household goods and by loans to cover emergencies such as illness or unemployment. "Today, personal debt is edging close to $200 billion; mortgage debt is approximately $140 billion, and consumer credit is about $55 billion." [5] This is encouraged by current economic practices in the United States. For many Americans, installment buying is the only means to the attainment of a material standard of living commensurate with their expectations and necessary for their self-respect. The increasing demands by young people in the United States for guarantees of economic security are related to the commitments

[5] Black, Hillel: *Buy Now Pay Later* (New York: William Morrow & Co., Inc.; 1961), p. xiii.

that family responsibilities impose on American breadwinners. Few of them can afford to take economic risks, even when young— a fact that also tends to limit the range of potential economic achievement for many.[6]

Occupational activities and associations in the United States are sharply differentiated from the activities and associations of the family. Families are not generally units of production. Residences are often located many miles from offices and factories. As men become more absorbed in their work, their participation in family life becomes limited. They leave their homes early and return late. The immersion of husbands and wives each in their own spheres leaves them with little time for each other. Fatherhood in the United States has the somewhat paradoxical effect of shifting husbands from the center of family organization. It ties them more and more to their occupational life by constantly increasing the economic needs that they are expected to satisfy.

While it tends to separate them in some ways, parenthood does bring other new concerns that both husband and wife can share. Young parents begin to view many aspects of their society in a new light. They begin to envisage the future in terms of a good community in which to raise their children. They become concerned about schools, adequate recreational facilities, proper companions. Parenthood tends to make conservatives of most people in many respects. The attractions of inadequate housing or bohemian neighborhoods fade once children are born. The childbearing period is the one in which many young Americans trek to suburbs, or at least seek better houses in better neighborhoods. They often become interested in politics for the first time because they see in it means for bringing about arrangements that they consider desirable for their children, or which will influence their own ability to provide for them. School systems become important and parents begin to take an interest in the selection of school boards. Church attendance is often resumed or increased as part of the religious training of children. In these ways, parenthood tends to tie parents to their communities as no other experience does.

Many values that their elders had urged upon them without

[6] Cf. *ibid.*, p. xiii, for extensive treatment of the subject.

much success are accepted by young American men and women when they begin to cultivate their own children. The need for social standards and restraints becomes apparent. Parenthood attaches young men and women more securely to the relatively systematic formulations of right and wrong, good and bad, desirable and undesirable that prevail in their society. Greater conformity is part of their new conservatism. In many societies young people are ready to "settle down" when they marry; in the United States this readiness is more likely to be manifest when they become parents.

The birth of children creates grandparents as well as parents. However, there is so little institutionalization of the grandparent-grandchild relationship in the United States that it is impossible to generalize about it. The two sets of grandparents have usually rearranged their own establishments and spheres of activity by the time their children have married. Unless the care of grandchildren devolves upon them—and this is not usually the case—the lives of grandparents are not significantly affected by the child-bearing phase of the new nuclear family.

The majority of Americans bring the child-bearing phase of their family life to a close after a relatively short time. They consider that family size is a matter of personal choice. This is consistent with the American emphasis on individual achievement and equal participation for men and women in extrafamilial activities. Limitation of the size of families promises release from the often severe restrictions of the child-bearing years and makes way for the realization of some of the personal expectations of parents. When the youngest child is ready for kindergarten, American nuclear families enter a new phase.

THE CHILD-REARING PHASE OF FAMILY LIFE

The child-rearing phase of family life is mainly concerned with the consolidation and development of family resources rather than with their expansion. It is more amenable to order and routine, less demanding of the energies of husbands and wives and, as a rule, is subject to fewer strains than the earlier phases of family life. Parents are usually freer to pursue their own interests than they have been for a good many years.

Decrease in the biological dependence of children, their entrance into school and relations with peers, and their increasing self-regulation release mothers from the need to supervise them constantly. Most women have mastered housekeeping skills by this time. They have learned the arts and techniques of child care and child training. Consequently, the child-rearing phase provides the American mother with some welcome leisure. As for the father, increases in income may be expected to have reduced his difficulties in meeting current expenses. Some of his basic investments in family goods and for family protection have probably been paid for. Thus, this phase of family life provides opportunties for the satisfaction of some of the needs of husbands and wives other than those that are associated with the well-being of their children. For their future comfort as individuals and as a couple, it is extremely important for American parents to take advantage of these opportunities. In the United States, total investment in children is a poor investment.

Not many American parents can return to anything that resembles their pre-parental freedoms. The various and changing demands of children require adaptations and modifications of relations with them. Parental mediation between siblings is often necessary. The material needs of the family, especially the growing wants of children in these typically child-centered families, preclude any great self-indulgence by parents.

Women whose husbands' incomes are low work when they can to improve their family's standard of living. Most of these women are employed in unskilled jobs, and so long as the country is prosperous they have little difficulty in finding them. Women who were professionally trained, or who had started business careers before marriage and full-time family care, can also manage during the child-rearing period to return to their earlier interests. Most of these women find it difficult, however, to extricate themselves from the complicated round of activities to which they have become accustomed. Furthermore, they face some obstacles from the professional and business world. Professional knowledge and techniques accumulate and change with great rapidity. An absence of ten or twelve years makes further training necessary. Business organizations do not generally consider the experience of running households and raising children an asset to their operations; they are seldom eager to re-employ a woman who has been out of the field for long. Another problem that confronts these women is the possible effect their working may have on their husbands. The reaction of husbands to wives who work for satisfactions other than increasing a low family income is not predictable.

More American women place high value on careers than prepare themselves for one. Some would personally be content to find their fulfillment within the boundaries of their family life, but the limited recognition accorded domestic accomplishments frequently moves even these to seek new sources of esteem. They are most likely to choose activities that are closely associated with their family life, such as membership in Parent-Teacher Associations and volunteer services in their communities. Some who did not go to college turn to Adult Education courses to enrich their personal lives and to equal what they hope their children will achieve in the realm of education.

During the child-rearing years American children are primarily absorbed in their school life and their associations with their peers. It is this separation of the children from their homes for many hours of the day that enables their mothers to pursue their own careers. Whether or not this kind of parting of the ways between mothers and their children is desirable for the children is a question that is much debated in the United States. Much seems to depend upon the success with which the child-bearing years are negotiated, the degree of harmony between parents, whether or not the economic level achieved by parents enables them to provide competent help in the home, and the personal integration and abilities of the particular children involved. There seems little doubt that the expansion of the lives of American parents beyond their family boundaries is good for parents.

Satisfactions for American men at this time depend largely on their successes in their careers. Their well-being is enhanced by wives who love them, provide for their comfort, share their leisure, and manage their homes and other activities in ways that command respect from other people. They are proud and happy with children who move from one stage of development to the next without too much difficulty and regularly succeed in those things expected of them. They are distressed when things have not gone well with their wives and children. But American men are not without solace for family difficulties, if they are successful in their work.

The self-respect of many American men is more dependent upon their reputation in their businesses and professions than it is upon their success as husbands and fathers. American women often complain of neglect by husbands who reserve little time for family members or family functions. This is one of the conditions that impel some American women to seek careers of their own. There are few rewards for Patient Griseldas in the United States; in fact, husbands often pay more attention to wives who command respect from others by achievements outside their homes. As fathers, the American men who are the most "successful" are often the least personally gratifying to their children since they are the ones who often have too little time to spend with the young. The economic practices and pressures in which American men are involved have moved many of them to the periphery of their family circles.

The goals of the child-rearing years in American nuclear families promise a great deal to all their members. For the young, development of their resources and expanding participation in the social realm provide immediate satisfactions and promise future ones. Husbands and wives are able to retrieve some of the individual and personal pleasures possible in their relationship to each other, and they may renew interests, activities, and friendships that they were forced to neglect when their children were small. The extent to which these things are done determines both the stability of families and the welfare of individuals. Although there are a number of almost unavoidable strains for American families during these years, they are neither overwhelming nor insurmountable.

The functional unity of the nuclear family itself reaches its peak during the child-rearing phase. Each family unit during this period tends to develop some of the characteristics of a closed group. Associations are largely restricted to a home circle made up of the nuclear unit, a few relatives, and a few close friends. Family solidarity is reinforced by what may be called a "family culture." This evolves to a considerable extent around the special occasions in the life-careers of family members—birthdays, graduations, promotions, arrivals, and departures. It includes family variations of national celebrations, such as Thanksgiving and Christmas. These shared experiences strengthen the mutual attachments of family members and probably evoke for each member an image of the family as a deeply significant unit. This image is fostered by the fact that each family is treated as a unit by the members of the community in which it lives. Successes achieved by any one member brings approval to all; failures bring disapproval for all. This kind of collective responsibility makes family members sensitive to the public performances of each of them.

The functional unity of the American family declines with the passing of the child-rearing period. In the United States, the future achievements of children depend upon their integration into other organizations and the establishment of nuclear families of their own. The next phase of family life is chiefly concerned with launching them into a network of relationships and organizations independent of the family. In the United States, the division between family and other membership is exceptionally wide. (Indeed, nepotism—preferential treatment for relatives in non-family organizations—is considered unethical by most Americans.) The concluding states of child-rearing bring changes that clearly distinguish a new phase in the family life of most Americans.

THE CHILD-LAUNCHING PHASE OF FAMILY LIFE

In any developmental series, the later stages are more varied than the early ones. Their character depends upon the successes and failures of particular people in early phases as well as upon general factors that affect everyone. This is true of the launching phase of the nuclear family in the United States. The economic achievement of the husband, the competence and maturity of both the wife and husband, the range and depth of their relationship, and the degree of social competence to which they have raised their children—all determine the accomplishments that are possible in the launching phase and the ease with which the transition from this to the next phase will be achieved. Nevertheless, there are general as well as individual factors that affect this phase of family life in the United States.

When children reach late adolescence, the future occupation of boys and the marriages of both boys and girls become of paramount concern to family members. Decisions concerning these matters are crucial for the transition of young people to full adult participation in their societies everywhere. However, in the United States the family elders generally have little control over access to other organizations. This is a result, in large part, of the division of labor common to a highly industrialized society. The American family is not an important functional unit in the economic and other major spheres, and can do little to help its children enter those spheres. In some complex societies (the Russian and Scandinavian, for example), non-family arrangements—political parties or state economic organizations—take over where family organization leaves off. Some of these arrangements seem to be efficient in helping to solve the problems of young adults.

American children must depend primarily on their own efforts to find membership in new relationships and organizations, most of which have no connection with those to which they have been attached. At this time, many of them leave home for schools or military service or jobs in different localities. Even when they are not geographically separated from parents, their schedules seldom coincide with family routines. Households become service stations of a sort, used at the individual convenience of each member. Only special occasions bring all members of the family together at one time. Unless the relationships between family members have been firmly established, this diffusion of activities and goals will mark the beginning of the disintegration of the family as a unit and of family relationships as well. When the launching phase is ended, meaningful family relationships between Americans persist primarily by virtue of affectional ties, since few widely accepted moral imperatives move Americans to maintain relationships that are no longer useful or pleasing.

In most technologically advanced societies parents are often unable to bridge the gap between the family unit and their children's jobs and marriages. Their position in relation to their children at this point is especially frustrating to American parents for whom the indulgence of children is one of their chief privileges. Their inability to provide what they know their children need is the beginning of their feeling of futility which increases with the progressive loss of their functional utility as parents. American children are variously prepared to make their way alone, though almost all of them are accustomed to a great deal of help from elders on demand. The failure of their parents to help them to solve their problems at this stage is sometimes profoundly disturbing to American young people, and currently there is a flood of writing about the crisis of American youth.

The experience of many American families during the launching phase supports the conclusion that serious inadequacies in our social order do exist. Some parents cannot cope with the overcomplexity that tends to characterize relations with children at this stage of family life. It is a period with a high incidence of rebellious and extreme behavior of many kinds among American young people, such as disastrous marriages and delinquency. Nor do the confusions of this phase of family life seem confined to any particular segment of the population. They are conspicuous in all classes, for most religious and ethnic categories, and for people at all levels of education. This conclusion is supported in a recent national Family Service survey:[7]

> . . . it is apparently the approach of adolescence that precipitates a crisis in parent-child relationships. For families whose oldest child is 12 to 17 years of age, parent-child problems top the list of worries brought to Family Agencies and marital problems drop to distinctly second place. (p. 17)
>
> A chart on page 4 shows the religious preferences of agency clients in relation to the religious distribution of the U.S. populations and concludes: "In general, the religious preference of the two groups are surprisingly similar. (p. 4)

[7] Beck: op. cit.

. . . agency clients tend to be somewhat better educated than the general population. Proportionately fewer
family heads in applicant families have not gone beyond
elementary school than in the case of the general population. On the other hand, many more have graduated
from high school and college.

Note that all social classes are users of Family Service. Roughly 9 per cent of the families applying were
defined as "upper class." The heads of families in this
category typically have graduated from college, hold professional or managerial positions, and have incomes of
$8,000 or more.

. . . the "middle class." The typical family head
. . . would be a small businessman, clerk, or sales person who had gone little if any beyond high school. . . .
these . . . contribute nearly half the total sample. This
proportion is well in excess of that suggested by the now
out-of-date image that Family Agencies serve primarily
the poor, the humble, and the unfortunate. (p. 9)

The remaining 43 per cent of the families served by
agencies belong to the . . . "lower classes." A typical
family head in this group would be a factory worker,
laborer, or domestic worker who has not gone beyond
elementary school.

These figures represent pooled national data that
average out local agency differences. (p. 26)

The positive side of the American situation is the openend-
edness of family arrangements. When opportunity is available,
there is little in American family institutions to prevent children
from taking advantage of it. The typical desire of American parents to see their children do better than they have done contributes to this freedom. Most parents are willing to do without
direct participation in their children's ultimate achievements and
are content in the knowledge that their sons and daughters have
attained a more ample life than they had. When American young
people do manage to find their way by means of associations quite
removed from their families, most of their parents do not stand in

their way. They regard this as the exercise of the individual's right to improve his lot.

The successful launching of children into the larger world has many positive aspects for parents, too. If the husband has been reasonably successful economically and if the wife has continued her personal development in areas outside motherhood and housekeeping, the couple may finally achieve something like their youthful image of their life together—namely, of a companionate relationship with a great deal of freedom to pursue their own interests. In this event, they have a period between family responsibilities and the inroads of age in which leisure, personal maturity, the knowledge of obligations well met, and social and economic means combine to make these the "best years of their lives."

Potentially, the launching phase of family life can be a period of rich and varied collaboration that provides pleasure to both parents and children. But family life in the United States is full of hazards and has few institutional supports, and the outcome of the long period of child-rearing is uncertain. When American parents and children bring this phase of their family life to a close, whether for better or for worse, the principal functions of the nuclear unit are ended. It may continue as an affectional center that reassembles from time to time as long as the parents live and have a household of their own; however, its assets and liabilities are dispersed. They are manifest in the personal competence of the children and in the ability of husband and wife to take up their life as a couple enriched by the knowledge of a family career brought to a distinguished conclusion.

THE AGING COUPLE—PERIOD OF RETIREMENT

Once the launching phase of family life is over, American couples are generally left to their own devices. In societies in which families are organized around several generations, there is no equivalent break in family relationships. The place of the members of the oldest generation is usually assured by some customary associations with children and grandchildren and by their own administrative functions as elders. American nuclear families provide no such security for their aging members. Instead, many of them face a period of drastic readjustments at a time of life when major adaptations typically become more difficult.

A felicitous old age in the United States depends largely upon individual effort and good fortune, not upon guarantees of support from children or services rendered by the state. The chief advantage in American family arrangements for the older generations is the absence of many institutional limitations upon their activities. Although they have no substantial guarantees of help from children, neither do they have many institutionalized obligations toward them after they are adult. When they have provided the means for their own maintenance, both economic and personal, American old people are freer than most people in other societies. For the men and women in the United States who have cultivated their own abilities, sustained their interest in each other and in friends, succeeded in evoking respect as well as affection from their children, and secured a reasonably ample income for themselves, the last years of life can be immensely rewarding.

Some categories of people in the American population are more likely than others to enjoy the freedom that old age brings. Professional people do rather well. Their work requires extensive development of personal skills and more opportunity to establish durable relationships with others. One of the great advantages for most of them is the fact that they are not forced to retire before they wish to, and so are spared the economic dependence and the loss of meaningful activity that are so damaging to many retired Americans. Those Americans whose family life is still patterned by the institutions of other societies have better guarantees for a rewarding old age than do more typically American families. Finally, since exceptional economic means go a long way toward mitigating the hazards of old age, many upper-class Americans spend their declining years in personal as well as physical comfort.

Many Americans cannot look forward to the last years of their lives with tranquillity, however. Ironically, their child-centered family organization, in which they invest so much of their own resources for so long, guarantees little to many of them when they are old. A moral presumption prevails that children will care for their parents if they are in need, but even if the children have the will, their ability to do so is often extremely limited. They have neither the income to support parents as well as themselves and their children, nor space in their homes for them. There is no functional place in nuclear households for grandparents. It is as unwelcome and uncomfortable for aging American parents to become dependent upon their married children, and especially to live with them, as it is for young couples to start their married life in the homes of their parents.

Physical disabilities are not the chief problem of aging parents in the United States today. A high standard of living and medical advances are not only prolonging life; they are improving health. Physical incapacitation, if it comes, tends to come later in life than it used to. The distress of the oldest generation is more likely to be due to social dislocations. When American women find themselves retired from family life at fifty-five or sixty and American men retired from their work at sixty-five, their plight is similar to that of unemployed people of any age. The attendant difficulties are similar: lowered income, depression and feelings of uselessness, isolation due to the loss of long-standing relationships, boredom, hopelessness due to the absence of commitments and the loss of a meaningful future.

The cumulative effects of changes in family and economic life that have dispossessed old people in the United States were largely unforeseen and unintended. Despite the conditions in American society that led to an emphasis on youth, older people were not easily displaced in the past, however impatient the young might be. Retirement was initially conceived as a benefit to aging men. But neither current pensions nor social security benefits are sufficient for their needs today. Increases in the cost of living and medical care, which have to be met with the lowered income that retirement brings, have reduced many aging people to a subsistence standard of living. Geographic mobility in the United States has contributed to the social isolation of old people. Children, relatives, and friends of early years are often widely scattered. There has been a great trek of old people to parts of the country where climate favors their health and their pocketbooks. Although these settlements of old and retired people provide new contacts with people like themselves, they are rootless associations and do not always compensate for the loss of contact with family and friends. For many old people, this move amounts to exile.

Current family arrangements in the United States seem to be inadequate to provide even a reasonably good life for enough of the aging members of the American population. The plight of the aging and the aged has become a matter of national concern. Reform of family practices is generally viewed as less feasible than support by non-family organizations. Some new provisions have been instituted by large corporations and labor unions. "Fringe benefits" are becoming part of many jobs. Economic organizations are providing housing, health services, recreational opportunities, and pensions as a regular part of their programs for employees. Voluntary insurance plans of all kinds have become widespread. At the same time, political agencies—city, state, and federal —are expanding social security benefits for the old and unemployed and will probably increase health services in the near future.

There is reason to hope that institutional programs of regular assistance to the old will relieve some of the anxieties about declining years that complicate family life and will allow more grandparents to live out their lives near their children and grandchildren. The life of American nuclear families could be enriched by augmenting parent-child and grandparent-grandchild relationships.

DIVORCE IN THE UNITED STATES

The high rate of divorce in the United States warrants special comment. Attitudes toward divorce are related to the general conceptions about marriage. It would be inconsistent for a population that places great stress on free choice for marriage, based almost exclusively on individual impulse, to impose many restrictions on access to divorce. So long as personal satisfaction is deemed the chief justification for continuance of a relationship, personal dissatisfaction is a logical justification for ending it. Although Americans have to formulate their grounds for divorce in terms that fit legal requirements, the main reason for the separation of American husbands and wives is their personal incompatibility.

As young people, many Americans are unprepared for the duties that marriage entails. As adults, they are often equally unprepared for the difficulties involved in obtaining a divorce, or for its consequences. The law is responsible for some of the initial difficulties that confront Americans when they seek a divorce. Divorce laws are not uniform throughout the United States. Legally, divorces can be granted only in the place of residence. As a result, Americans do not in fact have equal access to a right that many of them have come to assume should be available to every citizen. This has led to notorious evasion of certain laws and a kind of "bootlegging" of divorce. Like all black-market activity, this corrupts the legal profession and turns otherwise respectable people into perjurers. It also raises the price of the commodity. Divorce is expensive in the United States, another reason for the inequality of access to it. All of these factors contribute to a high rate of desertion, "the poor man's divorce."

Adjustments to divorce are at least as demanding for most people as adjustments to marriage. For both husband and wife, divorce is a manifestation of failure in some degree; this is likely to be unnerving unless a person is seeking a divorce in order to marry again. The fact that both spouses are rarely equally desirous of dissolving their marriage is another source of personal strain. The disruption of the circle of friends in which both husband and wife have moved is a common source of anxiety and tension. People take sides in a divorce. Newly divorced people experience a period of uncertainty concerning their acceptability to others that aggravates the damage divorce has done to their self-respect.

Except for the unusually well-to-do, divorce entails economic losses and burdens. For women, it usually means a sharp decrease in economic support, a fact that has been overshadowed by the glaring publicity given the divorce settlements of a few very rich people. Divorced women's expenses for rent, board, and maintenance are proportionately higher. They frequently have to supplement their alimony by going to work. If they are young and childless this necessity is no special burden, but women with children find it difficult to support themselves unless they have had special training before their marriage. In all but exceptional cases, divorce entails hardships on women with children. Neither alimony nor allowances for children are usually adequate for the maintenance of a suitable household and the growing needs of the young.

Divorce is also a financial burden for men. They, too, must provide for their own maintenance. The alimony that they pay may be insufficient for the needs of their ex-wives, but it is a large percentage of their incomes and curtails their own spending. Besides, payments made to a person from whom one is alienated are almost inevitably resented. If and when men remarry, the continued cost of their divorces often constitutes a burden that interferes with their new families.

Whatever the untoward effects of divorce on adults, it is the consequences to their children that make the high divorce rate a matter for national attention in the United States. Most divorced Americans remarry, and the reassortment of childless couples would not evoke great public concern. Nor does the stability of American society depend upon family control over an extensive range of resources and functions. Family units normally tend to break up anyway when parental functions are fulfilled. It is the fact that nuclear family units in the United States have become highly specialized agencies for the care and socialization of the young, and the fact that there is no dependable circle of relatives to which children can turn in times of trouble, that make the dissolution of nuclear families before children reach adulthood a social problem. Unlike their parents, children are not seeking greater personal satisfactions when their parents divorce, nor can they modify in their own interest the portentous changes and shifts in relationships that the divorce of their parents brings. Their inclusion in a new family is full of potential hazards. At best, a stepfather or stepmother, and step-sisters and -brothers, and half-sisters and -brothers, represent a family of great complexity for children.

It is true that a badly deteriorated relationship between a husband and wife may be more disturbing to their children than their separation. In the United States where the autonomy and isolation of the nuclear unit places the welfare of children almost exclusively in the hands of their parents, the child-parent relationship is continuously and directly affected by the relation of the parents to each other. Whatever affects the parents affects the children with almost equal intensity, although not in the same ways. Chronic conflict between husband and wife, therefore, seriously interferes with the welfare of their children. Under these circumstances, divorce may benefit the children.

Although their dependency makes the divorce of their parents profoundly disturbing to children, divorce law in the United States protects them less than it does their elders. Custody provisions vary greatly and are often pernicious. It seems reasonable to award children to their mothers when an extended family arrangement is lacking. Men are not homemakers and it is rare that their mothers or sisters can, or will, take over the care of their children. Yet there is no guarantee that the children's mothers are the more competent parent; frequently, too, their homemaking skills are unavailing because they must work. Children who are allotted to each parent for fixed periods of time suffer the consequences of having no stable center of organization for their lives. Further, they are subjected to constant shifts between sets of friends and relatives who are sometimes hostile to each other.

Child allowances awarded at the time of the divorce are often nominal in relation to the needs of the children. They seldom include arrangements for increase in proportion to expanding costs of the children's education, recreation, and material equipment. Legally, no provision is demanded for children once they reach their majority despite the fact that a great many young people in the United States need assistance for adequate professional training beyond that age. Furthermore, there is almost no supervision of the actual use of money allotted to children. Mothers can neglect them and spend their money on themselves. Fathers can fail to fulfill the legal contracts made at the time of the divorce. Appeal to the courts by either spouse is possible, but it is difficult, costly, not very productive for children, and is rarely made. In short, divorce procedures in the United States provide remarkably little protection for the children of divorced parents.

Parents can do a great deal to mitigate the strain that their divorce inescapably imposes on their children. They are equally capable, however, of ensuring that their divorce will be a disaster for their young. In the United States, the outcome of divorce, like almost everything else that concerns families, depends largely on the individual maturity and skills of the people involved, since there are no permanent family organizations to absorb the members of these disrupted homes. If parents are immature, or excessively bitter, or both, they may use their children as pawns and weapons in their own conflict. They may use their children as compensatory sources of affection and attention, bribing them to get preferential treatment. Such behavior is severely damaging to the development and well-being of children. On the other hand, people who are capable of recognizing that their parental relationship is not ended by their divorce are usually able to separate it from their marital dissatisfaction and to continue a sensible and cooperative association with regard to their children.

Gains and losses for family members following divorce are highly problematic. Yet, the right to divorce is consistent with American family institutions, and it has some general assets. When divorce is available to either spouse, this outlet tends to limit the potential abuse of one partner by the other and to facilitate compromise between them. Only large corporate families can absorb a center of serious inadequacy, and even in corporate families, rigid restrictions on divorce drive many women to escape intolerable marital conditions through suicide. This was not uncommon in traditional China.

> In 1935 when statistics were grossly incomplete, 1,353 suicides were reported in 244 counties and in 22 provinces. Of the total, 351, or 26.0 per cent, were caused by domestic discord or matrimonial difficulties, which contributed the largest single item among all causes of suicide in China. . . . Among the 351 cases of suicide caused by family conflict 253, or 72 per cent, were women.[8]

When family functions are concentrated in a nuclear unit, failure to consolidate the husband-wife relationship obstructs parental per-

---

[8] *Statistical Abstract of the Republic of China* (Nanking, 1935), pp. 360-1. Quoted in Yang, C. K.: *The Chinese Family in the Communist Revolution* (Cambridge, Mass.: The Technological Press; 1959), p. 107.

formance as well. Complete failure in the fulfillment of marital and parental functions threatens the persistence of any family, and every society makes the separation of husbands and wives possible under some circumstances.

Statistical correlations between high incidence of "broken homes" and delinquency, criminality, and mental illness have led some Americans to conclude that restrictions on divorce would curtail the incidence of these deviations. This conclusion seems unwarranted. In the first place, there are more "broken homes" than there are divorced couples. In the second place, analysis of family life in the United States suggests that the high rate of divorce is itself a product of the same factors that produce personal deviations and breakdown. Some of these are rooted in the relation of American families to non-family organizations.

THE RELATION OF NUCLEAR FAMILIES TO NON-FAMILY ORGANIZATIONS

Members of American nuclear families are less bound to each other than are people in societies in which families exercise more power over the resources and organizations of the society itself, and in which family obligations take precedence over individual achievement. In the United States, the characteristic emphasis on personal ends rather than on family welfare is made possible by the high standard of living and the differentiation of means to obtain what individuals need and want. The alternatives to family-provided goods and services are many, except for the very young.

Although this condition frees Americans from a great many personal obligations, it also deprives them of important rights. Among these rights are assistance in raising children, financial help in the early years of marriage and occupational experience or in crises, nursing in sickness, and care and protection in old age. These are all services that contribute greatly to human well-being, and people often have difficulty in supplying them by their own efforts alone.

The dependence of family members on non-family organizations for the satisfaction of many of their basic needs has not been advantageous to the maintenance of unity in American families. The needs of families as such have not been taken into account to any large extent by non-family organizations. For example, public school education has provided American society with a basis for consensus among the population as a whole, but often the values and goals it has provided are so different from those in some families that it has acted as a wedge between children and their parents. Economic organizations have not geared their policies concerning wages, hiring and firing, shifts in location, or production to the requirements of family maintenance. Despite all the sentiment about the sanctity of the family in the United States, the general assumption held by most Americans has been that the maintenance of the unity of particular families is almost solely the responsibility of each married couple.

Recently, responsible American citizens have begun to recognize that this is a frail basis for family stability, and too onerous an undertaking for only two individuals. The policy of organizations in the other spheres of life in the United States is changing. Business organizations, schools, and churches are all helping families by helping their members with fringe benefits, scholarships, marriage counseling, and other forms of assistance. Public agencies, at both the local and federal level, are becoming more and more involved with the study of personal disintegration and the family difficulties that are associated with it. New agencies are being added to old ones to help Americans who do not succeed in helping themselves. The federal government has begun to assist families by augmenting family income, providing housing and loans for education, assisting the children of unemployed people, and supplying food and clothing for people on relief. Agitation for national health services increases steadily. In short, the place of American families in the total network of organizations that service the American population is changing. The strains on the nuclear family that result from its isolation from a circle of relatives are being alleviated by reducing its isolation from non-family organizations.

Whatever the assets and liabilities inherent in American family practices, they are consistent with other American practices and widespread assumptions. Americans emphasize individual development, effort, and reward in all spheres of life. They demand freedom of choice in all relationships and expect to dissolve them when they are personally unsatisfactory. They are opposed to strict and stable hierarchical relationships and the compulsory assignment of tasks. They assume a right to social and geographic mobility and view the improvement of their lot almost as a duty. They do not consider themselves their brothers' keepers, except by choice. They pursue new techniques, goods, and associations, rather than cultivate and preserve old ones. In keeping with these sentiments and expectations, American families provide a maximum of individual freedom and fix few limits on the range of development or activities of their members. The correlate of this is that they tend to provide a minimum of individual security.

Since the autonomous nuclear family is eminently suitable to life in a large, complex, and industrialized society such as the United States, and is in harmony with American emphasis on individual achievement and freedom of choice, remedies for family ills in the United States will probably not try to change the nature of the family itself but will continue to take the form of support from economic and political organizations. Welfare benefits that provide families with assistance during the inevitable periods of strain that are associated with births, illness, unemployment, old age, and death would probably provide most American couples with enough security to enable them to meet the routine maintenance needs of their families. In this event, the majority of Americans would be better able to realize the exceptional potentialities for the enrichment of their personal lives that are inherent in their family arrangements.

SUGGESTED READINGS

CALHOUN, ARTHUR W. *A Social History of the American Family.* 3 vols. New York: Barnes & Noble, 1917-1919.

A detailed history of the American family from Colonial times to World War I.

CATHER, WILLA. *My Antonia.* New York: Houghton, Mifflin, 1961.

A vivid story of a Bohemian immigrant family in Nebraska.

HAGEDORN, HERMAN. *The Hyphenated Family.* New York: Macmillan, 1960.

Autobiography of an American writer, born in Germany, that clearly reveals the problems that face an immigrant family in adapting to American life.

LERNER, MAX. *America as a Civilization.* New York: Simon and Schuster, 1957.

In Vol. II, Chapter 8, Mr. Lerner provides a sound, generalized account of the typical life-cycle of many Americans, including their family life.

SIRJAMAKI, JOHN. *The American Family in the Twentieth Century.* Cambridge: Harvard University Press, 1953.

A readable discussion of the emergence of the prevailing autonomous nuclear family in the United States.

WHYTE, WILLIAM H., JR. *The Organization Man.* Garden City: Doubleday, 1956.

In Part VII Mr. Whyte presents a vivid picture of family life in the new suburbs. Based on extensive interviews.

THE CORPORATE FAMILY
IN CONFUCIAN CHINA

■

Characteristics of
Traditional Chinese Society
That Influenced Family Life

THERE IS perhaps no better contrast to the isolated nuclear family in the United States than the large corporate family that flourished in Confucian China for two thousand years. These two forms of family organization represent the smallest and the largest known family arrangements. The size and complexity of corporate families, their power over their members, and their influence upon their societies result in characteristics of family life that all but reverse the advantages and disadvantages of life in autonomous nuclear families.

Although large corporate families were never the most numerous in China, their influence and power were great and pervasive. As the fullest realization of the prevailing Confucian ideals of Chinese culture, the corporate form represented the normative family ideal to a majority of Chinese. The typical Chinese corporate family was a clan made up of a series of partially autonomous extended families guided by executive and administrative councils of elders. Thus the clan sometimes included thousands of members widely scattered around the country. Its chief functional unit—the one that most often constituted a single household—was the extended family of two or three generations. The *ideal* household was one in which several of these units were integrated into a complex organization that included four or five generations and all the collateral relatives in the male line. In these "great" families and in the more usual large extended ones, nuclear families of husband, wife, and their children were only a small link in a large network of family relationships.

In practice, this type of family could be fully developed only by the upper classes. The conditions of life among peasants and the many poor people in China could not support such a family or maintain, in full, the Confucian pattern of social relationships between young and old, and between men and women. In the first place, the poor could not afford to keep all their children together. Those who could not be gainfully employed in their family's occupations were placed as servants, apprentices, or even as slaves in the households and workshops of the rich. Secondly, since the mortality rate is always higher among the poor than among the well-to-do, more children of lower class families died in infancy and childhood and more of their parents died before reaching old age. In addition, poverty often reduced the application of the elaborate Confucian rules for family relationships to terms of address that denoted social distance, and such customs as the ones which prescribed that a wife must walk behind her husband and speak only when spoken to, and that parents must receive preferential treatment. Confucian manners were largely those of the Chinese gentry.

While the crushing poverty in which many Chinese lived kept the majority of Chinese households moderately small, the variety of relationships in them was still greater than that usually found in a nuclear family. Obligations between relatives were recognized even if they could not be fulfilled, and effective family relations extended beyond household units. The domination of parents over their sons and their sons' wives and children kept these families bound together even when they lived in separate households. Ties between brothers and between first cousins were intimate, and certain obligations to second cousins were recognized. The significance of this kinship circle provided collective strength for the common people whose households were small. Even for them, a semblance of the Confucian corporate family organization was effective.

> The structural principle of dominance by parents and stratification of status and distribution of function by sex and age is applicable to the organization of kinship units of all sizes, from the small family of the common people to the big family of the well-to-do, even to the clan with hundreds or thousands of members. Whatever the size of the unit, any individual member can readily find his or her specific place in this organizational scheme.[1]

Moreover, many of these smaller families in the villages worked for the local gentry and bore their names. Since in China all people of the same name were assumed to have had a common ancestor at some point in time, the people in the villages to a degree felt themselves to be part of the clans to which the great families belonged. Thus, the clan's influence on the lower classes was often direct and extensive.

The strength of the Confucian family ideal is indicated by the fact that whenever the economic plight of the lower and peasant classes improved, their families increased in size, their family relationships were patterned according to Confucian tradition, and, if their good fortune continued, they finally built their courtyards in the pattern of the gentry and became one of them. This phenomenon is succinctly described by C. K. Yang:

> A significant and well-known aspect of the Chinese traditional family is the integration of extended kinship circle, normally within three generations along the paternal lineage, into a single household whenever economic

[1] Yang, C. K.: *The Chinese Family in the Communist Revolution* (Cambridge, Mass.: The Technological Press; 1959), p. 10.

conditions permitted. The Chinese family in this sense was like a balloon, ever ready to expand whenever there was wealth enough to inflate it. As soon as there was enough land or other forms of production to employ the married sons, they would remain in the father's household, with property and income managed in common under the leadership and authority of the parents, and the process of expansion of the small household into a "big family" began.[2]

In Confucian Chinese society few aspects of life were untouched by family ties. The clans, through their extended families, controlled their members from the cradle to the grave. They were important units in political and economic life, and they were centers of education and religious ceremony. The pervasive influence of family relationships projected the family pattern on many non-family relationships. Teachers, government officials, scholars, employers, friends, and neighbors were addressed as "fathers," "uncles," and "brothers." Old people were generally called "grandmothers" and "grandfathers." The penetration of the clans and large families into all spheres of traditional Chinese society makes it imperative, for an understanding of the corporate family, to consider some of the general characteristics of that society.

CULTURAL HOMOGENEITY IN CONFUCIAN SOCIETY

It is impossible to do justice in a brief summary to a society that has been functioning for thousands of years. That one can generalize about it at all owes to the fact that for about two thousand years a remarkable cultural unity, based on Confucian principles was an important basis for its stability. By the Tang Dynasty (A.D. 618-907) the preference of emperors for Confucian philosophy made its principles the official doctrine of Chinese society. Knowledge of Confucian principles became essential for passing the competitive examinations for the Civil Service, the means by which the administrators of the realm were selected. Al-

[2] *Ibid.*, p. 9.

though this system of competitive examinations was modified and expanded from time to time, it remained fundamentally intact until the twentieth century. All formal education was oriented to the imperial examinations. The association of high office with scholarship gave the educated class exceptionally high prestige in China. Scholar-officials dominated the society. Their values and manners, largely Confucian, were the basis for a high level of consensus concerning proper public and private behavior for a heterogeneous and highly individuated people.

> Traditional Chinese society was composed of numerous semi-autonomous local units. . . . As a national system, these units were integrated, not so much by extensive functional interdependence and centralized control as by a fairly uniform institutional framework which enabled Chinese people everywhere to act together as a group on the basis of a common system of values.[3]

The cultural homogeneity in the Chinese political system was reinforced by Chinese family organization which also was based on Confucian doctrine. Traditional Chinese society was integrated by deliberate emphasis on family continuity. The individual life of a traditional Chinese was conceived as the prolongation of that of his father and grandfathers, and he assumed that his own progeny would transmit the individual in him to eternity. Hence time, which tends to be measured in terms of a single human life span in Western European societies and in the United States, was measured in centuries in China. This was a long view which helped to slow down the rate of change, but it provided a large measure of psychological security for a population that was often exposed to extreme physical danger.

POLITICAL ORGANIZATION IN CHINESE SOCIETY

Confucian doctrine prescribed a strictly hierarchical system of relationships, rooted in the family but extending to all other relationships, including that of the Emperor to his subjects. The

3 *Ibid.*, p. 20.

basic principles for this social order were formulated in the "Five Cardinal Relations." According to Mencius, in "the relations of humanity—between father and son there should be solidarity and affection; between sovereign and minister, righteousness; between husband and wife, attention to their separate functions; between old and young, a proper order; and between friends, fidelity." [4] The elaboration of the rights and duties associated with these relationships was the basis of education for young people. Within and without the family, traditional Chinese society was organized on the basis of a strict division of labor between the sexes and the subordination of women to men. There was also a fixed ordering of relationships according to age—the older always taking precedence over the younger.

Politically, China was (and still is) authoritarian. Dynasties changed, but government was highly centralized and emperors theoretically had absolute power, limited only by rigid ceremonial obligations to the gods, ancestors, and parents. They were expected to be meticulous in the fulfillment of these duties. If they were known to have been delinquent, they were, at times, held accountable for catastrophes. In practice, the emperors' power was restricted by the vastness of the territory over which they ruled and its limited means of transportation and communication.

The autocratic power of Chinese emperors was exercised through an extensive bureaucracy. As early as the Ch'in and Han dynasties (221 B.C.-A.D. 220) professional civil servants governed and administered the country. Recruitment for government positions was based, in principle and largely in fact, on scholarship. A series of traditional examinations in classical learning, caligraphy, art, and poetry was almost the sole means of access to office. Although most high officials came from those classes that could afford to provide the necessary education, a number of them originated in the lower classes, having succeeded in acquiring the education and passing the examinations that were prerequisite for office. Many peasant and craft families managed to send one son to a village teacher (usually a scholar who had failed in the final imperial examinations and returned home). If

[4] *The Works of Mencius,* Book III, Part I, Ch. 4.

their son succeeded in passing the examinations, his family moved on to the upper classes with him. There was always some social mobility in traditional Chinese society by this route.

Direct imperial powers did not effectively extend to the village and local level. There, the heads of large households and clans controlled the political, economic, and religious organizations in their own domains. But since they usually maintained a series of family scholars who occupied various official positions in government and at court, the great clans also played a large part in the administration of the vast land and population of China. As a partial but important check on the power of great families, the Civil Service prevented their sons, who constituted the bulk of the bureaucracy, from administering in their home districts. They were, instead, assigned to territories in which they would presumably not be subject to "conflict of interest." The interpenetration of political and family organizations was great. One can hardly overemphasize the importance of family relationships. However, the unity of the throne and the administration, with its division of labor, hierarchy of office, and professional qualifications, constituted an important check on the powers of the great families and clans.

ECONOMIC ORGANIZATION IN CHINESE SOCIETY

Overwhelmingly, the predominant economic basis for life in China was agrarian. By and large, craft production and trade were extensions of the interests and assets of the landowning class. This economic pattern supported and re-enforced Confucian Chinese family institutions.

In the first place, vast land holdings provided both living space and the raw materials needed for the maintenance of large households. These estates and the populations attached to them were the basis for much of the village life of China. The population of most villages was made up of clusters of a few "great" houses and their dependents, most of whom could trace some family connections to the landlords and to each other. All depended on the successful cultivation of the land for their support. Excess population, or natural or political catastrophe, meant disaster for a great many people. Many a "great" house fell and scattered its surviving members among the lower classes when crops failed. Frequently, lack of space and too great a burden on the land broke up large households. The need for more land impelled the clans to establish branches in new areas.

In the second place, the ownership of extensive lands determined a graded hierarchy of class and authority. The owner was a man with power over a large number of people. He controlled his sons through laws of inheritance, and others by distributing their share in both the work and the produce of the land. Thus, land ownership bolstered the hierarchy prescribed by Confucian doctrine for both families and society itself. It was a chief factor in class stratification. The power that the ownership of vast acres gave the owner over large numbers of manual workers on the land was the first object of attack by the present regime in China.

RELIGIOUS ORGANIZATION IN CHINESE SOCIETY

The religious life of China was very different from that of the Western world. For many centuries organized belief and ritual, concerned with the relations of men to the universe and to forces beyond their control, operated on two levels in China. On the one hand, there were systematic doctrines and practices associated not with revelation from supernatural sources but with the wisdom of sages whom the Chinese did not deify. There was, in addition, a large body of folk beliefs that did refer to a supernatural realm. The most important doctrines were Confucianism and Taoism. Buddhism, imported from India, had a widespread but not a dominant influence. Christianity was a much later importation from Western Europe and its impact was slight in comparison with that of the other systems of religious belief. Although hundreds of individual Chinese espoused the faith, Christian missionaries were ultimately more successful in inculcating ideas of individual achievement and technological development of natural resources than they were their religious teachings.

A folk belief in a spirit world existed alongside these systematized philosophies and religions. This was a form of pantheism that endowed everything with a spirit of its own—from rooftrees, chairs, tables, kitchen utensils, gates, and brooms, through the vegetable and animal kingdoms, to every man and woman, and to the earth and heavens. The eaves of the houses were built with upturned ends and decorated with appropriate symbols, and "spirit boards" and screens were placed in doorways as protection against the more mischievous of the spirit world. Adherence to Confucianism, Taoism, Buddhism, or Christianity did not eliminate belief in some part of this ghostly realm. This kind of belief is common in many parts of the world; in sophisticated populations it is likely to persist as notions about good and bad luck.

Unlike religions in the Western world, Chinese religious life was never a divisive influence among the Chinese. Although Confucianism became the basis for social organization in China, neither it nor any of the other systems (with the exception of Christianity) claimed exclusiveness. Nor did their doctrines so interfere with or negate one another that one system had to be abandoned if another was espoused. Thus many Chinese practiced several religions, including Christianity, simultaneously, without experiencing conflicts of conscience. Taoism, which advocates withdrawal from the practical affairs of daily life as a means to an understanding of eternal "ways" of the universe and considers ceremonies and formal relationships insignificant, encouraged the passive cultivation of individual insights and wisdom. It was not infrequently debased into magic and sterile mysticism. But in any case, Taoism counterbalanced Confucian emphasis on the subordination of individuals to collective forms and relationships. With its hierarchy of gods and saints, Buddhism provided a sense of otherworldliness and protection which was a source of personal comfort. Christianity, too, was a more personal belief that appealed to individuals as a counterinfluence to collective obligations. This religious eclecticism may in part account for the paradox manifest in many Chinese of a character at once highly individualized yet motivated toward the maintenance of collective units.

The special character of Chinese religious life and the religious attitudes of individual Chinese is recorded in a conversation between the Chinese scholar Siao-yu and Mao Tse-tung. They had been discussing the official establishment of the doctrines of Confucius, Lao-tse, and Buddha by the emperors of the Tang Dynasty during the period between the seventh and tenth centuries. Siao-yu is speaking.

It is interesting to note what realists the Chinese are! They may believe in a particular religion and guide their lives by it, but they seldom if ever become fanatics. That is why three different doctrines can exist side by side in perfect harmony. . . .

It's not only in this country that several religions can live together harmoniously, but also in the minds of individuals; . . . I know a very good example of this phenomenon in my own home: First, like everyone else, we had the *p'ai wei*, the ancestral tablet, on which was inscribed the order of worship or obedience—Heaven, Earth, Emperor, Parents, Teacher; but my grandmother wished to inculcate in us respect for the Sages, so she put up another tablet to Confucius. Then, as she had a certain weakness for Buddhism, she pasted up a picture of Buddha. Most interesting of all, however, is the fact that when she heard of the teachings of the European and American Christian missionaries, she supposed the doctrine of Christ must be important for people to have come from such distant lands to teach it, so she put up beside the Buddha another picture, of Christ on the Cross. I used to call my grandmother's tablet cabinet "the religious republic." This is quite typical of the religious beliefs of many Chinese.[5]

Both folk belief and systematic doctrines supported Chinese family institutions. Confucianism was their basis, providing the strict interpersonal regulations that were necessary for such large and complex family organizations. Ancestor worship, a logical part of this system, greatly facilitated the continuity not only of generations, but between lateral branches of the clans. Gen-

[5] Siao-yu: *Mao Tse-Tung and I Were Beggars* (Syracuse, N. Y.: University of Syracuse Press; 1959), p. 119.

ealogical records clearly defined relationships and the reciprocal obligations they entailed. Each family had its ancestral tablets, each branch of the family its ancestral hall, and each clan its great ancestral temple that encompassed them all and symbolized the collective unity of thousands of people. Over the centuries of political and economic turmoil, natural catastrophes, and invasions and occupation by foreign peoples, the great clans, bound through their common ancestors, recognized the needs of all members and provided protection for any who had a recognized place in the family organization. This protection extended to persons who came from miles away and whose branch of the family had maintained no direct contact with another, perhaps for a generation or more; it extended to people who were personally disliked. The clans operated in many important respects with the impersonality of large American business corporations; they had clear executive and administrative lines and formal designations of relationships and functions. Confucianism represented their constitution and by-laws.

Taoism, on the other hand, justified making exceptions to the Confucian rules. It was highly individualistic, scoffed at all formality, recommended the pursuit of individual ends and the heightening of personal satisfactions. Taoism formulated the more irrational and accidental aspects of life, and in so doing it provided relief from the reasoned, formal, and controlled behavior which Confucianism demanded. But although Taoism was a kind of safety-valve for the regulations of the Chinese family system and Buddhism was a source of personal comfort and security for the individual, neither doctrine withdrew the worshipper from the practices which bound him to his family and clan.

The folk "spirit" realm also reinforced the family by uniting individual members in propitiations of it. This operated on the immediate, everyday, household level of life. Every kitchen, every doorway, even fire and water and the house itself, had spirits to be pleased. Some were conceived as good, some as bad, many as merely amiable or mischievous. The welfare of all family members was felt to be tied up with keeping the spirits favorably disposed toward the family and its enterprises.

EDUCATIONAL ORGANIZATION IN CHINESE SOCIETY

No people have placed a higher value on education than the Chinese. It was not only the basis for the cultural continuity that bound them together but, since it was dominated by Confucian doctrine, it helped to perpetuate the hierarchy of relationships that characterized Chinese social order. Education was the foundation for the establishment of an elite class, some members of which constituted the core of the ruling class as well.

Access to formal education was not available to everyone, not even to all the sons of the well-to-do. Since students were economically unproductive during their years of study, scholarship was chiefly limited to the upper classes. Women were excluded from higher learning for the most part and the training of the majority of upper-class men was limited to the management of family properties and attention to family ceremony and honor. Upper-middle-class and upper-class men were not trained in manual skills, however; nor until the beginning of the twentieth century did their education include knowledge of science and modern technology.

The long history of the scholarly Chinese curriculum, and the fact that it was preparation for a series of thoroughly traditional examinations, resulted in its emphasizing orthodoxy and conformity. This had a stultifying effect on Chinese life in some ways. It encouraged a narrowness of view that excluded strikingly new information. The rejection by most educated Chinese of the scientific knowledge developed in the West has had particularly unfortunate consequences. Nevertheless, Chinese scholarship was rigorous and competition was keen; the training required tended to select the most intelligent from the mediocre and to channel the better minds into government.

The development of the Civil Service in China encouraged the establishment by the government of training schools. Middle and high schools were opened in district and provincial capitals as well as in Peking to prepare young men for the imperial examinations. There were three important degrees that represented ascending levels of academic achievement. If the analogy is not pressed, they may be likened to the series of degrees granted by Western universities. The first degree qualified a candidate to prepare for the second. It placed him in the class of scholars and gentry and allowed him attendant privileges. The second degree was much more difficult to attain and could lead to minor political positions. The third degree opened the way to offices of high rank and entitled its holder to a number of honors. Many candidates were eliminated at each step, and even of those who managed to qualify for the examination, only about one in ten received the highest degree. Almost no one achieved this goal before he was thirty, and he might be in his forties.

The men who passed these examinations constituted a class in Chinese society to which the highest respect was accorded. The great extent to which political office were held by scholars enhanced their prestige, and it also made the Chinese ruling class one of the most educated the world has known. Despite the intellectual rigidity that characterized a good many Chinese scholars and officials, and the corruption of some of them, the standards of behavior maintained by the scholar class as a whole were high. The exceptional value that its members placed on manners, ritual, and ordered relationships led to sterile formalism to some extent, but generally the scholarly life was one of good taste, ethical responsibility toward others, and great aesthetic achievement. To the extent that their ideals prevailed, they promoted harmony in Chinese society, and the esteem in which they were held assured them great influence.

But schools and formal education were not the principal means for transmitting the basic precepts of Chinese culture to the masses of Chinese. Family training in Confucian ethics was at the core of the upbringing of the children of all classes. Those who could neither read nor write were guided by its basic principles as a result of their experience in their households. The folkways and mores, which are always chiefly transmitted by families, embodied the philosophies of China. The oral literary tradition, preserved by professional storytellers and family elders, instructed the vast population in the basic values of the Chinese—their ideas of right and wrong, of proper relationships to superhuman powers and to their fellow men, of the qualities of the virtuous man and woman. The vast majority of Chinese were illiterate, but they were not uneducated.

In addition to the family rearing that helped to perpetuate cultural homogeneity in China, Chinese parents were obligated to see their children prepared for their future occupations. Apprenticeship was the most important means to this end. Those children who did not learn their skills from their grandfathers, fathers, and older brothers, or their grandmothers, mothers, and older sisters, were apprenticed to uncles, aunts, or cousins. Thus, family skills—manual among the lower classes, managerial among the upper classes—were handed down from one generation to the next.

In traditional China, education for most people was an integral part of their family life. At the same time, the principles, values, manners, and skills that were taught were of primary importance for the preservation of the patterns of Chinese family relationships for centuries.

CONFUCIAN DOCTRINE IN PERSONAL AND FAMILY LIFE

The customs that regulate the relations of men and women contribute to the style of life in all societies. In traditional China, Confucian doctrine greatly restricted the associations between the sexes, described men as superior, and placed all women in a subordinate position to men. Consequently, men were, in fact, dependent upon women for many services, and the reciprocity between them tempered the domination of one by the other. Among the poor, poverty itself imposed a kind of equality between husbands and wives. Wives who shared the manual labor of their husbands made decisions in their households; a poor man had less authority in his family than a rich one. In all classes women as well as men acquired prestige and benefits with increasing age. The sharp separation of functions between them produced a domain for women in which men seldom interfered and over which the older women ruled supreme.

Dymphna Cusack has recorded her interviews with women of all classes in China in an interesting book, *Chinese Women*

Speak. The following conversation with one of them expresses the hope of all traditional Chinese women.

> But mind you, a Chinese woman had her own place and dignity when she was old and the mother of sons. When the Lao Tai-tai went out all the household—sons and daughters-in-law and relatives and servants—assembled in the courtyard to see her go and rushed out to welcome her when she returned. In many ways, if she was a strong woman—and most Chinese women were!—she became a real matriarch. Lao Tai-tai means much more than its literal translation of 'Old Lady.' It was a term of honour that every woman hoped to hear addressed to her on her fortieth birthday! Dignity increased with age.[6]

The males' sphere in traditional Chinese society included politics, business, scholarship, religious ceremony, and the maintenance of the family lineage and honor. They alone dealt with the world outside the households. It was not uncommon for upper-class women to live entirely within the family courtyards. Their excursions beyond their gates were few, ceremonial, and well-guarded. Although peasant women worked in the fields and attended markets, they usually did so in the company of male members of their families who walked before them and did most of the negotiating.

The household was the woman's domain. The size and complexity of many of these establishments gave the women who managed them a great deal of prestige. In the large households the supervision of personnel, administration of real estate, social services to less privileged members of the family and clan, responsibility for order and discipline, and the assignment of tasks were added to usual functions such as child care and rearing, distribution of food and clothing, and care of the family property. Most important of all, motherhood was greatly honored in traditional China and virtually guaranteed a series of increasing rewards and protection.

Thus, Chinese women should not be thought of as slaves

[6] Cusak, Dymphna: *Chinese Women Speak* (London: Angus and Robertson, Ltd.; 1959), p. 19.

without personal significance. Chinese matriarchs had as much power as any in the world. Like women everywhere, Chinese women exerted an influence far beyond their households through their influence over husbands and children. In upper-class families, women were often trained in scholarship and the arts, as well as in domestic skills. There have been Chinese Empresses as well as Emperors.

Nonetheless, because women in traditional Chinese society were officially judged inferior to men and made subject to them, they could be exploited easily—and many were. The life of a young woman was particularly restricted. She was not only subject to the authority of her grandfather, father, uncles, and older brothers, but she had fewer privileges than even her younger brothers. In addition, she was subordinate to all older women. If she was a young married woman, she was subordinate not only to husband but to all her husband's relatives, and she was under the direct control of her mother-in-law. She would move up the ladder of privileges and power that age and motherhood would bring, but this was a slow process and for many years she could be exploited. If she was, she had no redress.

A double standard of sexual behavior was explicit in Confucian China. Men were assumed to be biologically destined to seek sexual satisfaction with a variety of women. Their romantic impulses, which had no place in the arrangement of their marriages, were given free rein in the practices of polygamy and concubinage. In Chinese opinion, women were not thought to be naturally subject to desires for variety in their sexual life; their biological destiny was assumed to be satisfied by motherhood. Both polygamy and concubinage were masculine prerogatives that were often enjoyed at the expense of the happiness and well-being of women. For the most part they were limited to the upper classes, chiefly because it usually takes some leisure to contract them and material means to support them. There was no aversion to them among the lower classes, however—merely inability to pay for them.

While polygamy and concubinage are offensive to most Western European and American people, their ill effects should not be exaggerated. They serve several important functions in the societies in which they are practiced, some of which are as important to women as to men. Both practices helped to preserve family lineage, a goal valued by all classes and by men and women alike. The state of medical practice and public health measures in China were such that infant and child mortality rates were consistently high. Heirs insured the continuity of Chinese families, and hence the well-being of everyone. Chinese wives who were barren, or who did not produce sons, not infrequently chose a second wife or a concubine for their husbands. The institution of concubinage also had the functional advantage of enabling Chinese men to gratify their romantic impulses within the context of the family. Whether the fact is admitted or not, sexual impulse frequently outruns the bounds of monogamous marriage, often to the unhappiness of everyone concerned. Furthermore, when there is no way to expand family arrangements to include extramarital relationships—in which many people everywhere are apparently involved at some time in their lives—such relationships tend to disrupt family units. Desertion, separation, and divorce are the methods for handling these situations in societies that impose strict sanctions against them, and there is no protection for children born of them.

Concubines were not full members of the family although they were members of the household. Their position was inferior to that of wives and they could be abused by them as well as exploited by their masters. Their children did not have equal rights with the children of ceremonial wives to opportunities and inheritance. But there was another side to this story. Most concubines were selected from the lower classes; indeed, they were often sold to the great houses by their parents, where their position was often a great improvement over life in their own homes. They were better fed, housed, clothed, and educated. If they were the object of romantic interest, they were often indulged. In other words, for many Chinese women, concubinage was a means to the improvement of class position.

Furthermore, the children of concubines belonged to their father's house and were protected by it. The exploitation of illegitimate children, who have no place in a family in most American and Western European societies, was largely eliminated in China. Although the children of concubines did not always share fully in the privileges of the house, if they were sons—and especially if the wives had no sons—they frequently became the heirs to the family wealth and prestige.

Nonetheless, it is true that the interests of women were officially subject to those of men and many of them were gravely at disadvantage. Many wives resented the presence of a second wife. They considered the taking of another wife justified only when they failed to produce sons. Their acceptance of concubines was ambivalent. If the concubines did not encroach upon the wife's domain, they were usually accepted with reasonable grace. The fate of concubines depended on many individual factors. It ranged from a position hardly distinguishable from slavery to one of power in a great household.

Both polygamy and concubinage were outlawed at the time of the establishment of the first Republic in China in 1912 with so little success that they had to be officially banned again in the new Marriage Law in 1950. There seems to be little basis for questioning the gain for everyone—men as well as women, societies as well as individuals—in change that makes possible for half the human race the realization of a greater range of their human potential. The Confucian Chinese family pattern imposed strict limits upon the potential development of women, with very few exceptions, for centuries. The subordination of women, however, was merely the most extreme example of submission to strictly defined limits in interpersonal relationships in a social order marked by a rigid hierarchy of relationships, feudal privileges, great discrepancy in the distribution of wealth, and domination of the young by the old.

CHANGING PATTERNS IN CHINESE SOCIETY

Family unity was consciously cultivated in China as the basis for its social order. Confucius believed that if an individual was taught to respect the authority of family elders he would automatically transfer the same obedience and loyalty to the emperor and the representatives of the state. He taught that the family is the root of the state and that to strengthen kinship ties is to strengthen the state as well. But for centuries, families commanded the principal loyalty of Chinese. Devotion to the state and to supernatural powers was chiefly manifest in the maintenance of family order and welfare. But contrary to Confucius' belief, however, this exaltation of the family did not insure loyalty to the state. In fact, it persistently impeded political centralization and coordination.

The new political regime is seeking to extend political control of Chinese life and resources, so it has attacked and suppressed both Confucianism and the large clans, which were the most complete embodiment of the Confucian family ideals. One of the great intellectual changes involved in the Chinese revolution is the substitution of the formulations of Marx and Lenin for those of Confucius as guides for the reorganization of Chinese society. The denial by the Chinese Communists of the applicability of Confucian ethics to political practice has removed one of the basic supports of the traditional family organizations.

But for two thousand years Confucian family values and organization were the principal means for the preservation of the identity as a society of a vast geographic area with a population of several hundred million people. Many other societies—Egyptian, Babylonian, Greek, Roman—have risen, and broken up, and have been reassembled. Western European unity under the medieval church dissolved into multiple national states. The populations of India and Indonesia have been variously divided by a series of conquerors. China, despite vast area and population, physical limitations and disasters, political invasions and conquest, has endured. Whatever the liabilities of the traditional Confucian order, one is forced to concede that it has had substantial assets for survival.

Traditional Chinese society did not evolve modern industrial techniques, nor succeed in making the state the principal basis for its unity. The present leaders of China are not only developing the scientific technological means for improving the material basis of life for millions of people, but they are also establishing political control over all aspects of Chinese society. At the present time, Confucianism is discredited in public life, though it is not directly attacked. The "great" families are being dispersed, prin-

cipally by the removal of the conditions necessary for their maintenance. Many of the patterns of living that characterized Chinese
society in the past are being extensively and rapidly changed.

Nevertheless, it is unlikely that Confucian family relationships will disappear, or even that the clans will lose all significance in China. Family organizations are always conservative,
and they were especially so in China. Confucian values are entrenched in the vast cultural store that is shared by all Chinese.
Many new arrangements introduced by the new political regime
appear to be old ones applied to new situations and given new
names. The People's Democracy under the direction of a completely dictatorial leadership is less of a paradox in China than
it might be elsewhere. Neither the traditional Chinese family nor
Chinese society was ever organized on the principle of equality.
Traditional order rested on a set of principles that supported a
graded system of duties and privileges and provision for all—not
merely according to their needs, but according to their position in
the order. Insofar as one can judge today, it appears that criteria
for the distribution of goods and services among the population
have changed, but not the principle of reciprocity within a
sharply graded hierarchy. Clues for understanding current events
in China are still to be found in knowledge of the traditional
order that prevailed for so long and the Confucian corporate family that was central to it.

SUGGESTED READINGS

CREEL, HERRLEE G. *Confucianism and the Chinese Way*. New York: Harper Torchbook, 1960.

A well-written account of Confucian doctrine and its influence on Chinese life.

HERSEY, JOHN. *A Single Pebble*. New York: Knopf, 1956.

A short and beautiful novel that has caught the nature and spirit of life along one of China's great rivers. Although China's rivers have been important determinants of her history, the river life of China is little known in the West.

LIN, YUTANG. *My Country and My People*. New York: John Day, 1935.

A personal survey of Chinese life by a Chinese scholar. An excellent picture of China as it was when the storms of revolution were brewing, before the shattering of traditional ways.

MAURER, HERRYMON. *The Old Fellow*. New York: John Day, 1943.

This fanciful reconstruction of the life of Lao-tse, the founder of Taoism, it is based upon the words of the philosopher and succeeds in communicating the spirit of Taoism better than more scholarly accounts.

PECK, GRAHAM. *Two Kinds of Time*. Boston: Houghton, Mifflin, 1950.

The special contribution of this personal account of life in China in the 1920's and 1930's is the author's perceptive analysis of differences in sentiment, thought, and values between Americans and Chinese.

PAYNE, ROBERT. *Forever China*. New York: Dodd, Mead, 1945.

This diary, written by an unusual English writer who was teaching in Kunming in 1942-1944, provides an exceptional glimpse of Chinese teachers, students, and farmers who were living at some distance from the violent events of the time.

————. *China Awake.* New York: Dodd, Mead, 1947.

Firsthand account of young people in China, especially students, and the impact of war and revolution on their lives.

————. *Portrait of a Revolutionary: Mao Tse-tung.* New York: Abelard-Schuman, 1961.

Excellent biography of the leader of Communist China. It includes a detailed account of the Communists' slow rise to power and a vivid description of the "Long March" and the years the Communists spent in the northern hills, which have become a saga in Chinese history.

· V ·

THE CORPORATE FAMILY
IN CONFUCIAN CHINA

■

Its Phases and Functions

THE CORPORATE family, sometimes called a *clan* or *tribe,* is the largest and most complex type of family organization. It is characterized by the inclusion of a number of partially autonomous extended family units, whose representatives form the executive and administrative councils of the clan. This integration of family units into an organization that sometimes includes thousands of people is a source of social and economic strength; it is most effective in societies that provide few social organizations other than families to serve the needs of individuals. Membership in a clan makes it possible for elders of families in largely agrarian and nonindustrial societies to provide more security for their dependents, thus compensating family units for some loss of autonomy. Also, these large organizations have advantages over smaller family units in competing for material resources and political power.

Nowhere has the corporate form of family organization been more fully developed than in Confucian China. In the past a highly centralized government did not reach into distant regions effectively. The development and control of natural resources, armed protection against invaders, police services, and most other public services had to be supplied locally. Individual families could not perform these functions, but families united into corporate organizations could and did.

The clans included or indirectly benefited small families in their districts, but they were dominated by the "great" families that owned large estates, ran large business enterprises, and manned the Civil Service. Their power extended far beyond the limits of clan, family, and village. Some of the lands and properties of the great families were ceded to their clans and the income provided was used for the benefit of communities served by the clans. Maintenance and control of the local militia, village schools, and roads and bridges; public recreation; poor relief, and the maintenance of genealogical records and ancestral temples were typically their responsibility. The gatherings of the clans for spring and autumn sacrifices to their common ancestors were at once the outstanding social events in the villages and the symbolic representation of the strength of the clans themselves.

The corporate family organization provided for the needs of about one third of the Chinese population. A few non-family organizations, such as fraternities, secret societies, and guilds, offered various services and some protection to a substantial number of people who did not benefit from clan membership. But, in the absence of effective state administration of public services in local areas, millions of Chinese who were without the protection of a clan lived precariously at best and on a subsistence level for the most part. The children of these masses are the principal heirs of the current revolution in China.

The operational units of the clans were their large extended families whose members dominated life in the villages, controlled a large proportion of the economic resources of Chinese society, constituted the largest segment of the educated class, and attended the Imperial Court. They were also the officials in religious ceremony, which in China was a major factor in the regulation of personal behavior and collective action. At all class levels in traditional China, family upbringing was the chief means for training and selecting individuals for active participation in the organized life of Chinese society. The upper-class extended families provided the foundation for the careers of the ruling elite.

PREPARATION FOR MATE SELECTION
AND MARRIAGE

Among Chinese in the past, marriage was a family affair, designed to maintain or improve the position of the family as well as the individual couple. Marriage was a contract between families and clans, and the suitability of a bride or groom was a matter for the family elders to decide. While a marriage was officially arranged by a professional matchmaker, the search for a suitable mate could be initiated by the parents of either the male or the female child.

What was sought in a marriage partner was a matching of many factors: family background, wealth, prestige, education, and all that could be ascertained about the personal attributes of the young people, such as age, appearance, special skills, and disposition. Brides were expected to bring a dowry commensurate with the wealth and position of their families. In this overwhelmingly agrarian society, dowries were not usually made up of cash, but rather of land, jewels, art and household objects, clothing, produce, and farm animals. Although the dowry went into the treasury of the groom's family, it gave the bride prestige and some of it was for her use.

Both the bride and the groom were well aware that their marriage was of more than personal significance. The choice of their mates was in the hands of their elders. Moreover, the bride's position as daughter-in-law in her husband's family was initially more important than her relation to him as wife. This eventuality was made clear from the beginning of the negotiations for her marriage. Part of the agreement was a payment, also in goods or cash, of a "bride price" by the groom's parents. This payment symbolically and realistically made the bride property of her husband's family, as well as a member of it. It ritualistically compensated her family for her removal from them, and severed their control over her. It kept her and her children bound to her husband's family in the event of his death. Thus the unity and continuity of his family were protected.

Once the marriage decision was made, and the details of dowry, "bride-price," date for the announcement of the betrothal, and date for the wedding were agreed upon, then contracts were signed. These were as binding as the marriage itself. This transaction was marked by exchange of gifts between families, gifts to the bride by the groom's family, formal ceremonies within the families, announcement to all clan members and to the ancestors. Often, contracts were made for young children, but marriage was not considered proper for girls under fifteen or sixteen or for boys under eighteen. It was considered equally improper for responsible parents or guardians to fail to provide mates by the time the young had reached these ages.

The young people themselves were explicitly trained for their married state. From the age of six or seven onwards, girls and boys were separated, the girls remaining in the women's courts, the boys moving to the men's. Except for formal family feasts, men and women traditionally ate apart unless the nuclear unit ate in its own rooms. Girls were educated for household tasks: cooking, cleaning, sewing, household management, and so forth. They were likely to know a good deal about child care since they lived in a group that included several generations to which babies were added at frequent intervals. They were instructed in detail concerning proper behavior toward males, toward their elders, toward their equals, and toward their inferiors. Terms of address reflected this precision. Every relationship carried a specific name and title denoting relationship through the paternal or maternal line, age, place in the nuclear family, place in their generation, place in the extended family, and place in the clan. All children were numbered as well as named. Since their ranking, and the conduct required of them in each relationship, was the same for all families, every girl was prepared for her position in the family of her husband by the time she moved into it. In upper-class families, girls were also often tutored in arts; they were taught to read, to write, to compose poetry, to know the classics, and to play a musical instrument. But these accomplishments did not excuse them from learning household skills and management as well.

Boys were instructed with equal precision in the formalities of interpersonal relationships. All were trained in ritual. They were assumed to be superior to girls, but like them had to await their turn in moving up the ladder of respect and privilege that was based on age. They were more often formally schooled than girls, who rarely received formal schooling unless they were members of wealthy families, and not always then. Where scholarship was a family tradition—or even where it was not—if there was ambition for the improvement of family status by means of government office, those boys who showed aptitude for study were intensively educated for many years to take the imperial examinations. The others were assigned to learn the skills required for family functions. They were taught to farm the land, to run the shops, to practice the crafts of their fathers, to manage businesses and estates. Choice of a boy's occupation ultimately rested with his elders—grandfather, father, uncle, or elder brother—but they duly considered the boy's aptitude and inclination. Since all income or produce went to the family treasuries as a rule, and family resources were distributed by the elders according to need and position, the young men were not called upon to finish their training before marriage.

Upon marriage, girls customarily left their own households and lived thereafter in the households of their husbands. There they were not given the customary name that indicated the generation to which they belonged in their own families, but acquired the name of their husbands' generation. Marriage for girls was an unusually sharp break from childhood and youth. This, more than the fact that their mates were chosen for them, was the real hardship associated with marriage for women. If their husbands' households were at a distance, they might rarely see their own families again. Because most of them had seldom if ever left their own courtyards, the separation was all the more acute. It was almost inevitable that the first months of marriage were complicated for the young wives by loneliness and homesickness.

The fact that a girl left home at the time of marriage tended to devalue her in the eyes of her family. Not only would she not be contributing to its maintenance, but her marriage would be an expense for the rest of the family. However, this disadvantage was offset by the fact that girls were exchanged, so to speak, and what went out with a daughter came in with a daughter-in-law. Marriages were often advantageous to both families, and grandchildren were prized by everyone. Happily, in many cases affection was not wanting for girls as well as boys.

As a general rule, males did not leave their homes upon marriage, but brought a daughter-in-law into the household. The couple was usually provided with a courtyard or room for their own use. Marriage conferred upon the groom increased status and a larger share of family benefits. These depended somewhat on his place in the family sequence. Whatever his position in the family, his wife shared in its rights and obligations.

Bride and groom usually met for the first time at the wedding itself. This seems a preposterous arrangement to people who choose their own mates, but Chinese young people had no other expectation. In practice, they often knew a great deal about each other. Relatives or matchmakers might have arranged for them to see each other at some family celebration, or in some cases they may have known each other as young children. Often, too, if the future bride and groom vigorously objected to each other, their protests were respected by their elders. In any case, the fact that they married as strangers seemingly did not prevent Chinese husbands and wives from developing mutual love and respect at least as often as people who marry after a period of personal acquaintance.

Of course, the power of elders to choose mates could be abused. Inappropriate matches could be made solely in the interests of family finance or status, but this was not the rule. Chinese parents were, after all, as fond of their children and interested in their welfare as any other parents. The selection of mates by parents resulted in an equality between the sexes, at least in this respect that does not exist where the initiative is a male prerogative. Another advantage to the Chinese system was that it guaranteed marriage for almost all females, and support for the early years of marriage. Thus it eliminated the highly competitive, uncertain, and, therefore, anxiety-ridden aspects of mate selection in places like the United States.

Weddings were elaborate and as costly as the groom's family could afford, for it was his family that arranged the ceremony and paid for it. The separation of the bride from her own relatives was emphasized by the fact that there were no celebrations in which the families of both bride and groom were joined. Where weddings were more or less elaborate, their function was as much the preservation of the status of the families in their communities as it was the legitimization of the marriage of the young couple. The groom's family sometimes went so far as to mortgage its property and income in order to enhance its prestige in the eyes of relatives, friends, neighbors, and its own child's family-in-law by making the wedding an impressive ritual display.

Traditional Chinese weddings were also designed to impress upon the bride and groom that their union was not merely a means to personal satisfactions, but a part of a complex organization which it was their duty to augment and preserve. The principal ritual consisted of paying homage to the groom's ancestors and to his parents. The toasts and good wishes on behalf of the bride and groom were not for their personal happiness, but for long life with many children—especially many sons.

THE NEWLY MARRIED COUPLE

The first years of marriage for newlyweds in the Confucian Chinese family were very different from those of a young American couple, or for any who live in a smaller, more personally oriented family organization. The life of the young husband was not greatly changed. He remained in his own household where his activities continued much as they were before his marriage. The major decisions concerning his welfare and that of his wife were still made by his elders. There was no sudden spate of new responsibilities and demands upon his personal abilities.

But the wife's situation was not an easy one. In the first place, she was completely separated from her intimate circle. Her loneliness and homesickness were heightened by the fact that in most instances she would see her own relatives rarely and would never again be part of the life of the household in which she had been raised. In the second place, she entered her new household as a stranger whose place was on the lower rungs of the ladder of authority and privilege. Her first obligation was to please her mother-in-law and to adjust to the hierarchy of new grandmothers, aunts, and sisters-in-law. She was, of course, trained to take her place in this group and was equipped with skills for the tasks to which she would be assigned. Besides, she had been chosen by her parents-in-law and approved by the elders. A daughter-in-law was considered to be an asset to the family since she was expected to insure its continuity as the mother of sons. Therefore, the bride was welcomed. Nevertheless, the importance of the formal and collective aspects of her new position limited any immediate expression of personal pleasure in her at first. She had to pass a tacit test of efficiency which had considerable influence on her ultimate personal acceptance by her new family. The economic situation of the family determined both the kind and amount of work she would be expected to do. Young brides usually assumed a traditionally determined share of the duties of the household. It was always a greater share of chores and included no part in the determination of what should be done, or how it should be done. When the family was prosperous, the ladies of the household were chiefly administrators. Servants did most of the actual work.

Since a wife shared her husband's status, her privileges varied in relation to his. The wife of an eldest son was in a more advantageous position than the wife of the youngest son. The relative status of the families of the bride and groom made a difference in the nature of the bride's reception in her husband's household. Ideally, the families were well matched, in which case the honor of each required the maintenance of suitable standards of behavior toward their daughter-in-law. Not infrequently there was an exchange of daughters between the "great" families which made each one a kind of hostage protecting the rights of the others. If, however, the match was unequal, a mother-in-law could make life very difficult for a daughter-in-law she considered to be beneath the family standards. If she considered the girl to be above her own station, she could be just as difficult for opposite reasons.

In the households of the Chinese upper classes, strict adherence to Confucian doctrine restricted the relations between husbands and wives. The companionate aspects of marriage were not encouraged. Custom, especially the practice of avoidance between the sexes, forbade both communication and contact between husbands and wives outside the privacy of their own quarters. Neither could support or defend the other in their relationships with family members. These were overseen by the family elders, male and female. Husbands and wives neither worked together nor ate together nor, for the most part, shared the activities of leisure. They subordinated their relationship to the round of family duties and associations, especially to the wishes and comfort of the husband's parents. This was especially true for a newly married couple. In time, and once they became parents, their own courtyards expanded and within them the intimacies of nuclear family relationships prevailed. Until that time, however, the relations between husbands and wives were centered in their private life together and opportunities for privacy were relatively few. On the other hand, there were no extrafamilial demands upon young married couples to interfere with their personal relationship. The fact that young Chinese couples had a limited number of personal associations available to them may have facilitated their union. They were more constrained to make the best of what they had.

Comparison of the position of newly married Chinese couples with that of American newlyweds illustrates the fact that variation in means for meeting recurrent human needs is limited by universal characteristics of the needs themselves. Personal and individual attributes influence the outcome of even the most formal arrangements; and the successful integration of a relationship in a collective unit, however loosely defined, is in part determined by constraints inherent in the nature of organization itself.

Although the actual obligations of a Chinese wife to her in-laws, especially her mother-in-law, were extensive, her own skills, charms, and the prestige of her family could lighten the application of formal rules. Although an American bride is confronted by no comparable set of services to be rendered, affectional ties that stem from the past make it almost inevitable that her relation to her husband will be significantly determined by how well she gets along with her in-laws. American husbands, unlike Chinese husbands, are subject to the same necessity of making approved adjustments to their wives' relatives. The tranquillity of either a Chinese or an American couple was and is often disturbed by a mother-in-law. The consolidation of the personal relationship between husbands and wives was and is importantly influenced by social differences between their families in both cases, and for the same reasons.

American women have the great advantage of continued access to their own families. Since neither husband nor wife is under the authority of parents, the families are equal in relation to the couple and exercise relatively little power over them in comparison with the traditional Chinese. In the event that family interference becomes intolerable, American women can dissolve their marriages and retain the custody of their children. These factors protect their personal well-being in ways that were not available to Chinese women in the past. But on a daily basis, most American women have far less help from their own families than Chinese women had from the families of their husbands. The Chinese bride's future was more predictable and secure, although more restricted.

Chinese husbands were expected to contribute to their support and to the support of their families, just as American husbands are. The means of so doing differed. Americans usually make their own occupational choice, whereas the Chinese were subject to the decisions of their elders in this respect. But once the choice was made for Chinese or by Americans, both were chiefly dependent upon their families for the means to prepare for it. In this matter, the Chinese had an advantage over the American because their families expected to support them and their wives and children until their training was completed, however long a time that took. This contribution is typically more limited in American families. The burden is usually shifted to the young people themselves when they marry.

American men have a wider choice of occupations and personal control over their financial resources. Chinese supported themselves indirectly by contributing to their family treasuries. They had little autonomy over the disposition of their earnings until they were well along in life. But Chinese males, like Chinese females, had much more security than the majority of Americans do. Their families provided occupational opportunities, care in illness, support in periods of unemployment, and regular personal help for their wives and children as a matter of course. The careers of Chinese were not hampered by heavy financial responsibilities for individual families. Americans are conspicuously lacking in these advantages.

The companionate aspects of the husband-wife relationship were not developed by young Chinese couples as a rule, but they often evolved as the couples grew older. The reverse is not infrequently the case in the United States. Young American couples are typically companions in many spheres of life, but the burden of their family obligations, which falls on them alone, often prevents them from continuing to share activities outside their family associations. The occupational demands upon husbands, and the requirements of housekeeping and child care for wives, can reduce the companionate aspects of the marriages of Americans to a range that is scarcely distinguishable from that traditionally prescribed for young Chinese couples. When this occurs, it is difficult for Americans to retrieve the companionability of their early years together. In China an increase in the number of shared activities between husbands and wives was assured with advancing years. This was a privilege of middle age.

Pregnancy and the birth of a first child changed the life of a young Chinese couple far less than it does that of an American couple. Nevertheless, the first child marked the end of an interim phase between marriage and parenthood, during which Chinese couples had been distinguished as "newlyweds" and treated in special ways. In the Confucian Chinese family, parenthood, rather than marriage, enhanced individual significance and moved the new parents up the family hierarchy of prestige and privilege. Hence, only dire poverty could make the birth of a child anything but a happy event. In the "great" families of China it was always welcome.

THE CHILD-BEARING PHASE OF FAMILY LIFE

The very great importance of family continuity in China in the past gave parenthood a significance that transcended its personal rewards. The future status of a wife depended on her becoming a mother, and her prestige increased with the number of her children, especially sons. A childless woman could almost be described as déclassé in a Confucian Chinese household. Her rights as a wife and those that went with age were often given merely nominal recognition. A bride's position was assured by the birth of her first child. Her principal obligation to the family was fulfilled. Her husband's status was improved and his regard for her as the mother of his child augmented his personal sentiments toward her. Many children were considered a sign of family felicity, and biological fecundity was the only limit to child-bearing. The corporate family organization was favorable to the maintenance of numerous children, since the households were large and flexible enough to make room for them and support was provided from the common family treasury. There was ample help for child care and supervision and neither parent was excessively burdened to meet the needs of their expanding brood. The child-bearing period was a rewarding one for parents.

How rewarding it was depended almost entirely on economic factors. Unlike the situation in the United States, in traditional China the number of children increased with wealth. There were no extra-family reasons for limiting the size of families. Chinese women did not pursue individual goals such as careers or volunteer services to communities; they were able to achieve personal satisfactions and self-respect through the competent performance of family functions. Since their families remained an all-providing organization for Chinese from birth to death, the individual satisfactions of both husband and wife were tied to the welfare of their families and clans. Therefore, the enhancement of family resources and honor, and their perpetuation through children, became an individual as well as a collective goal. A man's increase in wealth or advancement through scholarship did not lead to separation from family and the enhancement of an individual career, as it tends to do in the United States. It led to the expansion of households, and more children.

THE CHILD-REARING PHASE OF FAMILY LIFE

Whenever the span of biological fertility is the principal limit to child-bearing, there is no sharp division between the child-bearing and the child-rearing phases of family life.

In the Confucian Chinese family, child-rearing was itself so much a function of the whole household that the contribution of a particular set of parents was largely a partial fulfillment of a collective obligation. There was little variation in the rules and skills taught or the sequence and methods by which the young were coerced to learn them. Since the lives of the children were expected to follow the pattern of those of their fathers and grandfathers, or mothers and grandmothers, emulation of the elders, often unwitting, was an important and adequate part of training for adulthood. The family group as a whole provided the conditions for their socialization and acculturation, and children did not move out of the group. This arrangement not only ensured the continuity of each family, but also perpetuated the Confucian cultural patterns and ethics that dominated Chinese society. No alternatives were presented to the young. Children were less the offspring of their particular parents than they were a new generation in the larger family organization. They shared a generation name, and the relation between first cousins was almost equivalent to the relation between siblings. Since the children were so largely a collective responsibility in the Confucian Chinese family, the nuclear units within it were not child-centered.

In regard to sexual satisfactions, men were greatly favored by the system which, in principle, permitted them several wives and concubines, and did not condemn the sexual relationships they chose to make unless these threatened the resources or honor of the families. Any deviation from the strictest chastity by women was utterly taboo, however. Their adherence to this condition was almost assured by the pattern of strict avoidance of associations between males and females, except under carefully prescribed conditions. They lived in different courtyards. They ate at separate tables, except for husband and wife and small children when they chose to eat in their rooms. If they chanced to pass each other, neither spoke or looked at the other. Daughters-in-law and young girls rarely saw the father of the nuclear unit; older brothers were almost as much out of sight. Only important family ceremonials and feasts brought the men and women of a household together, and then they met in strictest formality.

This pattern limited the possible range of development of husband-wife relationships. It almost eliminated any very personal exchange between fathers and daughters once they were out of childhood, or sisters and brothers. It greatly intensified relationships between fathers and sons and between brothers and cousins of the same age group. It did not so greatly interfere with mother-son relationships, for sons were expected to pay their respect to their mothers daily throughout their lives. Mother-daughter relationships were apt to be very close, but were often shadowed by the knowledge that daughters would leave their own households for those of their husbands. If these were at any great distance, this meant all but permanent separation. Mother-daughter-in-law relationships were highly developed in the Chinese system. As time went on, daughters-in-law replaced the daughters of the household.

The women of these large households lived in exceptional intimacy with each other as a result of their regular co-operation in household tasks, management, and child tending. Each woman was expected to be clever enough to maintain her particular position with all its rights and privileges, and to prevent attempts to encroach upon these by other women. And, it must be added, men were expected to pay each woman the respect that was her due according to her station. Wives always had some precedence over concubines, and first wives over second. To ignore this hierarchy of rights out of infatuation for a perhaps younger and prettier woman was considered a breach of propriety and brought disciplinary action from both male and female members of the older generation.

It is not difficult to see that full participation in these complex households imposed great restraint upon individual satisfactions in the sense in which Americans and many Western Europeans view them. More than that, although the age-grading of privileges in the Confucian system guaranteed some rewards for everyone, the move up the line was slow. Talent and ability in China were often deflected to individual scholarship, the arts, or merely ingenious inventions for passing time, rather than being invested in constructive activities in the areas of politics and economics that might have improved the lot of the Chinese people and, perhaps, spared them the devastating effects of revolution. The conservatism and authority of elders effectively prevented their sons from undertaking large new ventures, and by the time they reached positions of power, most sons had lost their visions and ambitions and restricted their own sons in turn. Family training was consistent with both classical education and the autocratic political system.

THE CHINESE COUPLE IN MIDDLE AGE

In contemporary China new rights are being promulgated for young adults in general and for women. But under the traditional system, the long domination of parents and grandparents over sons and daughters who had reached personal maturity was a chief cause for rebellion. The advantages that the corporate Confucian family organization provided in the form of security and the sharing of the costs of maintenance were primarily to the young and the old. From the beginning to the end of middle age the arrangement could be personally frustrating. When their children began to reach marriageable age, however, and the older generation began to resign from some of its activities or to die, the Chinese couple entered into a period of transition that promised a fuller personal life at its end.

It would be inappropriate to apply the term "launching" to the beginning of the middle period in their lives. Child-rearing was largely a function of the "great" households and in this collective arrangement children of all ages were usually being trained for adult life at the same time. Decisions concerning marriage and occupation for young people—typical of the launching period in all societies—were usually made not by their parents but by the elders of the large family organization. Since these families were all-encompassing for their members for their entire lives, the separation of young people from their families that is usual in the United States was extremely rare. Except for women, who left their parents' households for those of their husbands, there were no abrupt breaks in family relationships.

This period in the "great" Chinese families is better described as an important move up the hierarchy of family organization for both parents and children. The newly married young people took precedence over their unmarried sisters and brothers and cousins. Upon the birth of their children, their parents became grandparents and entered the ranks of the elders. There were few occasions for upheavals in Chinese family life in interpersonal terms. The fine grading of relationships, and the rights and duties that went with them, made the life course of Chinese men and women a continuum of small changes. Therefore, the kind of strain and tension evoked by the lack of parental control over their children's marital and occupational choices, and the threat to family unity that these entail in a system like the American, did not arise in the typical Chinese family. Parents and elders were not powerless to provide the means by which their young people became full-fledged adults. As a result, the young people were not in a fiercely competitive situation with limited knowledge and skills for establishing the relationships they needed.

Because family ties and influence extended into all major areas of life in traditional Chinese society, young men moved as gradually into economic and political positions as they did into the higher levels of their family organizations. Women, of course, did not move out of the family circle. Participation in religious ceremonies began in earliest childhood for both sexes. For most Chinese, education was family-provided, although young men were sometimes sent away from home for special training. However, the adult activities of the Chinese were oriented to their families, even when they lived abroad. Typically, their earnings went into their family treasuries, and their honors contributed to the prestige of their families. Their powers over decisions of importance to their personal well-being increased, but chiefly by virtue of their inclusion in the higher councils of their families and clans. Their individual glory stemmed from their contributions to the prestige of their families.

This pattern of life, dominated by family relationships which regulated economic activities, is called "familism" or "feudalism" in China today, and is considered reprehensible. Certainly, such a pattern was incompatible with the requirements of modern industrial development and political techniques of social control. Nepotism often ignored prerequisites of knowledge and skill. Family control prevented the development of large-scale economic and political organizations based on impersonal standards of efficiency and performance that are the principal units of modern technology, economy, and political regulation. Furthermore, it tended to truncate the development of the talents of individual Chinese.

Nevertheless, in the past, this domination of the life of Chinese society by family organizations, and the consensus that prevailed by acceptance of the Confucian system of ethics, did provide a basis for remarkable unity in Chinese life. They imposed great restriction on individuals, especially on women and young men, but they also made their lives predictable, personally significant, and, within its economic and physical limits, secure. Thus, young people could move into full adult participation in their society without excessive personal anxiety, and Chinese of all ages faced few disturbing contradictions in values as they moved from one sphere of life to another. One of the important consequences of this system was that the Chinese could approach the final years of their lives with tranquillity, confident that they would benefit from the rewards to which their long years of service entitled them.

THE AGING COUPLE—PERIOD OF RETIREMENT

At around the age of sixty there were discernible changes in the lives of Chinese brought about by the passage of years and by new births. The push of new generations did not, however, threaten the aging with loss of functions, respect, and authority, or with isolation. On the contrary, it increased their security and surrounded them with people who respected and looked after them.

Consequently, there was little in the Confucian Chinese families that was apt to evoke the tensions experienced in American arrangements at the aging period of life. Just as young people could draw upon the economic resources of the large family and clan until they were old enough and sufficiently trained to add to them, so the aging could depend upon these when or if their ability to contribute to them came to an end. Once Chinese men and women became grandparents, they could choose whether or not they wished to continue to manage households (in the case of women) or to operate family businesses and property or hold public office (in the case of men). These obligations were theirs for as long as they wished, and no longer, once their grandchildren appeared as a visible guarantee of family continuity. Since early marriages resulted in grandparenthood at a relatively early age, retirement was often the choice only when great-grandchildren appeared.

Retirement did not mean loss of authority in decision-making. The elders were always consulted, and theirs was the final "yes" or "no" if they chose to take part in family councils. Withdrawal from some activities did not mean complete loss of other functions, such as scholarly pursuits and religious duties, art and hobbies, or the care and education of grandchildren. Certainly it meant no loss of position or status in the household, for the place of the elders was at the top of the hierarchy. The formal restrictions in relationships were often relaxed for grandparents. For example, although the relation of fathers to daughters was usually extremely formal, and there was little informality even between fathers and sons, the relations between grandfathers and grandchildren of either sex were often informal and overtly affectionate. Although a daughter-in-law might almost never see her father-in-law, it was not uncommon for a grandfather-in-law to teach a a favored granddaughter-in-law to read and write and to share his scholarly or artistic interests with her. The strict rules of avoidance between the sexes were also relaxed for the members of the households who had celebrated their sixtieth birthdays.

Thus, the end of life was typically a good harvest. The conditions provided by Chinese families guaranteed protection, honor, access to the exercise of whatever abilities each person chose to use, and an increase in significant relationships. Whatever threat there was came from outside the family organization. Natural catastrophes leading to economic collapse could threaten the survival of the whole family, but the best that any family could provide was reserved for its eldest members.

This prospect eliminated the conflicts that often attend the maturity of children in autonomous nuclear families. There was no reason for the Chinese to impede the forward movement of the younger generation. Parents were not threatened with the sudden loss of all the activities that had absorbed them for many years. On the other hand, they could resign from any they felt to be too burdensome without anxiety about their status. The division of labor and communal provisioning in large Chinese households made individual dependency, if it came, no cause for distress or loss of self-esteem. After all, the costs of dowries, "bride prices," weddings, and additions to the household to accommodate new married couples and their children were also shared. In short, in the corporate Chinese families, the final phase of family life was almost sure to be one of fulfillment. The Chinese could anticipate spending their old age in security and with serenity. In this respect, the assets of the Chinese family organization were very great, particularly in comparison with the unfortunate fate of so many old people in the United States. The limitation of choices and range of activity in early life, most keenly felt by those between thirty and sixty, was the price paid for felicity in old age.

THE FATE OF THE CORPORATE FAMILY
IN CONTEMPORARY CHINA

For two thousand years the institutional patterns of the Confucian social order prevailed in China. There were gradual changes and innovations, and there were devastations following natural catastrophes and invasions, but the major framework of social organization remained essentially unchanged. The Confucian large family and clan remained at the center of this social order. So long as it survived, the Chinese corporate family organization provided for the needs of its members and contributed to the stability of Chinese society with remarkable efficiency.

There were several serious weaknesses inherent in traditional Chinese society. The family and political arrangements were unable to improve the basic standard of living for the majority of people. The dependence of millions of people on agriculture condemns many to a sub-subsistence level of existence, and some to starvation, when it is inadequately balanced by industry and trade and when the techniques of production and communication are not highly developed. The old agrarian ruling class resisted the introduction of the means to change this condition in China.

The autocratic nature of authority in Chinese families imposed excessive restrictions on the development of the personal abilities of individuals and on the lives of young adults. The father-son relationship, although it included reciprocal obligations, demanded the subordination of sons so long as their fathers lived. There were many obligations to mothers as well. The commandment of filial piety, a compelling one in China, often placed excessive burdens upon young men and women. It also was the principal barrier to a more extensive development of husband-wife relationships in Chinese families. The subordination of women to men and their domination by older women, especially mothers-in-law, resulted in a good deal of exploitation and abuse in family relationships.

Parental authority and the grading of populations by age and sex is not unusual, but the Confucian Chinese were extreme in making these hierarchies major supports for Chinese social order. The hierarchical arrangement made the transmission of Confucian cultural patterns very effective, but in the long run this may have been a liability for the Chinese. It tended to block the adoption of innovations that could have benefited the vast and impoverished majority of the population. The gradual changes associated with the development of science and technology in the Western world were resisted, and native creativity was channeled into fields that would not disturb the old order, for example, art and literature. Floods and famine and epidemics continued to devastate large numbers of Chinese long after some means to prevent them could have been adopted. The restrictions under which women and young men lived often became unbearable and led to a large reservoir of resentment accumulating at the very core of the family itself.

It was largely the impact of Western peoples that cracked the ancient Confucian order of China. The principal ameliorants to a scarcity economy and marginal subsistence level for vast numbers of people today are industrialization and mechanization. This is the lesson that Westerners finally taught China. By the beginning of the twentieth century demands for the development of these techniques became significant, and they have steadily increased. Implementation of the demand began with a trickle of scholars sent out to Western countries to be educated. Not only were the scholars of China the first to learn the scientific principles and technical skills necessary for the economic rehabilitation of China, but they were foremost among the Chinese who added emotional drive to striving for economic improvement by associating it with new social ideals. The traditional prestige of intellectuals in China helped to persuade the masses to accept these new social and economic doctrines.

Changes were also fostered by the presence of Western business organizations set up in China to exploit the availability of cheap labor. Their presence was made possible by the military advantages enjoyed by Western powers. The establishment of Western political compounds in the port cities of China was one of the proverbial double-edged swords that have cut into historic social organizations and made way for new associations that in the long run have proved disadvantageous for the wielders of power. Western ideas and Western technology were introduced primarily by the missionaries and businessmen of European societies whose presence was, more often than not, forced upon the Chinese. The first Chinese converts to Western science and methods were people who saw in them the means to turn them against their inventors and so expel them from Chinese territory.

The unfortunate underestimation of Chinese people and Chinese civilization by most of the Europeans and Americans who went to China in the nineteenth century has produced consequences for their descendants in the twentieth century that they could not have imagined and certainly did not desire. Western science and power techniques are replacing Confucian ethics as the

means to social improvement in China, but the insult to personal
and ethnic pride by the people who introduced them has been a
major factor in Chinese acceptance of them. For the new regime,
the goal to make China at least a major and equal nation among
the great powers parallels the socialist goal to raise the standard of
living for the masses. Resentment toward Western societies for
their domination and arrogance in the past makes their reduction
to second-class powers a goal for some Chinese.

Change was not so sudden in China as many Westerners believe. A series of small social reform movements occurred as early
as the eighteenth century, but they were sporadic and abortive.
The first outstanding political movement in modern time was led
by Sun Yat-sen and culminated in the short-lived Republic of
1912, established after the Boxer Rebellion. This paved the way
for the Nationalist Movement finally represented by the Kuomin-
tang. In the 1920's, socialist and communist movements were organized. Following various struggles between these two groups and
the disorganization brought on by World War II, the Communist
Party under Mao Tse-tung finally triumphed in 1949.

The number of social movements in China during the last
seventy-five years or so is evidence of increasing discontent with
the old order and the inability of its representatives to preserve it.
All of these social movements sought the restoration of national
power and prestige, improvement of the standard of living for the
masses, and the liberation of women and young men from the
overpowering authority of their family elders. They differed concerning the means to achieve these ends, but by the consistency of
their concerted attacks on the old order, they were able to spread
uncertainty where it had not existed and to mobilize existing discontent.

The spread of new ideas, sporadic land reforms, wars and invasions, the infiltration of new industrial techniques, the training
of young men in other lands, the recruitment of young women for
work in factories that were growing up around the port cities—all
these factors undermined the powers of the family elders. Some
Chinese began to move out of their family circles by choice.
Strong support from many distinguished Chinese intellectuals,
who had been trained in Europe or the United States, led many

of the upper classes to join movements advocating change. Ironically, the rebellions of their own children did more to undermine the power of the "great" Confucian families, in the beginning, than attacks made upon them because of their economic and political domination.

The goals envisaged by the new political leaders in China will extend benefits beyond the limits of the ruling classes and raise the standard of living for the masses. The chief targets of the new political regime have been the old corporate families, who traditionally monopolized the resources of Chinese society, and the philosophy that justified their way of life. A government that intends to control the resources of the society, and to regulate the lives of the population, has to weaken the authority of patriarchal families over their members, and capture their loyalty by attracting them to new political, economic, educational, and cultural organizations. The current regime has done both. Although it has not been possible to eliminate an institution as deeply rooted as the Confucian family in so short a time, the Chinese corporate families are no longer important units in political, economic, or educational life. Changes in family relationships are extensive and will no doubt continue in a direction that will lead to the establishment of a new typical pattern of family life.

It was not necessary for the new regime to attack family and clan organizations directly. When the conditions for their maintenance were removed, these "houses" came tumbling down. It is conceivable that they will persist and retain some family significance in the manner of the clans of Scotland or Ireland, but it is extremely unlikely that they will ever again be the basis for order and stability in Chinese society.

Changes in land ownership, the collectivization of agriculture, and the nationalization of industry and commerce removed the economic props of the old families. With their economic losses, the authority of the family elders greatly diminished, since it had depended upon their control over the means of subsistence. Political power now depends upon a large, formally organized elite drawn primarily from the Communist Party which is even more tightly organized than the old ruling elite. By means of Party organizations in factories, on farms, among construction workers, in schools, in hospitals, and on city blocks, the population is being re-assembled and must rely on politically determined relationships for access to what it needs and wants. Family connections are currently more likely to be a hindrance than an advantage to individuals in the pursuit of a good life. The classical program of education has been abandoned in favor of training in science and modern tech-nologies. Art, literature, and theater are primarily in the service of organizations devoted to the dissemination of new values and new loyalties. The education of children and young people is no longer in the hands of family elders. Public nurseries and schools and uni-versities have taken over child training, and youth groups and other government and Party agencies provide recreation. Medical care is also supplied by government services, or is directed by them.

In addition to these basic changes that have progressively weakened the old family organizations, the new government has dealt them a fatal blow by espousing the cause of equality be-tween the sexes and the liberation of the young from the authority of the old. The traditional Confucian Chinese family was organ-ized on the basis of sex and age-grading; therefore, the elimination of these strictly maintained hierarchies completely undermined the basis for the authority of family elders. The new Marriage Law, promulgated in 1950, established equality between the sexes be-fore the law and in terms of economic and social rights. Husbands and wives now share family property and inheritance. Women are free to pursue any career and to control their earnings. Choice of mate is in the hands of each individual, and parents no longer have the power to control the lives of their married children. Both men and women may seek a divorce, and women may retain the custody of their children.

The traditional respect and privilege accorded to individuals on the basis of age alone have no place in Communist China. The only legal concession to the past is a law requiring children to sup-port their parents when necessary, and forbidding them to mis-treat or abandon them. The traditional authority of uncles and aunts and other members of the older generations carries little or no weight. Only the relationship to parents retains significance, and that imposes more responsibilities on parents toward their children than it does on children toward their parents. Revolutionary periods always enhance the prestige and importance of the young and even put the elders in their power. This reversal of the usual order has taken place in China, where it is even more of a drastic change than it would be in most other societies.

All massive changes in personal relationships and ways of life involve anxiety and hardship, and so they have in China. Many Chinese men and women, young and old, have suffered during this period of transition. But a large number of the people who benefited least, if at all, from the monopoly of the "great" families over the resources of the society, are better clothed, housed, and fed than they were before. They have better medical care and access to education. Their personal significance and dignity in the "new order" were beyond their reach under the old system. Hundreds of women view the change as a great liberation from intolerable domination by men and mothers-in-law. Feminist attitudes and organizations flourish. Women work beside men in every kind of occupation and profession and hold important posts in government, Party organizations, industry, and rural administration. Leadership is open to the young.

The Chinese do not find it hard to accept the fact that the new order is authoritarian and that a great many relationships are still subordinated to collective goals. Western concepts of individualism have always been foreign to them. They are accustomed to finding personal satisfaction in forwarding the interests of the larger organizations to which they belong. This facilitates the transfer of loyalty from their families to the Party and the State, and national pride has replaced family pride as a spur to individual effort for many Chinese.

Like the "trained inefficiency" of some experts, social institutions that embody the cultural patterns of a society most perfectly are the most useless when conditions change so greatly that something new is required. Modern conditions have turned the corporate Confucian family into a kind of dinosaur among institutions in contemporary Chinese society. The families of the majority of Chinese were never more than pale reflections of the Confucian family ideal, and it seems probable that the greater equality between men and women that existed in these families, and the attenuation of the authority of parents, may become the ideal as well as the typical pattern of Chinese life. Nonetheless, these families were oriented in many ways toward Confucian mores and sentiments, and it is possible that clan membership will survive as one of the links with the past that usually become important once revolutionary goals are attained.

Many of the changes that directly affect family life in contemporary China have been influenced by Western ideas. The spread of Western technology and industrial organization will probably bring China closer to the relationships and practices of Western societies. But the Chinese are not instituting Western arrangement as such, in family or any other organizations. The impact of Western culture upon the traditional organizations of nonliterate and technically primitive societies has had, for the most part, a disintegrating effect. A similar effect should not be expected in China. In complex societies like the Chinese, with rich and varied cultures of their own, new influences, however profound, do not destroy the traditional order or result in mere substitutions of alien ways. The impact of the West in China, as in other areas of the Far East, is certainly reflected in current changes, but the selection of ideas and techniques to be integrated into Chinese culture and social order is the prerogative of Chinese leaders. It is they who formulate the goals of current reform in China, and the new institutions they adopt will not be reproductions of Western ones but will surely be modified by traditional Chinese culture and practice.

At the present time, new patterns and old exist side by side in Chinese society. The distribution of change follows the penetration and effective control of local activities by Party organizations. China is vast, and extensive lines of communication are still in the process of construction. In remote areas, new laws and new ways are little known. But in cities and accessible districts of China, change has been rapid and extensive in many important spheres of life. The young, and the formerly dispossessed, readily respond to the indoctrination by Party organizations and adopt the new ways. Older people, and those who benefited from family organization in the past, continue to live in a network of family relationships as much as possible.

Social revolutions in Western European societies broke the

extra-familial power of many extended, aristocratic, and autocratic families a century or more ago. Many of them still maintain their identity and exert considerable influence over their members and even, in some cases, over their societies. Extended families are not without significance in the United States. Family sentiment in the "great" family organizations of China has been at least as profound as it is in these Western families, if not more so. It seems likely that although the unity of Chinese families will rest on new reciprocities, and their maintenance on non-family activities, the prestige of membership in "old" families will not altogether disappear in China. It seems certain, however, that family relationships will remain subordinate to the obligations of individuals to the laws and agencies of the new Chinese state.

SUGGESTED READINGS

BUCK, PEARL. *The Good Earth*. New York: Random House, 1931.

The rise of an extended family in pre-war China. It traces its history from the marriage of a poor peasant and a slave girl to the establishment of a great household.

————. *The Pavilion of Women*. New York: Pocket Books, 1949.

An inside view of the life of women in a great household.

CUSAK, DYMPHNA. *Chinese Women Speak*. London: Angus and Robertson, 1959.

A series of intimate interviews with Chinese women in many parts of China, recorded in the mid-1950's. Miss Cusak is an Australian writer, who is clearly on the side of the "new" China. Nonetheless, these reports communicate the variety of changes that are occurring in the lives of Chinese women of all classes.

MACE, DAVID AND VERA. *Marriage: East and West*. Garden City: Doubleday, Dolphin Book, 1959.

Excellent comparative study by the executive directors of the American Association of Marriage Counselors based on wide personal experience. Includes material on Chinese, Indian, and Japanese customs.

WONG, SU-LING AND CRESSY, EARL H. *Daughter of Confucius*. New York: Farrar, Straus, and Young, 1952.

Autobiography of a woman of the scholar-official and gentry class in China.

YANG, C. K. *The Chinese Family in the Communist Revolution*. Cambridge: The Technological Press, 1959.

One of the best scholarly analyses of the impact of the revolution in China on traditional Chinese family organization and institutions. It is based on field work and is infused with the author's knowledge of his country and people. Includes recent family legislation.

THE BILATERAL EXTENDED FAMILY IN LATIN-CATHOLIC EUROPE

■

Characteristics of Latin-Catholic Societies That Influence Family Life

THE BILATERAL extended family—which typically includes parents and children, and both maternal and paternal grandparents, aunts, uncles, and cousins—prevailed in Western European societies until modern time. Historically, this type of family has been associated with Western culture and the Christian religion. For many years the Catholic Church exercised profound influence in all spheres of European life. After the Reformation, nationally supported religious organizations were established in the Protestant countries of Europe. Differentiation in Protestant religious doctrine and the establishment of churches to support diverse beliefs broke up the unified Christian matrix that had prescribed a way of life in general, and family life in particular, for a great many people. A trend away from extended family organization was first conspicuous in Protestant European societies and has gone furthest in them. Today, the traditional bilateral Christian extended family is found in its most fully embodied form among people who are devout members of the Catholic Church, and more of these are found in the Latin countries of Europe than elsewhere. Except for an important Protestant segment of the French population, the number of Latins of any other religious affiliation is insignificant.

Actually, the geographic distribution of Catholic bilateral extended families is wide as a result of the fact that it was the predominant type among the Spanish, Portuguese, Italian, and French populations during their historical periods of exploration and colonization. These Europeans went to North, South, and Central America, North Africa, and parts of the Far East and took their forms of government, education, religion, and family life with them. In most of these places they found either no inhabitants or predominantly pre-literate or illiterate peoples whose technological strength was no match for their own and whom they subjugated. These Europeans became ruling elites in their new homelands and imposed the ways of their own societies on their subjects.

Distance from motherlands, frontier conditions in some places and plantation economies in others, and the mingling of indigenous populations with their own cultures and practices, inevitably modified the ways of conquerors and colonizers. Variation in the cultural practices of Latin-Catholic Europeans living in non-European societies is not so surprising as the fact that they have remained unmistakably and dominantly Latin in culture and Catholic in religion. Nevertheless, the presence of indigenous institutions in these societies and the modifications of European patterns that have resulted make it advisable to exclude non-European societies from this discussion.

On a theoretical scale of family organization based upon the degree of autonomy maintained by nuclear family units, the bilateral extended family lies about midway between the autonomous nuclear family that prevails in the United States and the corporate type of family organization illustrated by the clans of Confucian China. Unlike the corporate family pattern, nuclear units in the bilateral extended family have a good deal of autonomy. However they are consistently oriented toward a larger family circle that effectively influences decisions concerning the maintenance and activities of their members. These extended families also differ from the basic units of corporate families in that they are "bilateral," that is, the families of both husbands and wives are integrated into the kinship circle. This limits the power of the parents of each spouse with respect to each other, and of both in relation to the families of their children.

The family councils of these bilateral extended families are usually more informal than not, and the distribution of authority within them depends on personal factors as well as on fixed, traditional rules. The nuclear units are directly represented in these councils, and competition between them for dominance results in a shifting balance of power in the extended families themselves.

The integration of the nuclear units into the extended family is encouraged by several factors. One of the most important is ownership of property and its perpetuation through inheritance. Other factors are the ideals of family continuity and family honor which each generation is expected to protect and enhance. Also, family unity has been strongly supported by the Catholic Church. Important religious sacraments have given family values and the daily life of family members an aura of sacredness.

> As *rite de passage*, baptism, confirmation, first communion, marriage and death are all naturally subjects of religious ceremonial. But so also, by means of blessings and directed prayers for success, are other activities brought into the religious picture—agriculture or animal husbandry, journeys, the inauguration of new buildings or societies, as well as such implements of these activities as tools, means of transport, and the very foundation stone. Thus the Church acts as patron and protector not only during vital events of the life cycle but in ordinary daily activities of life.[1]

Finally, these families have been held together by the advantages they were able to obtain for their members in non-familial spheres of life. By pooling assets, such as capital, personal connections, and

[1] Kenny, Michael: A *Spanish Tapestry: Town and Country Life in Castille* (Bloomington, Indiana: Indiana University Press; 1962), p. 45.

information, extended families have been better able to secure material benefits and positions of power for the members of nuclear units than the latter could do by their own efforts.

Until the third decade of the twentieth century, the bilateral extended type of family was both the most numerous and the normative ideal in France, Belgium, Spain, Italy, and Portugal. Most people who belonged to the upper class, the *bourgeoisie,* and the peasant class lived in them. This type of family was traditionally tied to a rural pattern of life. As increasing numbers of the population moved to the city to swell the ranks of the urban proletariat, their ties with the exended family were weakened. The family loyalties of some of the upper and middle classes were also weakened or dissolved by modern conditions—particularly by modern education. Although education is still largely influenced by the Church in all Latin countries and controls all schools in some places, secular training is increasingly available. It is correlated with the expansion of industry, which requires scientific knowledge and technical skills. The education of young people is not as consistently oriented to Catholic opinion as it once was. The number of people in Latin-Catholic countries who follow the trend away from extended family organization has increased in direct proportion to the rate of increase in urbanization and industrialization.

But the extent of these trends in Latin-Catholic societies should not be overestimated. They are more conspicuous in France and northern Italy than in southern Italy, Portugal, and Spain. Many rural areas in all these countries have changed very little.

In actual numbers the bilateral extended family is conspicuous in rural areas in all these societies, and insofar as these populations have a normative family ideal, the extended family comes closest to embodying it. Despite geographic, ethnic, economic, technological, and political variations, the Latin-Catholic societies of Europe have shared a common cultural and religious heritage and have evolved similar patterns of living. Families in these societies have been greatly influenced by this Latin-Catholic matrix. In turn, they have been most important agencies for its preservation and transmission.

In the upper classes, the influence of extended families is greater than their numbers would seem to warrant because family membership is still an important means to positions of authority in political and religious life and to material advantages in the economic field. Such families achieve and maintain their positions through patronage, a common practice among Latin-Catholic people.

> When I speak of patronage I refer to a special and durable relationship between patron and client whereby the former acts as a protector, at times as a model to copy, and always as an intermediary to deal, in times of need, with persons or situations more powerful than the client. Everyone is at sometime or another both patron and client, and the richer and more influential one becomes the more clients one will acquire. God is the ultimate Patron and the Virgin and hundreds of patron Saints are thought to intercede with Him on behalf of their clients.
>
> The diversity of urban life produces complicated strata of power and authority which can be dealt with only by cultivated friendship and by patronage. Most bureaucrats themselves owe their positions to more influential friends and relatives. Thus they tend to perpetuate a practice to which they are indebted and committed.[2]

Although the control of Latin-Catholic extended families over the resources of their societies has been far less than that of the clans in Confucian Chinese society, it has been extensive enough to make them important to the social orders in which they lived. For the most part, they have slowed down the rate of social change. Whether or not they can survive drastic reformations in political and economic spheres is still to be seen.

Latin-Catholic societies have been aristocratically oriented. Position through birth and property ownership has been associated with fixed rights and privileges. Class divisions have been sharp, and "class" has meant a way of life as well as a category of occupation and income. People working in cities constitute a discernible stratum in these populations; the peasants in rural areas, another. A middle class made up of professional people, merchants, businessmen, craftsmen, and shopkeepers has been small, except in

[2] *Ibid.*, p. 135.

the industrial regions of Belgium, France, and Northern Italy. Until the end of World War I, the majority of people did not aspire to change classes, but rather to improve their economic situation within their own class.

Life in urban and industrial areas has been conspicuously different from that in rural districts and villages. Until very recent time, there has been no large flow of mass-produced goods from city to country, no networks of radio and television—not even a regular traffic of automobiles—to break down this distinction. In Spain, Portugal, and Southern Italy the land problem has been acute. Large estates have remained in the hands of upper-class families, many of whom have neglected their cultivation. These are densely populated countries that cannot afford the loss in productivity that has resulted from absentee landlords and inefficient agricultural practices. Among peasants, landholdings are frequently too small to support the families that till them. Masses of poor people have become poorer. The benefits of industrial enterprises have not reached the majority of these populations. The economic basis of these societies has largely maintained class divisions and differences that have long been supported by tradition.

Economic and technological changes are taking place at accelerating rates in the Latin-Catholic countries of Europe. They are breaking down class barriers and making class differentiation a crucial political issue. There can be little doubt that social stratification in these societies will change in important respects, but at the present time political conflict tends to sharpen their traditional divisions.

Another line of cleavage in Latin-Catholic societies is that between men and women. Despite current trends among the more sophisticated and urban members in Latin Europe, masculine superiority is assumed in matters other than the home and the spiritual aspects of the Church. The autocratic domination of men over women that once prevailed does so no longer, but many decisions are made for women by their fathers and husbands that are made by women themselves in societies where equality between men and women is stressed. In general, public affairs are a masculine domain and the training of men for their participation in political and economic life orients them to a much wider range of interests than is usual for women. Most families are willing to provide professional or university education only for sons; relatively few women seek this kind of instruction.

Latin-Catholic people still endorse a double standard of sexual behavior for men and women. Custom

> allows a much greater wandering in sexual relations to a man than a woman, who expects him to be 'naughty.' This is an attitude that condones adultery, but only when the sanctity of the home is not affected by it and the wife's honour is respected.
>
> Where it does not affect the unity of the household, a husband's infidelity is accepted with resignation by the wife; but the infidelity of a wife is the grossest degradation for a man.[3]

Access to prostitutes is relatively easy and provides diversion for peasant and working-class men. Among the *bourgeoisie* and upper classes, the institution of the mistress has been widely accepted. Latin men are not typically promiscuous. Even relations with prostitutes are often regularized to some degree. Those with mistresses are usually of relatively long duration.

A man may or may not provide totally for a mistress's support. It is not unusual for men to limit their contributions to occasional gifts, a fact which makes it possible for a good many of them to afford a mistress. Mistresses are frequently drawn from the category of women who work. A mistress does not have the status of a wife and a mother of legitimate children, but her relationship is generally respected and her children are usually provided with some protection by their father. Most women in these societies look forward to marriage, but if, for whatever reason, they do not achieve it, they seem to prefer a stable relationship with a man outside of marriage to none at all. They enter these relationships voluntarily and other people accept them.

Wives, for the most part, do not approve their husband's mistresses, but if they do not take too much of his time, do not threaten his economic performance or his bank account, if they are discreet and do not encroach on the wives' prerogatives or

[3] *Ibid.*, p. 82.

those of their children, they are accepted as one of the "facts of life." It is considered unwise to upbraid a husband about his mistress if he stays within the informal rules. In "worldly" circles wives and mistresses may meet socially and may even be good friends, but in these cliques wives are apt to exercise the same sexual privileges as their husbands. It is a tacitly accepted rule that a mistress will not embarrass a man's relation to his wife or threaten the unity of his family. Most of them do not.

Although the institution of the mistress is far less elaborate and formal than concubinage in Confucian China, it has served some of the same functions. It provides an outlet for romantic impulses that are not encouraged in marriage in Latin societies. It keeps the pursuit of extramarital sexual relationships within predictable bounds. In this respect it is more orderly and less exploitive than the unregulated relationships that are denied recognition in the United States. Mistresses, like concubines, are largely a privilege of the upper and middle classes, but there is no widespread opposition to this relationship even among those who cannot afford it. Latin women do not have the political, economic, or social freedom accorded American women, but they are by no means as subordinated and restricted as women were in Confucian China. They usually live in their own homes. They are not separated from their own parents and other relatives. They have rights that are protected by both the Church and the law. There is a great deal of collaboration between Latin husbands and wives in those things that concern the position of their family unit in the extended family circle, the rearing of their children, and the maintenance of their households. It is possible for women in these societies to have professional and public careers, though it is unusual. Latin women are explicitly praised by Latin men for the functions that they perform as wives, mothers, housekeepers, and even as sexual partners. Therefore, they take personal pride in these activities; they do not feel that they must undertake tasks outside their homes in order to win personal recognition. On the other hand, most Latin women take the position that the interests and comfort of men take precedence over their own.

The relations between old and young in Latin societies, rather than being guided by the emphasis on youth that characterizes the

American population, are typically a modified version of the pattern of Confucian age-grading. There is kind of informal hierarchy of relationships based on both age and sex, with respect rather than privilege for the older generation. Parents exercise authority rather than domination. Grandparents have a recognized place in family life, but the old do not impede the young adults from exercising their abilities, nor do they usurp positions of authority. Neither the old nor young, however, think of themselves as equals. The strength of relationships across the lines of age and sex derives more from the interdependence that results from a division of labor than it does from any achievement of equal rank or sharing of the same kind of activities.

> The real education of the child begins and ends in the home, and is the largely unconscious result of example and imitation. The child grows up in a society where the roles of each sex and age are clearly defined. Part of his training is directed to accepting the father's word as law and to viewing the mother as the source of all virtue. Respect for authority and virtue, embodied in the parents, is therefore instinctively acquired by the child and extended to all parents and adults, particularly close kin.[4]

The differences between young and old, men and women, and people of all classes and political persuasions in Latin societies are transcended by a set of common values and expectations derived from classical Greece and Rome, and from Christianity. Their chief embodiment is the Catholic Church. For centuries the Catholic hierarchy exercised political power. Although today the state apparatus in Latin societies is independent of Church influence in principle, and largely in fact, the Catholic Church is still nationally supported in all. While secular education has expanded greatly in the twentieth century, the education of the majority of children in these societies is still largely church-dominated. This tends to perpetuate the degree of fusion between religious, political, educational, and family institutions that differentiates these societies from the non-Catholic societies of Europe and North America.

[4] *Ibid.*, p. 62.

From the moment the child is suckled it is projected into a welter of ritual from which it rarely escapes in its lifetime. Baptism, Confirmation, first Communion, religious teaching in general and the cult of the Virgin and patron Saints in particular, fuse the Church and the child's everyday life into an indivisible whole which no amount of liberal or anarchical thought acquired in later life will fully destroy.[5]

Although fewer adults, especially men, are devout in Catholic practice, many who are not still insist on proper Catholic upbringing for their children and extol religious devotion in wives and mothers. The Catholic version of Christian ethics, and the patterns of relationships and daily activities that grew up under the aegis of Catholic regulation, are deeply embedded in the folkways and mores of Latin societies. This may strengthen Catholicism's chances for survival under the impact of drastic social changes.

As an institution the Church cannot be ignored, for in its sociological effects it has no rival. (p. 144)

Since the parish church cannot wholly exercise control by preaching from the pulpit or in the Confessional, or by *novenas* or Lenten Retreats, it looks to its associations to spread its influence. Of these, the most important today are the Catholic Action groups. (p. 148)

The women's groups are most active . . . They are the ones who dress and adorn the Statues of the Virgin and Saints . . . they constitute a little web of patronage by being virtually in control of organized charity in the area. (p. 149)

Opus Dei founded in Madrid in 1928 is an alliance of sacred and secular callings, marked by strict obedience to vows of poverty or chastity and distinguished by a pledge to God of all professional talents. The organization makes a far more active conscious use of patronage

[5] *Ibid.,* p. 56.

than do Catholic Action groups. Moreover, its movements are surrounded by an air of disciplined secrecy.
(pp. 150-1)

The men *en masse* will make at least a token appearance
at the services on important feast days. Although the authority of the Holy See in Rome may be recognized
merely by such formalities, this does not mean that a
wholly Catholic nation will not merge religion into the
totality of its general culture. Even the most cynical of
men will insist that his religion (although he may not
practice it) is an integral part of his existence, so that an
attack on his religion is also an attack on his way of life
and vice versa. Anti-clericism should be distinguished
from anti-Catholicism. (p. 46)[6]

While the Church has been the great institutional frame that
has encompassed Latin populations and preserved their moral precepts and traditions, the family has been the outstanding agency
for translating these principles into action. Traditionally, Church
and family have been the core around which the lives of Latin people were organized, and family life has, in turn, been organized
around Church doctrine and ceremony.

For Catholics, marriage, since it is a sacrament, can be dissolved only by the clergy. Although civil marriage and civil divorce
are now required in Latin societies, relatively few people would
consider themselves properly married without a Church service, or
separated without a Church annulment. The Church determines
attitudes toward child-bearing, child-rearing, and education.
Church rites are deeply imbued with family significance since they
mark critical moments in the lives of family members. Their celebration keeps families in close contact with the Catholic clergy
which is a source of instruction, advice, council, and comfort. Religious symbols are often family symbols as well. Family altars are
not uncommon. Children are given the names of Saints and their
Saint's Day is celebrated more elaborately than their own birthday.

[6] *Ibid.*

Finally, holidays in these societies are still mainly holy days. Church Days most often provide occasions for families to gather together for celebration, pleasure, and the renewal of family relationships.

SUGGESTED READINGS

BOWERS, CLAUDE. *My Mission to Spain*. New York: Simon and Schuster, 1954.

A personal history of Spain written by the American ambassador to Spain from 1933 to 1939. Mr. Bower's exceptional opportunities to meet people of all classes and parties and for travel throughout Spain make this a valuable source of background information.

MADARIAGA, SALVADOR DE. *Spain, a Modern History*. New York: Praeger, 1958.

Recommended standard history.

PADOVER, SAUL K. *French Institutions, Values and Politics*. Stanford: Stanford University Press, 1954.

A scholarly analysis.

SCHOENBRUN, DAVID. *As France Goes*. New York: Harper, 1957.

Despite its emphasis on political affairs in France since World War II, this report by a man who has lived in France ten years provides illuminating insight into the character and personal traits of the French people.

WYLIE, LAURENCE. *Village in the Vaucluse*, Cambridge: Harvard University Press, 1957.

A first-rate description of a French village and the life of its inhabitants based on a year's residence in the town. Mr. Wylie is a professor of Romance languages, but his talent for social analysis would be welcome in any department of sociology.

· VII ·

THE BILATERAL EXTENDED FAMILY IN LATIN-CATHOLIC EUROPE

■

Its Phases and Functions

THE LATIN-CATHOLIC extended family is made up of a number of nuclear units most of which live in their own homes. They are held together by a loose hierarchy of family relationships, usually associated with age, wealth, and potential utility, which culminates in an informal family council that can bring important pressures to bear on each nuclear unit to conform to family standards and contribute to family enterprises and welfare. The number of relationships typically included in the network of kin who regularly honor obligations to each other is fairly large, usually spanning three generations. Grandparents, parents, children, siblings, uncles and aunts, first cousins, and their children, in both the male and female line are all active members of this closely integrated family circle. Although each nuclear family lives alone by preference, obligations to relatives often expand their households. Aging parents, unmarried sisters or brothers, or orphaned cousins are not uncommonly provided for when the need arises by inclusion in the nuclear family.

The bonds of mutual responsibility between these people are permanent, whether they are reinforced by affection or not. Whatever their internal tensions, these families usually present a united front to outsiders. Furthermore, they are closed circles. The introduction of strangers is rare and not lightly undertaken. Children do not bring playmates or companions into their homes indiscriminately; men do not bring home their colleagues or business associates; neighbors do not drop in to introduce themselves. Children associate primarily with their cousins and the offspring of "old family friends." Marriages expand the circle of associations; occasionally, too, a long-tried friendship contracted at school or in professional life will be honored by introduction to the family.

These extended families constitute a private world which is a center of dependable relationships for life. They often make up the entire range of associations for women and children. Although the members of such families may be sharply divided on many issues, their public expression of differences and their public actions are constrained by a frame of family values and a sense of obligation to family honor, prestige, and social and material advantage. The potential contribution of the members to each other's personal satisfactions or careers, and the promise of benefits to nuclear units in the form of assistance in crises or of inheritance, are not the least of the factors that keep the members of these families together.

PREPARATION FOR MATE SELECTION
AND MARRIAGE

Preparation for marriage is explicit in Latin-Catholic extended families. In general, children in Latin societies are consistently oriented toward adult life. They are not allowed to become absorbed in peer groups or to put juvenile or adolescent interests ahead of the goals set for them by their elders. By the time they reach marriageable age, most of the young people are ready for the demands that their marriages and occupations will impose.

Young men usually postpone marriage until they have completed military training, are settled in an occupation, and have the means to support a family. Marriage is generally assumed to be the proper career for women. Unless they must seek employment, most girls in extended families do not continue their formal education after they have finished their high school at fifteen or sixteen. Housekeeping, baby-tending, sewing and cooking, and how to keep husbands comfortable are the subjects of the "higher" education of most of them, and they are trained in these performances in their own households. By eighteen or nineteen, most of the girls are ready for marriage; they are substantially assisted toward it by parents and relatives.

Contrary to their reputation for romantic courtship and alliances, Latins are more rational than many people about marriage. Family life is viewed with too much seriousness to leave marriage to personal choice unguided by instruction in its responsibilities. The religious significance of marriage, by emphasizing the contribution of family life to Catholic values supported by all Church members, reinforces awareness of the collective commitment that marriage entails and insures that it cannot be undertaken lightly by devout members of the Church. Although the choice of marriage partners is commonly an individual one, it is largely influenced by family elders, both directly and indirectly.

Indirectly, families influence the marriage choice of their children by inculcating their own standards of what is desirable in a mate early in their children's lives. The suitability of candidates for marriage is measured by the same standards that are ideally applied almost everywhere, whether the mode of selection is collective and formal or individual and informal. A marriage is considered a good one if the spouses are matched with respect to the economic and social position of their families, education, occupational promise in young men and domestic competency in young women, and religious membership. This ideal is not absent among Americans who typically give as little thought as any people to the collective consequences of their marriages. It was the goal of Confucian Chinese parents when they arranged marriages for their children. Among Latin-Catholic young men and women, their parents' ideal is often the self-imposed determinant of their actual marriage choices.

Furthermore, families indirectly limit the range of marriage choice by restricting the associations of their children to a circle of people who would be considered suitable candidates. Meetings between young people are supervised. Traditional chaperonage is no longer widely practiced by extended Latin families, but dating in the American sense is not common, either. The sons and daughters in these families are not typically allowed to play with children whose "connections" are not known by their parents, nor when they reach marriageable age are they permitted to have "dates" with such people. Parents are informed as to where their young people go when they are not at home. Gatherings and private parties that include approved circles of young people are common forms of entertainment. In the villages a kind of public courtship is still current. Young people promenade in the village squares, they follow each other to church, they meet at holiday celebrations. Under these circumstances, the preferences of young people become obvious to their elders and are encouraged or discouraged by them according to their own standards.

Directly, parental—and even grandparental—control of economic resources and access to education, careers, and desirable living arrangements is used by Latin-Catholic elders to coerce young people to give up relationships that they consider inappropriate. Parental approval for marriages is especially important in extended families because the young are deprived of a great many very practical advantages without it.

Once a choice is made by the young and approved by their parents, marriage arrangements are left in the hands of family elders. Dowries are still common. These are usually ultimately controlled by the husband, but it is generally assumed that they will be used to set up and maintain the new family unit. Since marriage is a sacrament of the Church and divorce is prohibited by it (except under exceptional circumstances and with papal sanction), approval by the clergy is important. Religious intermarriage is frowned upon. When the marriage is approved, the banns are read in church weeks in advance of the marriage and the young couple receive religious instruction regarding the rights and duties they are about to undertake in marriage.

Thus, when they marry, Latin-Catholic men and women are prepared for what lies ahead of them. They expect to love each other, but they are not usually "in love" in the American sense. Their marriages are more personal than those of the Confucian Chinese, but are like them in that they are approached with fairly realistic anticipations. Latin Catholics know that their years of relative freedom from responsibility are over when they marry. They envisage their lives together as undertakings that will be dissolved only by death. They hope for several children, economic security, good health, freedom from major catastrophes such as war and natural disasters, and the blessings of the Church. This is far from a romantic view.

THE NEWLY MARRIED COUPLE

In extended Latin-Catholic families young couples start their life together with as much material equipment as their families, the man's position, and the woman's dowry permit. Even if this is more than ample, it is not usually used for either personal indulgence or conspicuous display. If they can, the couple lives alone. If they cannot, for numerous possible reasons such as housing shortages or the needs of a parent, they will live with parents. Personal adaptations in a new relationship are always demanding, but strains are reduced when the participants enter it with similar expectations and with skills needed for their common endeavors. In this respect, Latin Catholics are generally well prepared and members of the more traditionally oriented families are especially so.

The education of these young people greatly reduces the importance to their marriage of a period free from the responsibilities of parenthood. The Latin marital relationship is one that can be realized without too much difficulty. The young couple conceive of their marital relationship as one of interdependence based on complementary needs, traits, and services, rather than as one in which equality is defined as alikeness and companionship as each partner disclosing all aspects of the other. Besides, these young couples do not strive for the degree of autonomy that, for example,

American couples do. Their independent households do not imply isolation from their larger family circle. Their marriages do not produce sharp breaks in the continuity of their ways of life, as marriages often do in the United States. At the same time, they are by no means as restricted by obligations to their elders as the Confucian Chinese were. They have considerable social latitude for the cultivation of their own life together. Latin-Catholic newlyweds in extended families are not likely to be subject to as many strains as young couples are in either autonomous nuclear or corporate types of family organization.

There are several factors that encourage the relatively early termination of the first phase of their married life. Parenthood is formally defined as the primary goal of marriage by the Church. For many Catholics, parenthood represents the fufillment of an important religious commitment and therefore is welcome. Emphasis on the continuity of their families further enhances the importance of parenthood for these people. Fatherhood brings new authority to young men in their families and in their communities. Motherhood has an aura of the sacred in the more traditional areas of Latin-Catholic societies and greatly augments the prestige of women in general. Under these circumstances, young couples hope for the wife's pregnancy as soon as possible.

THE CHILD-BEARING PHASE OF FAMILY LIFE

Church doctrine and emphasis on family continuity combine to encourage large families in Latin-Catholic countries. In principle, only the cycle of biological fertility is supposed to limit childbearing. Practice falls short of this ideal for many in these populations, but in the extended families four or five children are not exceptional. The social significance of parenthood makes it personally gratifying to individuals, especially women, and so the right is exercised more frequently than it is in countries like the United States where there are few socially guaranteed benefits to compensate for parental responsibilities. Besides, the extended family circle reduces the burdens of parenthood by distributing some of the costs of child-bearing, both material and personal.

In extended Latin-Catholic families the strains of life during this period stem from general economic conditions rather than from family organization. Natural resources have not been extensively developed in many areas in Latin countries. Mechanization of agriculture and industrial plants are lacking. Land has continued to be an important basis for wealth, in Spain, Portugal, and Southern Italy especially, and the largest share of its output has gone to landowners who represent a small percentage of the populations. There has been little class mobility in these societies outside of urban and industrial areas. The distribution of both cultural and material goods has been markedly uneven. There have been many poor, few rich, and a relatively small number of middle-class people in Latin-Catholic societies. Therefore, limited material resources make the maintenance of a growing family difficult for many families, especially in rural districts.

The problems of Latin-Catholic families at this stage do not arise from lack of personal help as a rule. Nuclear families are not isolated from relatives. While relatives are not indulgent and the young parents do not expect them to be, nevertheless they can be looked to for assistance if it is needed. Parents, unmarried siblings, aunts, and uncles expect to be useful. The women relatives help with household and child care. The men assist young husbands in their economic pursuits. In times of emergency they can be counted on for labor or produce or financial assistance.

Young married women are expected to keep a good house, live economically, spend money wisely, keep their family well fed and clothed, teach their children good manners and good behavior, and see to it that they are properly trained in religion. In Latin countries it is chiefly the women who are daily observers of religious practice and they take their young children to church with them. In urban France and Northern Italy religious observance by a growing number of adults may be more formal than devoted, but even when this is true, young mothers often see that their children are confirmed.

Except in agricultural areas, the work of young men takes them away from home, but their separation from the daily routines is not characteristically as great as that of American men. Businesses close at midday for two hours and the majority of men go home for a dinner at which family members are gathered.

While in some societies women exercise directly the power of decision in their homes, including the distribution of family income, Latin women usually do not. Latin men are typically the heads of their households. The routines of the household are organized around their needs and habits for the most part, and control of the purse is still a masculine prerogative.

Latin-Catholic men exercise authority as fathers, as well. They take pride in their children and are affectionate toward them, but they expect obedience from them. They take no more part in baby-tending or child care than they do in household tasks. Latin fathers make many decisions of a personal nature for their children. Their education and recreation, even their friendships, are often subject to paternal approval. In this regard, Latin fathers are closer to the Confucian Chinese than to Americans.

Although the ideal formulation of the relation between men and women in societies is not egalitarian and the division of labor between men and women is clear, husbands and wives cooperate in the supervision of their children and the dispensation of their households; their married life is usually one of collaboration. In contrast to the similar, but less explicit, division in the lives of American men and women, the arrangement in these Latin-Catholic families does not interfere with the consolidation of the husband-wife relationship or threaten the stability of families. There is a franker recognition of their interdependence by Latin-Catholic men and women that sustains their union. The more extended family circle to which they are consistently oriented, and Catholic doctrine concerning marriage, support it also.

> In the ideal pattern of husband and wife relationship the husband's distinctive role is that of the authoritarian head of the family who makes all the decisions; the wife's role is to be submissive, retiring, frugal, and uncritical of her husband. Though there may be a certain discrepancy between the ideal pattern and real behaviour, it is precisely the unquestioning acceptance of the ideal relationship that makes for tight-knit family stability and the sanctity of the home.
> From the ideal pattern one might well suppose that

the husband is the key personality of the family circle. As a figurehead he is, but the woman is the real power behind the scenes. The Church fully realizes this and depends on its domination over the women for eventual control of the family. Wives are nevertheless careful to perpetuate the myth of the all-powerful father figure in their children's eyes, because it tends to stability and, of course, to discipline in the home.[1]

The birth of children is not likely to be experienced as an interruption of a companionable life *à deux*. Despite the importance of children in these families, they are not child-centered in the way that American nuclear families are. Children are trained to give precedence to their elders. In Latin-Catholic families marital relationships are not threatened by the parental responsibilities of husbands and wives. On the contrary, parental functions are considered an integral part of the marital relationship.

THE CHILD-REARING AND -LAUNCHING PHASES OF FAMILY LIFE

Today in some extended families, parents limit the number of their children. But in the not very distant past this was not so, and even today many Latin-Catholic families do not voluntarily restrict the size of their families. When biological fecundity is the only limit to child-bearing, then a distinction between a child-bearing and child-rearing phase of family life is not useful, since these phases commonly proceed together. A last child and first grandchild can be approximately the same age in such families.

When individuals are effectively integrated into their family organizations for life, the concept of "launching" is also only partially appropriate. In Latin societies, however, young couples do usually move out of their parents' homes when they marry. Moreover, the men in particular are extensively involved in non-familial organizations, many of which are entirely independent of family influence. Thus, Latin-Catholic parents are faced with the need to

[1] Kenny, Michael: *A Spanish Tapestry: Town and Country Life in Castille* (Bloomington, Indiana: Indiana University Press; 1962), pp. 55-7.

provide access to an expanded network of associations for their young people, even though their move into new spheres of activity will not mean severance from many important family functions.

Changes from the time of marriage to middle age are more closely related to the complexities that follow on the birth of children and the stages of the life cycle of parents and children than to discontinuity in particular family functions. In autonomous nuclear families in which children are not expected to maintain functional ties with their parents and siblings when they reach adulthood, parents are not committed to parental responsibilities for life. Many Americans, for example, think of raising a family as a limited undertaking and look forward to middle years in which they can cultivate their own interests, as individuals and as a couple, free from responsibility for their children's welfare. Like parents everywhere, Latin-Catholic fathers and mothers acquire new concerns as time goes on, but unlike parents in autonomous nuclear families, their concerns continue as long as they live. The progressive educational needs of their children, their occupations and marriages, and the shifting needs of the older generation replace new births, the problems of infancy and early childhood, and the establishment of households as principal subjects of daily attention. In time, grandchildren make new demands upon their resources.

Indulgence of babies and very young children is typical in Latin families, but the life of children after the ages of five or six is highly disciplined. Parental authority is not usually autocratic, but it exists and is respected. In general, Latin-Catholic people believe that the conditions of life as it is actually lived whatever these may be must be understood and accepted and that young people must be prepared to meet them. To this end, training begins early and is rigorous and unremitting from childhood until the end of compulsory schooling at around fourteen or fifteen. Parents and teachers and the clergy are in accord about what they expect children to achieve and the means of coercion to be used to guarantee that they do.

In the home children are appraised early as to their potentialities. It is not assumed that everyone is capable of the same achievements. With a bluntness that would sound cruel to many American parents and teachers, children are subjected by their elders to verbal comparisons of their assets and liabilities. They are not all expected to do the same things, but they are expected to do what they can do as well as they can. If one child is doing his best, he is rewarded even though it is less than another is doing. If the other does twice as much, but his parents and teachers think that his performance falls below what he can do, he is punished. Punishment falls short of force as a rule. Increase and decrease in tenderness or, later, a show of affectionate respect are widely used. The granting and withholding of pleasure is common. Tongue-lashing, holding the child up to ridicule before others, is a chief means of coercing a youngster to conform to requirements and to do his best. Children soon use the technique among themselves. It is a potent weapon.

Children in Catholic extended families are generally taught to be quiet, neat, respectful to their elders, well-mannered, thorough, and to accept the facts of life as revealed to them without protest, sentimentality, or useless questioning. The proper use of their language is a matter of pride to most Latin people, especially the French and Spanish, and their children are taught to speak correctly and fluently. The daily life of children is almost totally devoted to school, chores, and homework; there are few hours for play. In lower-class families, children are from an early age assigned tasks at home which increase in responsibility as they grow older. Boys help their fathers, girls their mothers in a kind of apprentice relationship that stands them in good stead in adult life. In all classes, there is an early and clear division of labor between males and females.

The child-rearing years in Latin-Catholic families tend to be more personally demanding for both parents and children than earlier and later phases of family life. Except for the urban working class and some "sophisticated" upper- and middle-class families, nuclear households and the family circle remain the center of the lives of individuals. During the child-rearing years, the elders of the family are actively concerned with keeping the younger ones oriented to this center. They do not allow their children much social initiative. They even view their entrance into school as something of a threat to family regulation.

The peer groups of Latin juveniles and young adolescents do not usually replace their homes in importance. School relationships are generally kept isolated from the closed circle of siblings, cousins, and children of family friends. School peer activities provide an escape from family supervisions and an outlet for impulses that are not permitted expression at home, and consequently, tend to be rather conspiratorial and often rebellious. But they do not usually proceed to a point that would endanger either individual careers or family honor. While Latin youths often establish strong school ties, their school groups on the whole do not evoke the lasting loyalties which teams or clubs or fraternities do in some other societies. The sentiment of alumni toward their preparatory schools and colleges in the United States and England, for example, is absent in Latin countries. Success at school is expected in the interests of family reputation, but attachment to schools themselves is not encouraged.

The nature of the schools themselves mitigates against it as much as family sentiment does. Latin parents and teachers are allied in several important ways. Both are committed to teaching the young the "Latin culture" that is so large a part of the foundation for the unity of these societies and which is considered the mark of a person of worth. Tradition is transmitted by drill and conformity, not by educational experimentation or permissiveness toward the young. Schools are formal and entirely occupied with teaching a highly standardized curriculum. Sports and extracurricular activities are not part of these organizations. Competition is encouraged, but it is channeled into lesson learning. Each student is prodded by teachers and relatives to work hard to do better than his siblings, cousins, or schoolmates. Solidarity among the students vis-à-vis their elders is limited by their individual striving for advantage over each other which pays off in rewards in the family.

This competitiveness and individuation within formal limits is paralleled in other areas of life. Each nuclear unit competes with the others for a larger and better share of the resources of the extended family. Such things as inheritance from grandparents or unmarried aunts and uncles, or access to desirable positions, are not strictly determined by law or tradition. There is room for personal influence over the distribution of family benefits, and children are often an important means to this end. They are likely to be encouraged to learn to manipulate a variety of people quite early in life. A favored grandchild or niece or nephew not only has an ally with whom to resist parental pressure on occasion, but he or she builds up a power position in both the nuclear unit and the extended family organization. The advantages such a child brings to the nuclear family give him or her a limited equality with elders that is a foreshadowing of adult relationships in these societies.

Thus, the patterns of child-rearing, both at home and at school, gradually but cumulatively prepare Latin-Catholic children for adult life in their societies. They acquire a common culture along with skill in achieving personal satisfactions and advantages within a network of complex relationships without disrupting the network itself. Although the members of extended families continue to look upon them as the ultimate sources of security and individual benefits, their families are not centers of great personal freedom. Many American adults have no family circle to which to turn for assistance or support, but if they have, their relation to relatives is apt to be easy-going. In the Confucian family the corporate hierarchy guaranteed an accumulation of privileges. In Latin-Catholic families, no one is likely to be abandoned in need, but the achievement of full benefit from membership in them requires individual effort.

Whether young men and women, during the launching period, achieve desirable marriages and occupations is largely determined by their previous success with family elders and in school, and by the economic and social position of their families. These new relationships represent a branching out from the main family organization rather than separation from it. Many families in Latin societies still control access to positions in all spheres of life and consider it a family responsibility to see that their young members are well placed. This is one of the advantages that members of extended families have over their compatriots who do not have similar "connections." In return for this service, individuals are expected to keep the family council informed of opportunities in their spheres that might be useful to the family as a whole or to individual members in it. Coteries of people who belong to upper-class Latin families continue to preserve the economic and political and even religious power of their families through exclusive relationships based largely on direct family ties and inter-marriages.

Child-rearing and -launching in these extended families are not merely directed toward the cultivation of individuals who can provide for themselves and their own children. The elders in these families try to prepare their children to join with them to implement family tradition, enhance family resources and prestige. Even after their children are launched, neither parents nor grandparents—nor uncles and aunts for that matter—look forward to a period of relief from involvement with children or to an opportunity to develop their own individual interests, skills, or relationships. Wives and mothers do not look for activities outside their homes. Neither the general attitudes toward their domestic activities nor the conditions of life for aging people in these societies makes this desirable or needful.

THE AGING COUPLE—PERIOD OF RETIREMENT

In extended families there has been little occasion for aging people to be apprehensive about their welfare, unless the whole family is impoverished. Respect for parents and elders is taught to the very young and is re-enforced by respect for their authority and control over resources that influence the welfare of their sons and daughters, and grandsons and granddaughters. Cultural elaboration of privilege for older people has never been as great in Latin societies as it was in China, but a hierarchy of relationships based on age has been clearly discernible among Latin people, and still is. The relations between young adults and their elders in Latin-Catholic extended families does not tend to evoke the ambivalence on the part of both young and old that it often does in societies in which there are few institutional guarantees of continued personal significance and support for the old. There are few reasons for Latin parents to delay the social development of their children or their entrance into adult relationships and occupations.

Most men in Latin societies continue to be active in their occupations as long as they wish to be, or until they are physically incapacitated for them. Respect, honor, positions at policy-making levels in businesses and professions go to older men more often than to younger ones. Latin men are not suddenly deprived of the activities and relationships that have been important concerns for many years. Their prestige in their families is more likely to be enhanced than diminished with age, whether they choose to retire or not.

For most women in Latin societies, especially those in extended families, age poses far fewer problems than it does for many American women. They are not expected to compete with their daughters' generation in matters of physical appearance. They do not have to seek distinction in non-familial spheres to win respect from others. Latin women are recognized for their competence as wives, mothers, and housekeepers. As older women, they are proud of their life's work centered in their homes. When they become grandmothers, most of them have an important part in the rearing of their grandchildren.

In extended families the care of aging grandparents and parents, when it is needed, is given as a matter of course. If sacrifice of individual satisfactions is involved, the younger generation makes it. The self-respect of the old is not damaged when they find it necessary to accept assistance. Hardship for the old, when it exists, results from the economic insufficiency of the whole family, not from the nature of family relationships.

In extended families, relationships between husbands and wives, parents and children, and siblings, are not overpowered by obligations to a corporate hierarchy, nor are responsibilities to the extended circle usually such that personal pleasure in relations with others is sacrificed. On the other hand, relationships in extended families are intensified by the intrinsic importance of the families themselves. The fact that these relationships are expected to be operative for the lifetime of all members keeps individuals in these families from ignoring them merely because they may become inconvenient or because genuine affection for particular individuals is lacking. Family continuity is important, and individual impulses are not usually permitted to endanger family unity.

THE RELATION OF EXTENDED CATHOLIC FAMILIES TO NON-FAMILY ORGANIZATIONS

The integration of Latin-Catholic extended families has not been seriously threatened by organizations in other spheres of life. The unity of the family is almost as central to Catholic doctrine as to Confucian. School training supports the ideal that family obligations take priority over almost all others. These extended families are not so large and tightly organized that they control the major aspects of national life; they have probably slowed the pace of social change, but they have not prevented many important innovations. They have not provoked political attack. On the contrary, people of all shades of political opinion, from that of Communists in France and Italy to that of conservatives like the followers of Salazar in Portugal or Franco in Spain, have supported family institutions. They have all instituted legislation for family welfare. In combination, the major institutional arrangements in Latin societies still tend to reinforce family life rather than to interfere with it.

For these many reasons, Latin-Catholic extended families are remarkably stable. They serve as islands of private relationships that provide both material and psychological security for their members throughout their lives. The strains that do occur with some frequency in these families derive from three main sources. In the lower classes, they stem chiefly from material poverty. In the upper and middle classes, they are evoked by potential fluctuations of power within the extended families themselves and by the highly competitive nature of life in Latin societies at these levels of the populations. But on the whole, in terms of potential capacity for survival and the fulfillment of basic family functions in the face of rapid and drastic social change, the bilateral extended family—generally characterized by moderate size, moderate power over members and societal resources, and a moderate number of obligations to relatives—seems to justify the great respect accorded the "Golden Mean" by Latin-Catholic people.

SOCIAL CHANGE AND THE FUTURE OF
BILATERAL EXTENDED FAMILIES

Since the end of World War I there have been massive social changes in Latin societies which have influenced the family life of more and more members of these populations. The destruction of property and loss of life in two devastating wars in Europe and fighting in the Far and Middle East broke up many old extended families. The development of industry, stimulated by the requirements of war and reconstruction, has continued. The need to replace manpower by women workers in all areas of economic life during the war years took many women out of their homes and villages, and a large number of them have not returned. Those who did return were changed by their experience, especially with respect to traditional acceptance of masculine privilege.

Cities have grown, and occupational opportunities have been expanded by new industry. Both have attracted more and more young people who are thus removed from the consistent influence of the family circles that preserved common values in the past. In addition, they have become independent of family authority by virtue of their economic self-sufficiency. Increasingly widespread revolt against the unequal distribution of goods and services that prevailed in these societies, especially for the impoverished working and peasant classes, has led to the organization of a series of political parties and movements dedicated to drastic reforms, and also to the chronic instability of political organizations in Latin societies. These movements for political and economic change have been associated with anticlericalism that is only sometimes anti-Catholic as well, but in all cases they attack traditional powers of the Church.

All these factors have disturbed the general acceptance of the cultural matrix of common values and social arrangements that has been conspicuous in Latin societies in the past. They have produced a cleavage, relatively recent, between people who are still strongly oriented to tradition and those who are energetically opposed to it. The majority of the people in Latin societies probably do not belong to either of these categories. But if they follow their habit of adapting to things as they are, they must of necessity modify the ways taught them by their elders. Many of these modifications have been unwitting. In general, new means for earning a living, technological innovations, and new emphasis on science and secular education, added to the dislocations of war, have redistributed these populations physically and socially, with the result that in the personal relationships of many of them there are widespread changes.

Nevertheless, the Latin cultural tradition, now centuries old, is deeply entrenched in the folkways and mores of the people. The nature of Christian doctrine as embodied in the Catholic Church, which has made its communicants dependent upon an elaborately organized priesthood, has given the Church a strong hold on its members, and those who withdraw from it usually cannot do so without experiencing profound personal conflict. Organized encroachment upon the powers of the Church in Latin societies is countered by the mobilization of its own extensive international organization. Political unrest has not produced political unity. Localism is still vital in these countries, and the reluctance of people from different regions to band together, especially in Spain and Italy, keeps them politically weak. There is some support for family-determined, aristocratic leadership, and a number of extended families have managed to survive and to influence events in the political and economic spheres of life. Feminist striving is not strong in Latin countries; there is still relatively little demand for higher education by women. Since most of these countries are plagued by unemployment, the women have not been encouraged to participate in economic activities traditionally dominated by men as they have in countries, like Russia, that need labor.

And so the persistence of the old is about as conspicuous as the introduction of the new in Latin-Catholic societies. Confucian Chinese society, dominated by great families and clans and regulated by a system of ethics that was the same for personal life and for political, required reorganization of every sphere of the society if it was to be significantly changed. Latin-Catholic societies appear to be able to absorb radical changes in some spheres of life and for some people without greatly disturbing the patterns of life for others. There are a great many people in these societies who do not question the basic values and customs that have long been incorporated in the Church, the schools, and their families. They do not want changes in these spheres of life and they view with suspicion proposals for economic and political reforms that threaten to evoke them. Many people in all areas in these countries, but especially outside of their principal cities, have continued to maintain traditional family, educational, and religious institutions in the midst of extensive, even revolutionary, changes in political and economic life.

The history of the Latin countries of Europe suggests the possibility that a relatively clear separation between private and public spheres of life may protect the one when important modifications are made in the other, if private arrangements do not seriously interfere with new public organizations. Although Latin-Catholic extended families have frequently been influential in the economy of their countries, they are not essential economic units. These economies include both public and private control. Although some extended families have retained power in the political life of their countries, monarchical forms of government have disappeared in all of them and the significance of their aristocracies as such is largely limited to the realm of social prestige. The Catholic Church has compromised with political organizations in these societies also. By so doing, it has kept much of its power in personal, educational, and spiritual matters and has even maintained a large proportion of its material wealth and its influence in political affairs.

It is conceivable that the very consistency and homogeneity, which is reflected in individual character traits and values shared by many Latin-Catholic people, may have impeded the development of arrangements that might have benefited these societies. It seems highly probable that these people would be profoundly disturbed psychologically if they were confronted by conditions that opposed their religious convictions and/or their cultural consensus. But their actual histories suggest that this combination of religious and cultural support so greatly reduces anxiety in the private aspects of their lives that they are capable of radical and extreme behavior in the public spheres of politics and the economy without suffering personal conflict or disintegration. This seems to be indicated, for example, by the anticlericalism of staunch Catholics and by the exceptional individuation of many Latin people in their personal affairs, even including their family councils.

It may be that institutional combinations that provide extensive satisfactions for important individual needs without impeding the maintenance of collective order can continue largely unmodified for long periods of time even when other institutional areas, with which they are interrelated, undergo drastic change, so long as the formulations that make for personal security are not attacked. Comparison of the relations between church and state in the Communist regimes in Russia and Poland seem to support this conclusion. In Russia the close connection of the Orthodox Church with a discredited monarchy and aristocracy had apparently alienated enough people to enable the new revolutionary regime to disestablish the Church without mass opposition. But in Poland the vital significance of Catholic practice to a majority of Poles has forced an atheistic government to permit the Catholic Church to perform its rites and even to continue religious instruction in public schools in return for its tacit support of the political policies of the State. In any case, the extended family institutions and organizations in Latin-Catholic societies in Europe, closely allied with the Church and with Church-dominated schools, have apparently been successfully insulated from the effects of extensive changes in their political and economic arrangements to a remarkable degree. They have even survived the devastating impact of modern wars.

The current increase in the actual number of autonomous nuclear families in these societies does not necessarily foreshadow the elimination of the importance of extended ones. Even in highly industrialized and urban societies like the United States, where there was never strong traditional support for them, extended families have persisted among immigrants and have developed among people in the upper classes. These larger family units are often able to provide advantages for their members that isolated nuclear units cannot.

In Latin-Catholic societies there are still a good many extended families that have advantages to preserve. It is unlikely that the traditional ideal of family continuity will disappear from these societies for some time to come despite an increase in the tempo of social change. The benefits that extended family organization provides to individuals may well be especially advantageous in a period of political and economic uncertainty and the threat of extinction in the event of war. The instability of organizations in other spheres of life is likely to revive traditional sentiment for families as the most dependable sources of protection and support. It seems highly probable that bilateral extended family organization will continue to be an important part of the social order in Latin societies.

SUGGESTED READINGS

BEAUVOIR, SIMONE DE. *Memoirs of a Dutiful Daughter*. New York: The World Publishing Co., 1959.

Although the author's fascination with her own musings makes this heavy going in part, she does provide a good picture of a French middle-class extended family.

GIRONELLA, JOSE MARIA. *The Cypresses Believe in God*. New York: Knopf, 1955.

A detailed story of a Spanish middle-class family through which the author provides a panorama of Spain, the Spanish people, and the social and political events that preceded the Civil War.

LAMPEDUAS, GIUSEPPE. *The Leopard*. New York: Pantheon, 1960.

Excellent account of an Italian aristocratic extended family by one of its members.

METRAUX, RHODA AND MEAD, MARGARET. *Themes in French Culture*. Stanford: Stanford University Press, 1954.

Report of a study made by a team of social scientists based on interviews and tests. It deals with some important aspects of French family life.

PITTS, JESSE. *The French Bourgeois Family and Economic Retardation*. Cambridge: Ph.D. thesis. Harvard University, 1957.

Some penetrating observations on French family life by a sociologist who is familiar with France.

PART THREE

■ ■ ■

The Influence of
Different Cultural and
Social Settings on
Family Organization

■

THE AUTONOMOUS NUCLEAR FAMILY IN SCANDINAVIAN SOCIETIES

■

Comparison with Nuclear Families in the United States

THE NUCLEAR family is by no means the only form of family organization in Norway, Sweden, and Denmark. In the past the majority of families in these societies were of the extended type and controlled property through family inheritance. The extended type of family persists today, particularly in rural areas. Where it does, parents tend to cling to control of family property. Their children chafe under their regulations, which often continue long past childhood and youth; if these children defect to pursue their own careers, it is seriously disturbing to both the older generations and to the young.

In urban and semi-urban districts today, however, the autonomous nuclear family is the normative ideal for the majority of Scandinavians and it is the most common type of family unit among them. Scandinavian nuclear families are similar in many ways to their counterparts in the United States. Individual choice of marriage partners, stress on the companionate aspects of the relationship between husbands and wives, their combined autonomy over the management of their households and the rearing of their children, and the gradual emancipation of children from regulations by their parents are characteristic of family experience in both Scandinavian and American societies. But while Scandinavian and American nuclear family units are detached from a larger circle of relatives, the resulting strains on individuals and on family ties are not so great for Scandinavians as they are for a conspicuous number of Americans. Since this advantage for members of Scandinavian nuclear families is related to their political, economic, religious, and educational organizations and to the size and homogeneity of their populations, it is necessary to summarize some of the outstanding features of the cultural and social settings in Scandinavian societies.

GENERAL SOCIAL CHARACTERISTICS THAT INFLUENCE FAMILY LIFE

The many similarities among the social organizations, culture, and people of Norway, Sweden, and Denmark are the justification for combining them under the title "Scandinavia." They were once politically unified and, although they are independent nations today, they remain a recognizable political bloc. They are relatively small in size, unusually homogeneous in population, are technologically advanced, and have a very high standard of living. The languages spoken in all of them are similar enough to make it possible for people from one country to understand those of the others. Finally, the major social institutions in these countries are essentially alike.

Politically, Scandinavian countries are constitutional monarchies, and an aristocratic class is still recognized. Their parliaments are powerful; they specify and grant the executive functions of the Crown. For about thirty years they have been dominated by Socialist or Labor parties. Despite the presence of a Royal House and an aristocracy, there is less differentiation in the range of income and material resources in Scandinavia than there is in the United States. The royal families participate extensively in the ordinary, daily life of these populations—far more, for example, than they do in England. They do not indulge in much pomp and display.

Norway, Sweden, and Denmark are all "welfare states" and have been since the late nineteenth century. They are Socialist, but their socialism derives from nineteenth-century French and German socialist thought rather than from more recent formulations of socialist doctrine. Although the dominant political parties chiefly espouse economic planning and the interests of working people, they are far from revolutionary. Labor and Conservative parties, despite conflicts of interest, have frequently cooperated and supported programs in the interest of national welfare. The majority of Scandinavians currently assume that no one should have too much or too little in material resources and that everyone, regardless of individual fortune, should have reasonable security and well-being. In large measure, they have succeeded in achieving this goal by means of extensive welfare legislation, most of which has been widely supported on a nonpartisan basis. Labor and employer unions and cooperatives participate in many government programs.

There are minor variations in the organization and dispensation of welfare benefits in these societies, but the basic provisions are the same. National health insurance provides medical, dental, and maternity care for everyone. Unemployment compensation and cash income during illness are available. Low-cost housing is supplied by the government and cooperative agencies, and housing loans are increasingly obtainable. Extensive and specifically family benefits are a conspicuous feature in these countries and will be discussed in connection with family life. Provisions for illegitimate children are supervised or supplied by the Courts. At the age of sixty-five or approximately, all Scandinavians receive an old-age pension.

In addition to these insurances against individual crises, the Scandinavian states provide other benefits to their people. There are State theaters, ballets, and orchestras whose members are required to tour the provinces. There are state-supported art and craft exhibits, many of which are sent by boat as far as the North Cape of Norway. The money from national athletic pools is equally divided between public athletic facilities and national support for artists and scientists.

Because of the universal availability of social services in Scandinavian countries, there is no loss of self-esteem for those who accept them, as there frequently is in the United States where public services of this order are relatively new and not universally applicable. Scandinavians take advantage of social services as a matter of course since all have—through their taxes—contributed to them. The very high level of taxation which sustains these benefits has greatly narrowed the range of differences in income and way of life between classes. There are few rich—no very rich by American standards—and few very poor.

In comparison with those in the United States, cash incomes in Scandinavia are greatly reduced by this extensive program of tax-provided services. The universally moderate income level, along with the sharing of so many supportive facilities among Scandinavians, probably accounts for the absence of that competitiveness, manifest in conspicuous display, that is common in the United States, and for a notable decrease in social distance between classes in Scandinavian societies. There are very few rich living in exclusive and isolated circles; the upper classes, and even the king himself, mingle in public places without special ceremonies. These democratic situations are the logical outcome of greater actual equality in Scandinavian life.

In many respects their economic practices are an extension of their political arrangements. There is national control of a large percentage of the natural resources, industrial plant, and public utilities in Scandinavia. The principal economic base differs somewhat in each country. Sweden is the most highly industrialized. Fishing, forestry, and shipping dominate the economy of Norway. Denmark is one of the important dairies of Europe. Since there is a high level of technical proficiency among these people, nonindustrial activities are intensively and scientifically developed.

The state does not control the total economy. There is still a good deal of private business and enterprise, and small family farms account for the largest proportion of Scandinavian agriculture. About half the economy is run by means of private cooperative associations. This is especially true for all phases of farm production and distribution. Many trade unions, especially in the building trades, run consumer and production cooperatives.

There are strong worker and management unions, both of which have evolved policies of responsibility, not only to their own members, but toward each other and the national welfare. After an early period of conflict which was ruinous to workers and nonworkers alike, the unions established schools to provide workers with the knowledge necessary for understanding the wide aspects of economic life as well as with their more specialized interests and problems. These schools were originally organized for adult education, but workers schools in the cities and folk schools in the rural areas have become an important part of the national educational systems of these countries. They emphasize the general economic aspects of dominant occupations and provide advanced technological training, but they have expanded their curriculums to include basic training in the humanities and the arts. Educational standards in these societies are very high and educational facilities extensive. Education is free and universal. There is no illiteracy, and Scandinavians are the best-read people in the world. Teachers' salaries are relatively high. They are paid for overtime work and receive full pensions after twenty years of tenure. The educational system includes seven years' compulsory elementary schooling; secondary schools include the folk and worker schools, technological schools, and universities. Training is both more formal and more disciplined than in the United States. The requirements at each level are stringent and so are the prerequisites for moving up the educational ladder. The Scandinavians follow the general European pattern of education in which every child receives similar basic training to the approximate age of fourteen. At this point differentiations are made according to past performance. Those young people who show aptitude for more academic pursuits, including the professions, are encouraged to go on and are directed to high schools that train for the universities and professional schools. Those who do not are directed to vocational schools.

The Lutheran Church is the Established Church in all Scandinavian countries. It is fully supported economically by their governments. Training for the clergy is state-provided and so are ministers' salaries. The Catholic Church is the only other religious organization to which a substantial number of Scandinavians belong, but the proportion of Catholics in these populations is small. The religious monopoly of the Lutheran Church does not interfere with religious tolerance in these countries, however. Scandinavians strongly support freedom in this regard today.

Religious life among Scandinavians is not as uniform as the presence of an Established Church might suggest. In the not very distant past the Church was more powerful and less tolerant. It was largely Fundamentalist in doctrine and reinforced the patriarchal authority of the then prevailing extended families. It was, in turn, supported by them. Churches were centers of social life in towns and villages and the clergy exercised considerable control over the life of these communities. Lay leadership was a conspicuous feature of religious observance in Scandinavian churches and homes, however. This practice could impose limits upon the power of the clergy, and did so when differences between the advocates of Fundamentalist and Liberal interpretations of Church doctrine developed. Some lay leaders of the Church were among the first to demand the extension of secular regulation in their societies. The ability of the clergy to attract almost universal support for the Church was weakened.

Scientific and technological developments have secularized many aspects of living in Scandinavia, as they have in other Western European societies and the United States. Increased urbanization and the break-up of many of the old extended families have detached many Scandinavians from traditional ways which were closely associated with religious doctrine and practice. The Church remains a routine part of the daily life of Scandinavians chiefly in rural areas. In urban centers, the separation of religious practices from other routines is clear-cut.

Nevertheless, the doctrines of the Lutheran Church are deeply imbedded in the culture of Scandinavian countries. The majority of Scandinavians are Church members. Although this membership is nominal for a great many adults, most Scandinavian children are baptized and confirmed in the Church. Religious education is still part of the curriculum in elementary schools. The majority of marriages are celebrated by Church weddings. Funerals are presided over by the clergy. Thus, although regular Church attendance is sparse outside of agrarian communities, crucial events in the lives of Scandinavians are still marked by religious ceremony. For the vast majority these ceremonies are the same. Heterogeneity in religious life, which is characteristic of the United States, is unknown in Scandinavia.

Finally, two very general and attractive aspects of life in Scandinavian countries that are not precisely part of their basic establishment must be mentioned to complete this brief description of the social setting in which family life proceeds. It is insufficient merely to say that the standard of living is high. It is really enjoyed by a great many of the inhabitants. Public parks are served by distinguished artists and are well equipped with facilities for public pleasures. The Milles Garden in Stockholm is one example. Tivoli, in Copenhagen, is the most famous. Music and theater and dancing are made available along with the usual features of amusement parks. Enjoyment of the out-of-doors in general and active participation in sports are widespread. Sea and mountains are readily accessible almost everywhere in Scandinavia. Almost everyone swims and boats and hikes and camps and skis, not merely during a brief vacation period, but throughout the year. These activities are typically shared with families and friends.

In general, it is easier to maintain a comfortable balance between work and recreation in Scandinavia than it is in many countries, especially in the United States. The Scandinavians are industrious and place a high value on work. Nevertheless, their daily routines are interspersed with frequent and generous hospitality and recreation of many kinds and they take uninhibited pleasure in both.

PHASES OF FAMILY LIFE

Preparation for Mate Selection and Marriage

Nuclear families in Scandinavia are not child-centered. Young children are provided with good, rather than indulgent, care. Parents are not usually authoritarian, but they exercise authority.

Their children are more consistently supervised and regulated than children are in the United States. Homes are more likely to be centers of recreation for the whole family. Communities, neighborhoods, and housing projects frequently provide a setting for children's play that enables their elders to keep track of what they are doing. The cultural homogeneity of Scandinavian societies makes it easier for parents to prepare their children to meet the demands that will be made upon them than it is for many American parents.

The life of pre-adolescent children is family oriented to a high degree. Schools are more disciplined than they are in the United States and they do not offer a large number of extracurricular activities that keep students away from home. Sports and other recreation are usually provided by families and are shared by young and old.

After their uniform elementary school years, Scandinavian children are given more specific occupational training than American children. There are apprenticeships for those who do not go into the professions, and the system of folk schools in rural districts and of industrial schools in urban areas extend their educational opportunities. Advanced study in academic and professional schools is provided only for those who demonstrate ability for them. On graduation, students must serve internships in the field as part of their contribution to government services.

Girls have access to all these facilities and many avail themselves of them. But more Scandinavian than American girls are taught domestic skills and are, therefore, more likely to be competent housekeepers when they marry. The majority of Scandinavian women devote the better part of their lives to homes, husbands, and children, by preference as well as necessity, just as women do in the United States. It is their advantage to be trained for their tasks and to enjoy respect for their performance.

Premarital sex mores in Scandinavia are not as restrictive as they are in the United States. A pattern of sexual experimentation among adolescents exists, especially in rural communities and for engaged couples. This probably encourages marriages at a later age than is typical in the United States since it eliminates the tension that drives many young Americans into marriage at an early age and before they are ready for it. It certainly contributes to the relatively high rate of illegitimate births and probably accounts for the enlightened legislation concerning illegitimacy in Scandinavian societies.

"Despite legal and public lenience in Scandinavia, there are still sufficient difficulties in emotional strain, reputation, economic support, legal procedure, and child care to make non-wedlock child-bearing less popular than abortion or legitimation by marriage or adoption as a solution to extra-marital pregnancy." [1] But there is no overwhelming stigma attached to either an unwed mother or her child as there is in the United States. When marriages are precipitated by pregnancy, they are still celebrated by Scandinavian families and by the Church. If the mating is considered unsuitable in personal terms, little pressure is put upon the parents to marry. Illegitimate children are wards of the state. In most instances the parents jointly support their child, but if the father is unknown the state provides assistance to the mother.

The usual expectation for Scandinavian young people when they approach late adolescence, however, is that they will settle down and choose their work and their mates. In many important respects, mate selection among Scandinavians involves fewer risks than it does for Americans. The circle of friends and acquaintances in which they move is usually known by their parents and is so homogeneous that the risks encountered by American young people owing to differences in ethnic or religious backgrounds are largely eliminated for young men and women in Scandinavian societies. They could almost pick a partner at random and be matched in these characteristics. More young Scandinavians are prepared for householding and occupations when they marry and many are more mature sexually than their American counterparts. Not least among their advantages are the state-provided marriage and housing loans which help to subsidize their marriages and ensure their independence.

Once Scandinavian young people make their selections, engagements are usually announced and banns are read in church. Civil marriages are permitted and are common among some pro-

---

[1] Eliot, Thomas D., Hillman, Arthur, *et al.*: *Norway's Families* (Philadelphia: University of Pennsylvania Press; 1960), p. 271.

fessional people and people who have been divorced. But marriages are typically viewed as occasions for ceremony and family rejoicing in Scandinavia. They are preceded by the same kind of preparations and festivities that occur in the United States, and most young women and their parents look upon a large church wedding as the appropriate celebration of so important an event.

The Newly Married Couple

The life of newly married couples in Scandinavia is similar to that of American couples. Marriage typically marks their emancipation from parental authority. They look forward to the satisfactions of setting up their own households and making their own plans for life together. Marriage is considered a partnership by Scandinavians, as it is by Americans, and the early education of girls and boys is similar enough to ensure their capacity for companionship when they marry. Some brides continue to work if they held jobs before they married, and some support themselves and their husbands while the latter complete their occupational training. But most Scandinavian women, like most American women, do not choose to work after they marry. The division of tasks between husbands and wives is even clearer in Scandinavia than it is in the United States. Housekeeping is overwhelmingly the work of women and most of them view it as a full-time occupation.

Whatever the particular circumstances in which individual marriages take place in Scandinavia, marriage in general does not precipitate as sharp a break in the life cycle of young people as it does in the United States. Their training for vocations and domestic skills, often their premarital sex experience, their relatively consistent orientation to homes and families throughout childhood and youth, and cultural homogeneity combine to make the approach to marriage more rational for Scandinavians. Marriage itself is more likely to be one of a series of events that mark the transition from youth to mature life than a sudden induction into adult responsibilities. Consequently, the impact of marriage imposes fewer strains on individual Scandinavians than on individual Americans, a condition that makes it easier for them to stabilize their marital relationships.

The general welfare programs in Scandinavian countries also reduce the responsibilities that confront newlyweds. They need not worry about the cost of medical and dental care, and they are protected if unemployed. These tax-supported services facilitate the shift in child-parent relationships that marriages evoke. The emancipation of children is not impeded by their maintenance needs or those of their parents. Both are assisted by the state. Thus family ties are apt to be less encumbered at this time than they are in the United States, and many of the psychological strains that are common in this country are eliminated for both young and old in Scandinavia. Serious breaks in family relationships, especially estrangement between parents and children, are less common. The security that continuity of close personal relationships provides is better protected in Scandinavia. This is an asset for individuals and for their marriages.

In this social setting, early pregnancies do not threaten the well-being of Scandinavian couples in the way they frequently do that of Americans. Prenatal and obstetrical care are included in national health insurance programs. Maternity leave is granted women who work. Family ties provide women with personal support. They are less often among strangers when their first child is born. It is unlikely that the careers of young husbands will be drastically altered by the prospect of parenthood. For many reasons, in Scandinavian countries, the welcome afforded a first child is less frequently diminished by distress due to the consequences of its birth than it is in the United States.

The Child-bearing Phase of Family Life

Although many first pregnancies are unintended in Scandinavia, planned parenthood and the deliberate limitation of family size are at least as common as they are in the United States. There is no special emphasis on family continuity and the status of women is not dependent upon their becoming mothers. Childbearing is not fraught with collective significance. Scandinavians have children, or do not, for individual and personal reasons.

The expectations and goals of Scandinavian families during the child-bearing phase are similar to those of Americans. The differences in their lives during this period stem primarily from differences in general social conditions. In the long run, the Scandinavians have the advantage. State nurseries and kinder-gartens and child allowances are added to the other welfare bene-fits that lighten the burdens of family maintenance in these countries. Registered baby-sitters and exceptionally good park fa-cilities for children are important aids to young mothers. These arrangements make it easier for those women who wish to con-tinue careers to do so. They also enable Scandinavian couples to be—as they expect to be—companions to each other as well as parents to their children.

Scandinavians, like Americans, expect a great deal of their children and are prepared to invest a large proportion of their personal and material resources in their young. They are en-couraged to do so by the high educational standards and intel-lectual achievements associated with the advanced technology and high standard of living in the Scandinavian countries. Scandi-navian populations are not large and their material resources are not abundant. Only by intensive cultivation of both can their phys-ical security be maintained. Their extensive state-provided benefits certainly do not eliminate the need to encourage individual achieve-ment. Rather, their democratic way of life and its guarantees for personal freedom require an adult population that is highly edu-cated and capable of self-regulation to an exceptional degree.

Even with their social legislation it would be difficult for most Scandinavian parents to provide many children with the training and education necessary to produce the kind of adults who can both maintain and benefit from Scandinavian life. Therefore, large families are not the normative ideal for urban Scandi-navians. The child-bearing phase of their nuclear families is rela-tively short. It is usually ended by choice after two or three chil-dren are born.

The Child-rearing Phase of Family Life

The fact that the protection of family life has been made a central goal of state planning in Scandinavian societies makes the child-rearing years different in many important ways from those in the United States. To date, direct family assistance in the United States goes to the disorganized and indigent, for the most part. It is directed toward rescue and repair rather than to regular support to prevent the need for rehabilitation. Scandinavian governments have recognized that household maintenance and parenthood in modern societies impose too many responsibilities for two people to meet solely by their own efforts without hardship to themselves and danger to the stability of their families. The governments, therefore, have accepted responsibility for providing families with regular assistance.

The value of housework is included in annual estimates of national economic productivity. Domestic efficiency is fostered by encouraging women to take courses in domestic science which are given by state agencies. Vacations have been assured for housewives by the organization of a registry of visiting housekeepers who are also available to help in case of family emergencies. Recently, a program of part-time occupational training for women has been advocated. All these measures relieve many of the strains of family life for women and enable them to cultivate and pursue their own interests with less cost to themselves than American women have in so doing. The fact that domestic tasks are officially recognized as an important part of the national resources of Scandinavian countries and that housekeepers are increasingly provided with the same benefits commanded by other workers make the work that absorbs most women a greater source of self-respect for Scandinavian women than it is for American women.

The tensions experienced by Scandinavian men as family providers are greatly reduced by the insurances provided for personal crises and by direct state support for the performance of family functions. Scandinavian men are not released from the need to make a good deal of individual effort if their families are to enjoy many of the opportunities available in Scandinavian societies. Their social security is achieved at the expense of cash income; therefore, personal success is likely to be measured in terms of individual skills or position. But the demands upon Scandinavian men, like those upon their wives, do not prevent them from sharing family pleasures as well as family responsibilities to a much greater extent than is generally the case for American men. They also have more opportunity to indulge their own interests.

Scandinavian men and women can afford to live as well as their immediate resources permit; unlike so many adult Americans, they do not need to curtail immediate satisfactions to provide for future needs. Reduction of anxieties about the future enriches their family life by enhancing their individual well-being. The family goals envisaged by people in Scandinavia and in the United States are much the same; however, the political and economic arrangements in Scandinavian societies make their achievement easier. More Scandinavian couples reach the end of the child-rearing years with their marital relationship intact.

The Child-launching Phase of Family Life

The autonomy of Scandinavian nuclear family units and their limitation of family size make the phases of their family life as distinct as those of families in the United States. When children have completed their education, family concern centers on their marriage and occupational choices. Again, the differences between Scandinavian and American families are not essentially in their goals, but in the circumstances in which they pursue them.

The launching of children in the United States frequently initiates a period of tension for everyone involved. American mothers who have devoted their energies to their children at the expense of their own interests and personal relationships are often destructively ambivalent toward their children's moves toward independence. The departure of children from their parents' homes not infrequently exposes bankruptcy of the relationship between husbands and wives who have been too absorbed in their own spheres to cultivate the companionship they envisaged when they married. Increasing economic demands upon men approaching retirement and a curtailed income often strain their physical powers and increase their personal anxieties. Fortunately, all these conditions rarely obtain for any one family. But in the absence of regular non-family sources of assistance they are a threat to many families in the United States, and a large number of families do experience some of these tensions.

The Scandinavians fare better for the most part. Since Scandinavian mothers are not as tempted as American mothers to find their chief satisfactions in the lives of their children, they do not view the departure of their young with apprehension. Since Scandinavian marital relationships are less frequently sacrificed to parenthood, Scandinavian men and women more often regard the launching of their children as the opportunity for increased leisure to pursue their mutual interests. Government aid to students, to young people who wish to marry, and to the old, relieves Scandinavian parents from some of the additional economic demands that are a source of distress for many Americans at this time of life.

The transition from the activities of youth to full adult participation in their societies is easier for young Scandinavians than it is for young Americans. Not only are they generally better prepared and provided with a wide range of welfare benefits, but they do not usually go far afield in pursuit of their careers and, therefore, are not subject to the disturbing effects that the loss of familiar relationships induces in a society like the American where geographic and social mobility are more common. New and adult experiences are not so sharply divided from those of childhood and youth in Scandinavia.

In Scandinavian as in American societies, the persistence of close associations between parents and children, between siblings, and between these and other relatives, depends largely upon the strength of the affectional ties that have been engendered in the child-rearing years. But many factors in Scandinavia make it probable that these associations will be more numerous and stronger. Therefore in Scandinavia, neither the young nor the older nor the old are likely to be seriously threatened by the dissolution of the household that is common practice when children leave it to establish their own.

The Aging Couple—Period of Retirement

Many individual factors determine the degree of felicity experienced by aging and old people. Illnesses and deaths bring emotional impoverishment as well as physical losses, and the presence or absence of interests and the skills to implement them make the difference between life enjoyed or endured. Personal resources are always an outcome of individual effort. They can be encouraged, but they cannot be conferred. Individual ability to meet the adjustments required by retirement and age in Scandinavia varies greatly, as it does everywhere. However, there are a number of social factors that make the terminal years of life easier and happier for more people in these societies than in the United States.

Differences between the lives of young and old are not as great in Scandinavia. Many activities are shared by grandparents, parents, children, and grandchildren, and their friends. Consequently, the aging are less often threatened with distressing isolation and do not suffer its detrimental effects. Pensions, health insurance, and special housing in some cases not only insure physical maintenance, but eliminate strain on personal relationships for old people. The democratic system of social legislation in Scandinavia places its benefits in the category of rights rather than relief or philanthropy. Scandinavian elders are not especially privileged, but they are paid respect by the young. Most aging people in Scandinavia continue to live in an environment that is familiar. The drastic changes in living arrangements and personal associations that so many Americans are forced to make as they grow old, and the anxiety they often have about physical support and care, are not common. Not all old people in Scandinavia reap a rich harvest, but few of them are left isolated or in want.

GENERAL CONCLUSIONS

Comparison between Scandinavian and American family experience clearly illustrates the fact that the assets and liabilities associated with a particular form of family organization can be changed if the general social conditions in which the family operates are different. Autonomous nuclear families do not incur the same hardships in Scandinavian societies that they do in the United States. American experience suggests that isolated nuclear family units cannot, without great strain, provide adequately for the needs of their members in a large and heterogeneous industrial society. In Scandinavian societies, nuclear families are not only relieved of some of their responsibilities by the state but the general social conditions in which they live are also more favorable to their success in achieving their ends.

This does not imply that the arrangements that favor family life are uniformly felicitous or that everyone in Scandinavia is personally well integrated, content, and happy. In many ways the Scandinavians seem to have come close to the realization of some of the ideal prescriptions for social welfare advocated by a variety of social philosophers, reformers, and revolutionaries. They have a high standard of living coupled with exceptional maintenance security for all. Their political arrangements include a great deal of rational planning along with the unifying sentiments associated with popularly supported monarchies. They are highly sensitive to the civil rights of every citizen and encourage exceptionally democratic relationships. Cultural achievement and distribution are distinguished. Educational systems are first-rate. Religious organizations do not impede developments in other spheres. Family units receive a great deal of support from outside sources. This bolsters their stability and enables them to provide psychological security for their members. Scandinavian families generally succeed in rearing their children to a fairly high level of adult competency and independence.

Yet there is ample evidence that these Scandinavian societies have not been more successful than others in eliminating major problems in collective life, or in the lives of individuals either. One of the things about which social scientists are agreed is that rates of suicide, divorce, and addictions are indices of the presence in a society of unsatisfactory conditions which are sufficiently widespread to condemn a number of its inhabitants to serious forms of personal incompetency, regardless of their individual potentialities. Suicide and divorce rates are high in Denmark and Sweden, and alcoholism has been called the "curse" of Scandinavian societies.[2] The rates of alcoholism have been so high in these societies that their governments have passed laws to limit the consumption of alcoholic beverages. Government centers have been set up for the cure of alcoholics. Alcoholism is cited as the principal cause for divorce in Scandinavia.

[2] Cf. *Norway's Families*, chap. xiv.

SUICIDE RATE PER 100,000 POPULATION

Year	U.S.A.	Denmark	Sweden	Norway
1952	10.0	22.9	16.7	6.9
1953	10.0	24.1	18.6	7.7
1954	10.1	23.3	17.0	7.4
1955	10.2	23.3	17.8	7.4
1957	9.8	22.1	19.7	7.4

DIVORCE RATE PER 1000 POPULATION

Year	U.S.A.	Denmark	Sweden	Norway
1952	2.52	1.55	1.15	0.64
1953	2.46	1.49	1.17	0.62
1954	2.35	1.52	1.20	0.62
1955	2.30	1.53	1.21	0.58
1956	2.28	1.46	1.18	0.60
1957	2.24	1.43	1.20	0.58

SOURCE: *United Nations Demographic Year Book,* 1959.

Family life *per se* does not seem to be a major source of trouble in these societies, however. Divorce rates are almost half what they are in the United States in Denmark and Sweden, and one fourth in Norway. The suicide rate in Denmark is double that of the United States and is the third or fourth highest in Europe. Sweden is not far behind in this respect. But suicide is usually highly correlated with the *absence* of family ties. In countries for which records are available, the category of people with the lowest suicide rate is that of people who are married and have children. If there is a causal connection between the family ties and low suicide rates, as many social scientists have assumed, one must look for non-family factors to ascertain what it is that drives Swedes and Danes to suicide. It appears that relatively stable family organization alone does not always protect individuals from stresses in other spheres of life.

The very great difficulty involved in an attempt to identify the factors in societies that precipitate an exceptional number of cases of personal disintegration and asocial behavior among their populations is illustrated by the example of Norway. Norway is as like Sweden and Denmark as societies can be like each other in population, geography, history, and political, economic, educational, religious, and family arrangements. Yet the Norwegian divorce rate is one-half of the rates in Sweden and Denmark. The suicide rate is less than one-half that of Sweden and is one-third that of Denmark. In all the manifestations of personal problems, except alcoholism, that are believed to be connected with general social conditions, Norway is close to the bottom of the list.

It is doubtful that any actual organization of a large population can be satisfactory, let alone optimal, for all members, or even for all large categories of people included in them. But comparisons between societies reveal that some institutional arrangements, or combinations thereof, cope with particular human needs better than others. Adequate means to protect and rear children, ready assistance in the inevitable personal crises of human life, and some guarantees of access to employment and aid during periods of unemployment are among the minimum requirements for family maintenance and competency. In pre-industrial social orders, these conditions were provided by extended and corporate families. In modern industrial societies in which autonomous nuclear families prevail, many family units are unable to meet these requirements without regular assistance from non-family sources. This assistance is regularly provided in Scandinavian countries. It is not routinely available for all Americans.

As a result of the homogeneity of the Scandinavian people and culture, of the small size of their countries and populations, and of their social legislation, nuclear families in these countries can perform their functions without excessive strain on family members. In a country as large as the United States, however, it is difficult to provide the kind of social security for families that Scandinavians have. American nuclear families are less successful than Scandinavian in maintaining their unity and providing for their members. Comparison of American and Scandinavian family experience suggests that the number of social problems that stem from family failures will continue to be large in the United States unless some similar assistance is made available to the American people. In modern, technologically advanced societies, the autonomy of nuclear units leaves too many of them with decreasing means to meet the increasing demands of their members. Unless non-family organizations supply some of the support formerly made available in extended families, a great many nuclear families in industrial societies will fail to perform the functions which are chiefly their responsibility.

SUGGESTED READINGS

ELIOT, THOMAS D., HILLMAN, ARTHUR, *et al. Norway's Families.* Philadelphia: University of Pennsylvania Press, 1960.

An excellent Fulbright study by a team of social scientists. The authors have used the data collected in interviews and their observations to establish connections between family life and other major spheres of Norwegian society. They have also used historical records to support their conclusions about changes in Norway since World War II.

HAMSUN, KNUT. *Growth of the Soil.* New York: Knopf, 1921.

A portrayal of farm life in Norway.

LAGERLÖF, SELMA. *Marbacka.* New York: Doubleday, 1927.

Memoirs of a Swedish novelist that deal extensively with her family and home life.

MYRDAL, ALVA. *Nation and Family.* New York: Harper, 1941.

Deals chiefly with social legislation and family welfare in Sweden.

SHIRER, WILLIAM. *The Challenge of Scandinavia.* Boston: Little, Brown, 1955.

This is a concise and readable survey and analysis of the economic, political, and artistic life of Norway, Sweden, Denmark, and Finland by a distinguished journalist. It includes summaries of the social legislation that influences family life in these countries.

· IX ·

THE CORPORATE FAMILY
IN MOSLEM SOCIETIES

■

Comparison with Confucian

Chinese Corporate Families

THE LARGEST dry zone in the world is an area that extends from the Atlantic Coast of North Africa to the western borders of China. The Arabian Peninsula is in the center of this expanse and it is in this physical environment that Moslem societies and culture evolved. Arab conquest, and with it Islam, added Syria, Persia, Iraq, and Egypt to the Arab core. Later periods of Moslem expansion included Armenia, the Balkan Peninsula, Afghanistan, and parts of India, Malaya, North Africa, and Spain. Some of these areas are fertile, especially those watered by the Nile, the Tigris, and the Euphrates Rivers, but much of this territory imposes special difficulties for human settlement.

Physical resources and cultural development and distribution in a society can modify the efficiency of particular social arrangements as much as the interrelationships of its social organizations do. The comparison of Scandinavian with American nuclear families revealed the influence of these conditions to some extent, but they are more vividly exposed by comparing corporate families in Moslem countries with those of Confucian China.

Like the Chinese clans, Moslem tribes have controlled a large part of the material wealth in their countries and their members have had almost exclusive access to the cultural opportunities and the positions of authority. Vast number of Moslems who have lived outside the protection of these family corporations have been condemned to a meager life that the hazards of climate, terrain, wars, and the whims of the powerful often reduced to a sub-subsistence level or slavery. But the natural and cultural resources of most Moslem countries have been poorer than those of China and their use has been greatly influenced by Moslem religious doctrines. The effects of these differences on the performance of corporate families in Moslem societies are the principal concern of this chapter.

GENERAL CHARACTERISTICS IN MOSLEM SOCIETIES THAT INFLUENCE FAMILY LIFE

Although Moslem countries differ markedly in physical characteristics and although their populations are heterogeneous, their common religion sets them apart from other peoples and binds them to each other. Islam, which has often transcended differences of race, nationality, geography, and culture, is in this respect similar to Catholicism and Confucianism. The ability of religious organizations to perpetuate themselves for long periods of time by their control over the education of their members is very great. Political and economic organizations are often powerless against them. At present, political parties are challenging traditional religious beliefs and social relationships in Moslem societies, as they are in so many others, and the ultimate place of Islam in relation to the other major institutions in Moslem countries is yet to be determined. But it was Islam that gave form to a typical, traditional family life among Moslems and its fate depends upon the outcome of current political conflicts.

Change is in process or is brewing in many Moslem lands. Untraditional leaders, all of whom are at least nominally committed to the improvement of the life of the masses, are urging rapid technological innovation and the secularization of political, economic, and educational institutions. Since Islam prescribes a way of life in all its aspects, just as Confucianism did in China, it is under attack in parts of the Moslem world. The division between religious and secular organizations has become sharp in some places. Moslems are beginning to be characterized by their degrees of religious involvement as well as by differences in the interpretation of doctrine—the basis of their disagreements in the past.

Contemporary social movements have created rifts in the religious and cultural unity of Moslem peoples, but they have not yet destroyed it. Moslems remain at least as homogeneous as Latin-Catholics and still present a solid front to non-Moslem people. Even in areas that have established modern secular institutions, such as the large cities of Turkey, Egypt, and Iraq, innumerable habits of living that were shaped by religious doctrine persist. Most of the rural, mountain, and desert regions of Moslem countries have changed very little since Biblical times. Up to the present, the new governments in Moslem societies have not been as successful as the Chinese in diffusing new knowledge and technology. In countries like Saudi Arabia, Yemen, and Iran, modern transformations are just beginning. As always, family customs change more slowly than all others, except religious institutions; they change first, when they do, in urban rather than rural areas. The traditional corporate family is still conspicuous in the Moslem world.

The center of the Islamic institutions which regulate the lives of Moslem families is the Arabian Peninsula. The Arab society in which Mohammed lived shaped most of his opinions concerning the proper conduct of daily life. The life of Mohammed remains the model, and his words the guide, for all aspects of living for approximately 500,000,000 Moslems. This Arabic influence on Islam has left its mark on all Believers, many of whom are not Arabs. Although Islam spread far beyond Arab borders and, from its early history, included populations whose civilizations were more advanced than those of the Arabs, the religious significance of Arabic countries has made them exceptionally important to Moslems of non-Arab lands. Arabic is the language of all members of the Faith. Mecca is the shrine toward which all devout Moslems face five times a day and to which they must travel at least once in their lifetime.

When geographic and physical conditions are generally favorable to human maintenance they can be largely ignored as determinants of what is possible for the populations that live in them. Along with the biological limitations of human organisms, they are more or less assumed to be universal and, hence, of equal significance. But extremely limited and humanly unfavorable physical conditions impose special hardships on people. By greatly restricting the means for maintenance, they limit the variety and complexity of the social arrangements that people can evolve and they modify social institutions that people import. This phenomenon has been a conspicuous factor in the historical development of Arab people.

Variety of terrain and division between desert and fertile oasis underlie the distinctive complexity of Arabian social orders. The people of the Near East evolved a way of living that took advantage of the contrasting features of the land. They came to live chiefly in three kinds of organizations, each of which was concerned with different kinds of production. Villages, located near adequate supplies of water, were agricultural. People in nomadic camps were primarily herders of animals and providers of transport. The cities were centers of trade, the production of processed goods, and the formulation and recording of knowledge. Each type of unit was dependent upon the other for supply and, in combination, they made up an economic system and political unity of sorts. This rather loosely integrated arrangement prevailed when Mohammed was born in 570 A.D.

Mohammed, like Confucius, appeared during a "time of troubles." Both were reformers who sought to diminish strife in their populations and to provide a set of rules and a program by which order could be established and peace and prosperity achieved. To do so, they codified a good many of the prevailing customs and patterns of relationship, and they supplied a new religious and ethical basis for the order and reforms they advocated. They were also alike in their conviction that every phase of their societies and the minutiae of daily life are properly included within the jurisdiction of the administrators of ethical regulations.

The materials that Mohammed and Confucius worked with were different in important respects, however. The practices codified by Mohammed included those of nomads and semi-nomads whose cultural level was less evolved than that of the Chinese at the time Confucious formulated his doctrines. The physical resources of the Arab terrain were much poorer than those of China. Finally, and most important, the religious and ethical influences on the two men were most unlike. Since the new religion founded by Mohammed became the chief basis for unity among his followers, as well as the basis for their family life, it is necessary to know something about it.

Islam draws extensively from Judaism and Christianity. Its emphasis on the records of the Old Testament brings it closer to Judaism. Mohammed did not assume divinity, nor has it been ascribed to him by his followers. He simply called himself a Messenger of God. He did not himself claim to be one of the Prophets. He believed that the Angel Gabriel had conveyed a Message from God to him commanding that he set it down for his people. This Message, as recorded in the Koran, is believed to be the revealed Word of God, not the ideas of His Messenger. Islam, like Christianity, is based on revelation.

In the face of widespread disunity among Arabs at the time, Mohammed proclaimed the doctrine of Islam—the complete submission of every individual to the Will of God. Serving God required adherence to a rigid and positive program based upon compulsory religious and legal duties. Unlike Christianity, which encouraged asceticism and withdrawal from the world, Islam contends that the way to God is by means of the proper regulation of worldly living. To this end, Mohammed formulated rules for daily life in great detail.

Mohammed did not institute either an organized priesthood or sacraments. He prescribed a number of ritualistic observances which are known as the Five Pillars of Islam. First among them is acknowledgment of the unity of God expressed in the words: *la ilaha illa' Allah; Mohammed rasul u'llah* ("there is no God but Allah; Mohammed is the Messenger of Allah"). The second is the call to prayer five times daily. Prayers are said facing Mecca wherever a person might be. On Friday, noon prayer should be said in the company of other Moslems. Regular almsgiving as an act of piety is the third injunction. The fourth is the observance of the fast of Ramadan during the entire month. Ramadan is the ninth month of the Moslem lunar year in which Mohammed received his Revelation. Finally, a pilgrimage to Mecca must be made at least once during the life of every Believer. These religious injunctions are practiced by all devout Moslems wherever they may be. The absence of a priesthood as a necessary adjunct to religious observance facilitated the spread of the doctrine and its persistence for observance is entirely within the capacities of each member of the Faith. In large part, it has been perpetuated as an essential and regular part of family life.

In addition to the basic rules governing the relation of every individual to God, Mohammed formulated a larger body of ethical and legal rules to regulate the relation of people to each other. Some of these are included in the Koran. The rest are collected in a supplement to it called the Tradition. The Tradition is based largely upon pre-Islamic folkways and mores that were codified and explained by Mohammed and his followers. Originally it was a record of orally transmitted accounts of Mohammed's words and deeds. These were gathered and written down in the ninth century and a final version was completed in the eleventh century. The Koran and Tradition are the source of Islamic Law and, until recent time, there was no other law in Moslem societies.

Moslem communities have been theocratic, a characteristic that differentiates them from the Chinese. Although in the beginning Islam was a political as well as a religious entity in all Moslem communities, and has been so in many places and times, periodic political decline led to the differentiation in some of them between the religion of Islam and the Moslem state. Nevertheless, at no time have these spheres of life been far apart in any Moslem society. A predominantly secular state, such as Turkey or Egypt, is a contemporary phenomenon among Moslems and is not yet an ideal for all of them. The sacred source of the Law of Islam makes it theoretically an infallible record of moral obligations regulating not only the religious and domestic life of all Moslems but their political activity as well.

Over time, differences of interpretation concerning the application of the Law arose. Consensus was achieved by appeal to learned men in the communities. This practice led to the differentiation of a class of scholars, called the Ulama, who became professional teachers of the Law. They were consulted for opinions concerning the correctness of views in the event that conflict arose between Moslems. Like Jews, Moslems have maintained their own communities and ways of life based on their own Sacred Law whenever they have lived in non-Moslem societies.

Education in theocratic societies is regulated by their sacred documents. Moslem schools were, and in many places still are, religious schools, and formal training has consisted largely of learning the sacred documents by rote. Although modern knowledge and technology have been introduced in many Moslem lands, all religious Moslems are instructed in the teachings of the Koran. Today there are numerous scholars employed to reconcile traditional doctrines with modern conditions and innovations, as there have been Christian scholars to harmonize early Christian tenets with the changing circumstances of succeeding periods. One of the problems for reformers in Moslem countries is the conflict of opinion between them concerning the place that religious teaching is to have in the new orders they endeavor to create. In the past, sectarian differences did not include the question of whether or not sacred law should prevail. The introduction of secular laws has raised this problem and by so doing has introduced a source of sharp division between Moslems.

Educational programs vary in relation to religious convictions. To begin with, foreign schools—French, German, English, and American—and foreign economic organizations brought secular training into Moslem societies. In revolutionary areas, local religious schools were restricted and secular ones established. But the latter have not been supplied to areas very far from urban centers. In the more conservative Moslem states, secular training has been limited to the children of the small ruling classes who were sent abroad, there being no sources for such instruction at home. In all these societies, acceptance of "Western" schools has waxed and waned in response to the tides of political opinion of the leaders who controlled them at the time. The education of most Moslems, especially women, remains largely parochial. This is an important factor in the maintenance of traditional patterns for living and of unity among Moslems with respect to other populations.

In the Koran itself women are described as inferior to men. Their chief functions are designated as motherhood and contributing to the pleasure and comfort of men. However, a good woman is deemed one of man's blessings, and men are admonished to treat them well. They are guaranteed one-fourth share in inheritance.

But the patterns of life for men and women are sharply differentiated. Traditionally oriented women live in seclusion in their households. In some respects this pattern is similar to the Confucian Chinese. Like the latter, a Moslem woman's status is related to her motherhood, her age, and the position of her husband in the family hierarchy. Like the traditional Chinese, Moslem women are subordinate to their fathers, their husbands, their husband's fathers, and their sons. Like the Chinese, they exercise considerable authority in their own sphere. However, in practice their sphere of respect and influence has been more meager than that of Chinese women. This may be due to the generally lower level of cultural elaboration in Moslem societies. Moslem households at their best have not provided women with the scope for individual cultivation that Confucian Chinese households did. The same degree of respect has not been paid to Moslem women that was accorded to Chinese women, and among traditional Moslems, women have been more easily cast aside than they were among the Chinese. Divorce is easily obtained by Moslem men and they have exercised this right far more frequently than Chinese men did.

Traditional Moslem women have not been formally educated. They have been apprenticed to their mothers and female relatives who taught them domestic skills, their proper relations to men and elders, and their religious duties. While this was also the general pattern of education for Chinese women, those in the upper classes were often educated in caligraphy, poetry, literature, music, and the arts as well. The seclusion of Moslem women in their households has been much greater than it was in China. Typically, they know less about the world beyond their walls than Chinese women because their men have shared less with them. In nomadic villages Moslem women have participated in the lives of men much more extensively than women in agricultural villages and in the towns and cities. But life in nomadic camps has imposed great limitations upon both men and women. The organization of all knowledge around the teachings of the Koran and Tradition has kept the general cultural range much narrower for all Moslems than it was for the Confucian Chinese for whom Confucian doctrines were honorable but not sacred, and which competed for their attention with a great variety of other sources of knowledge and ethical guidance.

In the economic realm, land, production, animals, trading rights, and even people needed for labor of many kinds have been controlled principally by corporate families in Moslem countries. The importance of oil to Western nations, and the accident of its concentration in the most traditionalist Arab lands, have augmented the resources and power of ruling families. The impact of foreign intrusion into these societies has been disruptive in many ways, but mostly by intensifying the power struggles within the powerful families and between them. Currently there are signs that, unless they are undermined by their own internal conflicts, Moslem ruling elites will move into a position of ascendency over Western economic invaders. Their future struggles will probably be with their own subjects.

This is the general social background in which the traditional corporate families have operated in Moslem countries. Technological innovation and political revolutions are introducing massive changes into most of them, but the rate of change is uneven, not only in each country, but between countries. As usual, the rate of change is much faster in urban districts and along the routes of trade and communication than it is in rural or desert areas. Among Moslems, the religious issue greatly influences susceptibility to the modification of traditional ways. Where strong religious conviction exists it is difficult to initiate new rules and practices. Where Sacred Law is the only law of the land, resistance to change is stubborn. Innovation is almost inevitably accompanied by bitter strife and severe social dislocations.

To date, families as such are still viewed as the basis of society, even by revolutionaries in Moslem countries. It seems likely that the very weaknesses of Moslem corporate families, as compared with the great Confucian Chinese families, protects them now. Their control over national resources has not been as extensive, nor the subordination of individuals to family authority as strong, since all are subordinate to God. And so corporate Moslem families have not been so great an impediment to political and economic change that the leaders of contemporary social movements have felt impelled to try to eliminate them. Rather, reformers have focused their attacks on the ruling families and try to persuade the many other corporate families to support their policies.

PHASES OF FAMILY LIFE

While the corporate family, or tribe, is both the most typical family organization and the normative ideal in Moslem societies, the functional unit is the extended family. This includes the nuclear families of brothers, sons, nephews, and sometimes male cousins. Not all male relatives and their families live in one household, but extended households are made up of several nuclear families under the authority of the oldest male. Extended households are in turn united in large tribal organizations, numbering hundreds of members, that are regulated by councils of elders. Ties between extended families related by blood are strong, and tribal organizations include all the descendants from common ancestors. Although ordinarily each extended family is self-sufficient and keeps its own interests paramount, yet for some purposes and under some circumstances it may draw upon the assets of the whole tribe. In times of need or threat, extended families close ranks in the interest of their own survival as well as that of the tribe.

Moslem tribal organizations are not typically as tightly meshed as the Chinese clans were. They are confederations rather than monolithic corporations. This looser organization has often been a source of trouble for Moslem families. Competition for tribal leadership not infrequently breaks into open conflict and may be ended only by force. Families can be destroyed in these contests. Furthermore, the position of a leader who has fought his way up is not secure. Sooner or later it is likely to be challenged and conflict begins again. The happier alternative is a kind of democratic leadership that is common in the tribes. Chieftains are elected by the heads of families who make up the tribal councils. In these cases, tribes are governed with their consent, and the greater autonomy of each family is an asset.

The general pattern of family relationships in Moslem societies is similar to that of the Confucian Chinese. Like them, Moslems place great emphasis on kinship. Traditional reciprocities between grandparents and grandchildren, uncles and aunts, and nieces, nephews, and cousins, as well as those between members of nuclear family units, create close family ties. Lineage is reckoned by kinship through the male line. Family continuity through sons is a prime value and all children belong to their father's house. Moslem families are patriarchal; authority is a male prerogative. Children are subordinate to their elders and women to men. Age-grading and a very sharp division of labor between men and women characterize Moslem households.

Traditional Moslem family life is based on Islamic doctrines, just as traditional Chinese families lived according to Confucian doctrine. Mohammed condemned celibacy and enjoined all Moslems to marry. The laws and regulations concerning marriage, divorce, inheritance, proper relations between men and women, the treatment of widows and orphans, the training of children, and the position of the aged are inscribed in the Koran and Tradition. Midwives resort to verses from the Koran to assist a mother in the delivery of her child. The "Call to Prayer" is recited into the child's ear as soon as it is born. Chanting of the Koran is a frequent accompaniment to the activities and festivities of households. The Koran is held before a bride's face as she enters her husband's household. Family routine includes prayer five times daily. There is hardly a transaction in the course of the day for which the name of Allah is not invoked and the Word of the Prophet quoted. Finally, the pain and sorrows of death are eased for the dying and survivors alike by the recitation of verses from the Koran.

Similarities between traditional Chinese and Moslem corporate families are many. But their doctrinal basis and the physical and social settings in which they operated are different and result in variation in the same type of social organization.

Preparation for Mate Selection and Marriage

Marriages between Moslems are traditionally arranged by elders, with family interests kept prominently in mind. The arrangements are sealed by a contract between the families. They are often made for very young children, although marriage usually awaits their maturation. Matching, among Moslems, is almost exclusively limited to family and economic background. Very early betrothal rules out considerations of the individual attributes of the couple. Kinship marriage is not uncommon. Unions between uncles and nieces are frequent and first-cousin marriages are considered the most desirable. This latter practice has two advantages. It favors the bride by providing her with parents-in-law who are also an aunt and uncle and who, it is assumed, will be predisposed to treat her well. It benefits everyone involved by protecting and consolidating the economic resources of families. Dowries are part of marriage arrangements and are chiefly financial contracts.

Polygamy up to four wives at one time is allowed by the Koran. Mohammed insisted upon equality in the treatment of wives; each is to have her own and equal quarters, each is to receive the same amount of affection. This is a difficult assignment, and more often than not it is not fully carried out. Concubinage was well established in Mohammed's time and has continued to be a part of Moslem family life. Polygamy and concubinage have been accepted in all classes of Moslem societies and have been much more widely practiced than they were in China.

The functional utility of these practices to corporate families are many, despite their disadvantages to family members, especially women. The continuity of families depends on the birth of sons. Consequently, in traditional Moslem families childless women are frequently divorced. Even if they are not, their barrenness almost certainly leads to the addition of another wife or a concubine to bring sons to the family. Women who have borne only daughters are subject to the same treatment—witness the divorce and remarriage of the Shah of Iran in 1959. Extra wives are economic assets in agricultural and desert villages where women are needed to augment the labor force. In upper-class families, multiple wives and concubines enhance a man's prestige; insure the continuity of his family by the birth of many children; enlarge his kinship circle and, thus, his sphere of economic advantage; and keep property in the family. Among ruling families and nomadic tribes, marriages are used to forge political ties as well as for economic benefits.

The political leaders of recent revolutions in Moslem states have outlawed polygamy and concubinage. In such states as Turkey and Egypt, liberation from these practices has won the support of hundreds of women for new regimes. But there is no strong feeling against such practices among many Moslems, including a great many women, and they persist. Before the laws were enacted many polygamous relationships and relationships with concubines were contracted, and new ones are still being established by the wealthy and powerful, especially in the more traditional states like Yemen, Saudi Arabia, and Iran. Both polygamy and concubinage are supported, after all, by Sacred Law.

In addition to these forms of mating there is another: marriage for a limited and specific time. This is a convenient arrangement for men who are separated from their homes for long periods for business or study or any other reason. Under the contract, the women with whom they temporarily cohabit have the privileges of a wife during the term agreed upon. Any children of the union belong to the father. At the end of the period the woman returns to her parental household and is free to enter into any other form of marriage without loss of status.

Whatever the arrangement, women after marriage leave their parents' homes and move into the usually large households of their husbands. Once the betrothal contract is signed, the couple may meet under formal circumstances in the company of their elders. Preparations for the wedding, exchanges of gifts, arrangements to fulfill the agreements with regard to dowries and bride-prices are elaborate. Two ceremonies are involved, usually separated in time.

The first is of an official nature and, except in modern Moslem states, is presided over by a religious official. The bride traditionally takes no part in this ceremony. Its chief function is the signing of a legal agreement by the groom, a guardian of the bride, and witnesses. A bride-price and dowry are included in the contract, as they are in Confucian agreements; however, the function of the bride-price in the two societies differs. In China, the bride-price served to emphasize the bride's separation from the jurisdiction and protection of her own family and to bind her to that of her husband. In the traditional Moslem arrangements, however, women remain more closely oriented to their own families, and the bride-price and dowry serve to provide some protection for the bride. The Moslem groom and his family pay a part of the bride-price when the marriage takes place, but if the marriage ends in divorce they are obligated to pay the woman the entire amount. Moreover, when a man divorces his wife he must return a large portion of her dowry to her. It may be that the frequency with which men divorced their wives in pre-Islamic lands, and the plight of divorced women left without material resources led to these arrangements. In any case, they place an economic restraint upon men and alleviate the threat to women that their extreme dependency has engendered. For his time, Mohammed was unusually concerned about the welfare of women and children, especially of widows and orphans.

A celebration is the second occasion that marks a marriage. It is as elaborate as the families can afford. As is the case almost everywhere, these celebrations provide entertainment and, at the same time, reinforce the status of the families in relation to each other and in their communities.

Traditionally, young Moslem couples resemble young Confucian couples in their training for marriage and in their relationship to each other at the time of marriage. Family interests take precedence over individual satisfactions in Moslem matchmaking, and romantic love plays no part in marriage. Young people are trained to accept the marriages planned for them by their elders as one of the natural conditions for reaching full adult status in their societies. Like young people everywhere, they hope for personal returns from their marriages, but these are to a great extent envisaged in terms of institutionally defined achievements.

The enhancement of family welfare and parenthood are conspicuous sources of individual satisfaction for Moslem men and women, as they were for Confucian Chinese. The companionable aspect, present in American and Scandinavian marriages, depends upon the assumption that husband and wife are equal; it is lacking in the marriages of Moslems, who traditionally do not hold to this assumption. But a cultural definition of the inequality of men and women does not preclude satisfying personal involvement, and young Moslem couples have achieved it in their own ways, as the Chinese did in theirs, and probably as often as people do who seek it on the basis of individual choice.

The Newly Married Couple

Moslem husbands and wives have limited expectations of each other. They do not share the same daily concerns. The task of Moslem women is almost exclusively to please men sexually, to attend to their physical comforts in the household, and to bring children to the house. Whether a relationship that includes respect and love and more extensive communication develops between husbands and wives depends on how well the wife performs her basic functions, and on the personal characteristics of her husband. But unlike the Chinese, Moslem couples even in wealthy families do not have their own quarters that are relatively isolated from the rest of the family. Moslem men have their own rooms in their households where they receive visitors. The traditional Moslem bride enters the household of her husband's family where she takes her place in the secluded section called the "harem," the women's quarters. Like the Chinese, Moslem women are as obligated to their mothers-in-law as to their husbands and must establish harmonious relationships with a hierarchy of female relatives. Their contact with males is limited to their husbands, their fathers, and, to a restricted degree, their uncles and brothers. They are more secluded than Chinese women were and are therefore more dependent on each other; in fact, Moslem women are almost never alone.

On the whole, the life of Moslem women is not without interest and satisfactions. Their family circles are large and varied. The women's quarters and baths are centers of news and gossip and the kind of indirect manipulation of relationships that is characteristic of enclaves of women everywhere. They influence events beyond their walls through their husbands and sons in important, though incalculable, ways. Nonetheless, extreme seclusion combined with a low estimation of feminine potentialities for learning or activities outside domestic and religious spheres impose great limitations on the development and use of the abilities of women. The majority of Moslem women have been stunted by their family arrangements. Their seclusion even in public has been symbolically maintained by the wearing of the veil. The disappearance of the veil is a conspicuous mark of social revolution in Moslem countries. "Modern women" have been, and are being, emancipated from seclusion in their homes and from its symbol in the outside world. But such women are still relatively few among Moslems. The degree of seclusion varies with economic level. Among the very poor, of which there are many, and among nomadic tribes where women travel with the men, sharp division between the lives of men and women is not possible.

The Child-bearing, Child-rearing, and Child-launching Phases of Family Life

Since one of the chief purposes of marriage among Moslems is the insurance of continuity of large families, the birth of a child is hoped for as soon as possible. A Moslem woman's security and prestige are greatly enhanced by the birth of her child, especially when it is a son, but not to the same degree as they were for Chinese mothers. Wherever children are highly valued for collective as well as personal reasons, child-bearing is encouraged as long as it is biologically possible. This phase is then more or less concomitant with that of child-rearing. This is especially the case where multiple wives and concubines contribute to the number of children born to a single father. Early marriages augment the number of children also. In traditional Moslem households, the range of ages among the children is so great that some of them are being launched into full participation in adult activities at the same time that others are born.

The chief means of training for Moslem children is their immersion in the life of their households. Children are not excluded from the presence of their elders; thus, they learn by emulation and by the exhortation of their mothers, fathers, uncles, and aunts, older siblings, and cousins. In traditional families, only boys are formally educated. Moslems are indulgent toward infants and young children, but boys and girls are separated when they are around six or seven and from then on they are expected to comply with adult rules of behavior and are constantly corrected to this end. They are given increasingly responsible tasks in what amounts to apprenticeship to their elders. Households are all-encompassing for the young. There is no sharp break between the lives of children and those of the adult members of their families.

Traditionally, Moslem children are expected to carry forward the activities of their elders. Therefore, these elders can serve as adequate models for them. There is little to incite the young to rebel or to leave the family circle; there is little opportunity for "delinquency." So long as Moslem societies remain theocratic, thus keeping the rate of change slow, Moslem families can perform their functions of socializing and acculturating their young without strain. On their part, children rarely break away from home. The majority of those from the upper classes who are sent abroad for training return home to contribute their expanded capacities to the augmentation of family resources. The notion that children must be better than their parents is foreign to Moslem families. Improvement is not conceived in individual terms. Bettering one's lot depends upon improving the position of the whole family.

However, the improvement of family position is beginning to depend upon sending sons out of their households, often out of their countries, for a modern, secular education. It is even becoming important to provide daughters with formal training, if for no other reason than that educated men increasingly demand educated wives. Good marriages for traditionally reared girls are becoming difficult to arrange. The development of Western industrial plants in Moslem countries, chiefly for oil and military installations, has provided technical training for lower-class youth. Individual enterprise is encouraged in the interest of maintaining secular states and modern technological economies. Revolutionary organizations are mobilizing young people and providing them with goals and the means to achieve them. Often these run counter to the principles of their elders, encouraging the young to escape from strong family influence.

These developments have brought the seeds of change to Moslem societies, but have sown them unevenly. Even where changes in family relationships and in the rearing of children have gone furthest, in Turkey and Egypt for example, they have not broken up family organizations for the most part. They have increased tensions between the old and the young, but family interests themselves have seemed to reconcile family elders to changes and so preserved the unity of families to an extent that has not occurred in modern China.

The launching phase of family life among Moslems is not sharply differentiated from its other phases. The continuity of generations in corporate families prevents the often shattering adjustments that produce so much strain in the autonomous nuclear family. Among Moslems the occupational placement of sons and the marriages of both sons and daughters are usually family affairs, as they were among the Confucian Chinese. Individuals are not put under strain to achieve them. The life of most young people is expanded within the family framework. Daughters are exchanged, and a new generation is born to guarantee the continuity of the family and its enterprises.

Although the Moslem world is in a period of transition, political disunity has slowed down the rate of change in many other phases of life there. The political spectrum ranges from the fairly well-established new order in Turkey, through the less stable ones in Egypt and Syria, to traditional ones in Saudi Arabia and Yemen, which are still governed by old ruling families. The trends in Moslem societies bode significant change for traditional Moslem family institutions. However, at the present time the absence of stable social orders and the conflicts among Moslem states and between them and non-Moslem countries have increased the importance of the family as a source of individual security. Governments in Moslem societies have not yet replaced families as the chief means of access for most people to education, occupation, marriage, and personal protection and support.

The Aging Couple—Period of Retirement

The position of aging and old people in Moslem societies is usually as comfortable as their families can make it. Both men and women move up the ladder of their family hierarchies, thereby increasing their importance in determining policy. Their withdrawal from some of their customary activities is voluntary. Threat to their well-being is primarily tied up with threat to the continuity, honor, or economic position of their whole family. When these are assured, the aging are content and secure. In Moslem families, the old have not usually been accorded the power and status of their comparable age group in Confucian families, but they have been given care and respect.

Unlike the Chinese, whose ideal was five generations, the average Moslem household had three generations living in harmony under one roof. Large Moslem households usually break up when the oldest generation begins to die. Brothers and their families, who have lived together under their father's authority, separate and establish households of their own in which they become the undisputed heads. The system of respect due elder brothers in China that kept male siblings in an hierarchical relation for life does not obtain among Moslems.

In Moslem societies, brothers frequently fight for supremacy in the tribe or for control of the economic resources and positions of power of extended family units. An arrangement made by a parent can be challenged after his death. This has resulted in strife within extended families and tribes that was not characteristic of Confucian Chinese families and clans. The absence of stable regulations for fraternal relationships introduces a threat to aging family elders and to the continuity of the families themselves. In the case of ruling families, fights over succession between brothers, between uncles and nephews, and between cousins have had disastrous consequences for their people.

Another factor which has weakened Moslem society in general, and the powers of elders in particular, is the extraordinary use of marriage for tribal advantage that has characterized the most powerful Moslem families. The following description is typical for ruling families twenty-five years ago. While it is only a somewhat extreme example of upper-class Moslem families today, it is still a valid picture of some of them in the less technologically developed Moslem states.

In the formation and consolidation of the Saudi kingdom, the bed was as important as the battlefield. The late king forged links of kinship between himself and every major Bedouin chieftain in his realm by taking a wife from every important tribe. Most of his hundred-odd political marriages lasted no more than four wives at a time, but the sons they produced were all endowed from birth with princely offices.

Today there are more than three hundred male members of the royal family on Saudi Arabia's "civil list," and since most of them have little to do other than scour the Near East for wives and concubines, they are breeding faster than any other section of the population.[1]

In part, and aside from the sometimes exceptional number of their sons, the control of Moslem elders over their sons has been weaker than that of the Chinese because their resources were more meager and sometimes insufficient. To the extent that the elders could not satisfy the desires of their many descendants, they fostered conflict between them. In part, the impoverishment of Moslem families has been the result of religious conflicts and the Moslem custom of resorting to the sword to settle them. Over and over again, learning and the arts have flourished in rich and splendid cities only to be destroyed in extremely bloody struggles between rivals for political and religious power. What has been true for cities has been true for families. Moslems have tended to be wasteful of their assets.

As for women, Moslem families do not generally provide them with the same degree of security that women in traditional Chinese families had, and their position is not greatly enhanced as they grow old. Divorce has been frequent and unpredictable among Moslems; in traditional Moslem countries a

[1] Alan, Ray: "Saudi Arabia: Oil, Sand, and Royalties," in *The Reporter*, December 1, 1955.

Moslem husband can discard his wife without stating a reason. The husband's obligation to return her dowry has been a deterrent to divorce when the dowry has been a significant economic asset to his family. In these cases, the divorced woman's loss of status in her own family is somewhat offset by the economic gain she brings with her. But if a Moslem woman is divorced, she rarely has an opportunity to see her children again. Unless she remarries, she is deprived of a respectable position in a household and the important rewards of motherhood. She can reach old age without assurance of care and homage from her children, a condition that was extremely rare among the Chinese.

Patriarchs in traditional China were often matched by matriarchs who were sometimes powerful enough to subordinate even the men in Chinese families. But few if any Moslem women, even in the upper classes, can approach the position of prestige and honor that was given to Chinese women who reached the top of the hierarchy in great households. The sacred nature of the statements in the Koran and Tradition about the inferiority of women have apparently reinforced traditional practice to an extent that the much-honored, but secular, statements of Confucius did not. Moreover, in Chinese families the rewards of motherhood were greater and more secure. Few Chinese women could be deprived of the protection of their children, even if they were neglected and mistreated by their husbands. They were rarely divorced.

Neither men nor women in traditional Moslem societies are guaranteed as much by the simple process of growing old as they were in China. Their authority as family elders is not bolstered by unusual privilege for age itself. Family solidarity is conceived to be one of the principal foundations of social order by Moslems. But the bonds within families are looser than they were in Chinese families and, by and large, the potential harvest from family life by aging Moslems is not as great as it was for Chinese.

THE FUTURE OF CORPORATE FAMILIES IN
MOSLEM SOCIETIES

Family organizations alone, however extensive and powerful they may be in a society, are insufficient to provide a large range of opportunities or protection for *many* people, even under favorable material and cultural circumstances. When, as in Moslem countries, physical conditions are inhospitable to human life and cultural development is limited, corporate families provide a better way of life for their own members than is available to people who do not have such family support, but they cannot under such circumstances provide amply for them. This is seen by the fact that corporate Moslem families have been able to realize the potentialities of the corporate family organization less often than Confucian Chinese families, who existed under more favorable physical and cultural circumstances. Richer natural resources; the nature of Confucian doctrine with its emphasis on harmony in relationships, personal cultivation, and order; the absence of theocratic authority; and the existence of a centralized political system that imposed some limits on the control of national resources by families—all combined to keep the Chinese united as a people and made for a richer social fabric. The great families benefited from the stability of Chinese society, to which they also contributed in no small measure. Competition for material and cultural wealth and power was suppressed within Chinese families and competition between them was kept from flaring into devastating conflict by the presence of strong central political organization. The administration of Chinese families was more efficient than that of Moslem families. Authority based on the hierarchy of age and sex was firmer. Divorce was rare, and both polygamy and concubinage were limited and regulated by family supervision. Chinese women had more scope for the development and exercise of their abilities. Thus, owing to many general factors that influence family life, corporate families were more effective in providing for their members, in maintaining their own unity, and in contributing to the unity of Chinese society itself.

Nevertheless, even with their comparative weaknesses, corporate families have provided vital support for Moslem societies for fifteen hundred years. Not the least of their contributions has been their ability to train generations of young people to perpetuate the culture that has united heterogeneous Moslem peoples. Today, however, it is precisely this cultural basis for unity that is being undermined by the impact of modern technology and non-Islamic social philosophies. The leaders of social movements in some Moslem lands envisage a secular state. In religious terms, many of the changes they advocate are heretical. But support is growing among Moslems for the renunciation of Islam as a political ideal, for a reinterpretation of the Koran and Tradition in the light of modern knowledge, for the limitation of religious regulation to spiritual and ethical matters, and for the establishment of secular law as a basis for Moslem states. The recognition in the Tradition of contingencies in which some things are permissible that are not strictly defined and authorized by the Koran provides a small opening for change within the framework of Islam. But it is very small. Most of the changes advocated run counter to traditional molds.

And so revolution is the prospect for the future in most of the Moslem world—if not today, tomorrow. The fate of Moslem corporate family institutions will depend upon their ability to maintain themselves without seriously colliding with political and economic organizations. Among Moslem states, revolution has gone furthest in Turkey. What has happened there is probably a useful guide for events that are happening, and are likely to happen, in other Moslem countries.

The Case of Turkey: A Tentative Guide to Changes in Other Moslem Societies

The first successful revolution in the contemporary Moslem world took place in Turkey and, although other Moslem countries will change in ways that reflect their particular societies, some of the features of the Turkish reorganization will probably be duplicated. Insofar as religious formulations and practice have determined the life of Moslems—and that is very far indeed—change will be of a similar order. Events in Turkey since the end of World War I provide a kind of natural experiment for observation.

Drastic change in social orders rarely occurs unless the society has reached a condition of impasse. The Turkish Empire had been in turmoil for years before 1914. Turkey proper, on the mainland of Europe and hence in extensive communication with the West, had come under French, and, later, German influence. Some trends toward the development of Western technology and economic practices had begun. In particular, modern schools had been established on the German model, and Germans had been in charge of the training of a modern army. When war broke out in Europe in 1914, Turkey sided with the Germans who, in return, promised to shore up the crumbling Ottoman Empire.

The oft-repeated situation of warring factions had been undermining the Sublime Porte for years. German defeat, added to this essential enfeeblement, left Turkish society in chaos. The caliphate, weak and corrupt, was no bulwark for the declining traditional order, and the economy was bankrupt. The only vital organization capable of maintaining itself and some general order was the army. Small social movements for modernization, which was also westernization, and the elimination of widespread corruption in the political-religious hierarchy, had had sporadic successes and influence. By 1922 a man whose education and personal development had drawn heavily upon European sources emerged as the leader of what proved to be a successful revolution. He was called Kemal Ataturk. Significantly, he had the army behind him.

Conditions were so chaotic that Ataturk had little effective opposition and the change that he wrought was remarkably bloodless. He proclaimed a Republic, temporarily run as a military dictatorship. He wisely abandoned claims to empire on the grounds that the Turks could ill afford one. His goal was a secular, technologically modern national state. He promised a constitution and representative government, but he ruled by decree while these were being written and arranged. The major changes that he instituted probably represent the minimum program for all Moslem states that reach the point of reformation.

Politically, the first step was the separation of religious and political powers. The new constitution was to guarantee a secular democratic government; state-provided, universal, secular education; freedom of religious expression and limitation of the national Moslem religious control to religious matters; and political equality for men and women. An intensive program was set up to train the Turkish people in the principles and techniques of representative government. Ataturk was aware that people who have always lived in social systems in which all areas of living—political, religious, educational, and familial—are organized as rigidly authoritarian hierarchies, cannot set up and operate self-regulating organizations. This fact is unfortunately often overlooked by aspiring political leaders and their supporters. A desire for freedom from unsatisfactory arrangements does not automatically imply the ability to operate new arrangements. In the case of the Turks, a constitution and representational assembly were evolved and, about twenty-five years after the proclamation of the Republic, an election was held. The Turks are remarkable among new states set up by decree in that Ataturk's revolutionary party permitted itself to be voted out of office. The difficulties in setting up democratic forms of government for populations that never had them is illustrated by the fact that in 1960 the party voted into office was accused of dictatorial administration and was arbitrarily deposed by the army.

Ataturk set up an administration that emphasized and enforced the elimination of ancient patterns of life that interfered with the new order. Women were forbidden to wear the veil and men the fez. Religious holidays, which had almost equalled nonreligious days, were restricted in number in the interest of economic and educational efficiency. The exclusion of females from educational organizations was forbidden.

Ataturk's economic goals were the establishment of effective means to improve agricultural techniques and life in the agrarian villages in general. Technological development and the expansion of industrial plants were to be encouraged and aid sought from abroad to this end. The appropriation and redistribution of land had top priority. Since the old system of land ownership had been intimately connected with the corporate family system, land reform brought changes in the traditional family organization as well.

Old family arrangements were further undermined by the program that secularized education. The new administration's proclamation of compulsory secular schooling for all children both removed children from the absolute and exclusive control of their families and eliminated religious schools. A large program for the building of schools throughout the country and for providing teacher training was initiated.

No phase of Turkish life remained untouched by the revolution. Interest here is in the effect of these changes on family life. Families, and especially extended and corporate ones, are generally conservative. They resist conspicuous change. Nonetheless, under the new conditions in Turkey the old families could not escape many basic modifications, both direct and indirect.

The new secular laws attacked the traditional family directly. By law, multiple marriages and concubinage were forbidden. By law, women could no longer be forced into seclusion and denied education or political participation. By law, marriage and divorce had to be performed by civil officers. Whatever the rights and duties of the marital state, men and women were to share them equally. By law, children had to go to secular schools. By law, redistribution of land broke up family holdings and reduced means for corporate family support. These requirements were not achieved without dislocation and conflict. The disposition of existing wives and concubines had to be settled. Elders, especially men, fought to maintain their privileges and powers. A large number of women resisted exposure to the outside world. Some voluntarily stayed within their four walls rather than appear in public with their faces exposed to strangers. Children were thrown into conflict and uncertainty by the opposing demands made upon them. Men and women were embarrassed in each others' presence in situations for which they knew no rules. The relations between husbands and wives became strained as new attitudes were unevenly established among them. A great deal of tension was generated between the first generation that grew up after the revolution and their parents.

Nonetheless, after more than thirty years, the modification of the old family form has been widely established. In general, change has been in the direction of decrease in the size of families, the break-up of large households, decrease in parental controls, increase in the education and political and economic participation of women, decrease in male domination, and increase in individual marriage choice. These changes have not, however, led to the pattern of family life that is increasingly predominant in industrial societies—namely, that of the nuclear unit living alone in almost complete autonomy and the elders bereft of significant influence. Rather, the bilateral extended family has become the common type in modern Turkey. More and more nuclear units live in their own households, but husbands and wives and their children remain oriented to the parents and grandparents of them both. Regulation by the older generations has become informal as compared with the past and it is less extensive, but it has not disappeared.

The lives of young people and women in Turkey are much freer than they were before the revolution. More of their time is spent outside of their homes. Girls and boys, and young men and women, mingle at school and for recreation. However, the type of dating that is common in places like the United States is not usual in Turkey. Turks more frequently choose their own mates now, but parental consent is important and some young people still prefer family-arranged marriages. Although equality between the sexes is the official order, Turkish women, unlike Chinese women, have not flocked from their homes to undertake every kind of occupation. Fairly militant feminist organizations exist in Turkey and they strongly support movements for change. In the cities many girls expect to complete secondary school and some to go to college. More women have jobs and a good many work in government agencies, social service agencies, and the professions. But most Turkish women devote themselves to their families and their homes, taking a subordinate position even in the making of family decisions. Finally, a great many Turks are only nominally Moslem. The rigid constraints on family relationships that Islamic doctrine imposed in the past have been cast off by many educated people in the urban areas of Turkey. Family life has been secularized.

Diffusion of change is always uneven. In the Turkish case, the centers of innovation are the principal cities. Rural areas have changed most where special training projects were set up and where transportation lines are most numerous. In remote rural areas the old forms can be found almost intact. In Istanbul and Ankara the saying goes that in the center of the city the women wear scarves. By the time they reach its outskirts, they have moved the scarves to cover their mouths. Once they reach the country they are veiled. What is true of the veil, for centuries one of the basic symbols of Moslem life, is probably true of most of the new ways. Particular organizations and laws can be deliberately enacted and imposed by force or persuasion. For these to become institutionalized in a society takes time, and this process produces its own modifications, unforeseen and unintended.

Nonetheless, changes in Turkey in the short time since the revolution are impressive. It is doubtful that social scientists, in the relatively naive days of thirty years or so ago, would have predicted that a theocratic society, centuries old, could change so much so rapidly. Historical events since 1918 have provided dramatic lessons. Much of what happened in Turkey has happened, and is happening, in other Moslem countries. The patterns of change are by no means identical, but the conditions leading to revolutionary change in each country and the innovations established follow a generally similar pattern.

Long-impoverished masses become aware that human effort can modify many conditions that in the past were assumed to be matters of Fate. Foreign contact, political or economic or both, introduces the knowledge that there are techniques for improving living conditions for masses of people. A growing number from these populations learn modern skills and technology. The old political-religious regimes are forced to rely more and more on modern trained professionals for their armies, their administration, and their economic activities. As a result, a middle class grows up in societies where populations were largely divided between the few rich and educated and the many poor and illiterate. Some of these middle-class people become spokesmen for their class and for the vast needs of the masses. In time, one among them succeeds in organizing support for radical change among the masses and, usually with the assistance of an army, assumes political power.

This is the general course of events that have transpired in countries like Egypt and Iraq and that seem likely to occur in the majority of Moslem lands. In all of them, the programs for reform are similar to those effected in Turkey. When and if these reforms are achieved, the fate of corporate families will probably be much the same as it has been in Turkey. Domination of a society by powerful families cannot be countenanced in modern states. Traditional *ruling* families will come under attack by revolutionary governments. Many of them will find it impossible to maintain their unity in reformed Moslem societies. Aside from ruling families, many corporate families will probably survive, but their members will become citizens subject to the regulations of their states. Their domination by family elders and their lifetime subordination to family interests will end.

In direct relation to the degree of stability in each Moslem country, corporate family organizations will probably break down into bilateral extended families. The relative looseness of Moslem corporate organization in the past favors this, as does the need of family members for wider scope for individual choice and action under the conditions of contemporary life. Modern technology can overcome some of the physical disadvantages that have made corporate families almost essential to an adequate standard of living in many Moslem countries. Irrigation, improved transportation, and industry can provide a broader economic base for masses of people. The economic services of families to their members will probably be limited. But the heritage of a theocratic state and the interdependence of religious and family life makes it unlikely that the normative ideal of family organization in Moslem societies will become the isolated nuclear family. In the foreseeable future, Moslem family life is more likely to resemble that of Latin-Catholic countries than that of more secular, technologically advanced countries like Sweden and the United States.

SUGGESTED READINGS

ASAD, MUHAMMAD. *The Road to Mecca*. New York: Simon and Schuster, 1954.

An autobiography of an Austrian Jew who became a Moslem and lived with the Arabs in the Middle East for many years. Asad's personal encounters vividly reveal the heterogeneity of Moslem life and people. Asad's special contribution is his comparison of Islam, Judaism, and Christianity.

HITTI, PHILIP. *The Arabs: A Short History*. Princeton: Princeton University Press, 1943.

Standard history.

MEHDEVI, ANNE SINCLAIR. *Persian Adventure*. New York: Knopf, 1953.

Account of the marriage of an American girl to a Persian and her impressions of her husband's Moslem family.

ORGA, IRFAN. *Portrait of a Turkish Family*. New York: Macmillan, 1950.

An autobiography that brilliantly describes a traditional Turkish family and the shattering effects upon it of World War I and the subsequent revolution.

PAYNE, ROBERT. *The Holy Sword*. New York: Harper, 1959.

A popular but well-informed history of Islam and Islamic civilization. Eminently readable.

———. *The Splendor of Persia*. New York: Knopf, 1957.

A writer's history of Persia which provides insight into a civilization as well as giving historical facts.

VAN ESS, DOROTHY. *Fatima and Her Sisters*. New York: John Day, 1961.

Mrs. Van Ess lived and taught in Iraq for fifty years. This account of a recent visit with personal friends not only provides a glimpse into the intimate life of Arab women, but describes the changes that are affecting their lives today.

X

EXPERIMENTS WITH
FAMILY LIFE IN
RUSSIA AND ISRAEL

■

LEADERS OF movements to bring about revolutionary political, economic, or religious changes frequently have very explicit attitudes toward the family organizations that prevail in the societies that they are eager to reconstruct. Whether their attitudes are positive or negative depends in large measure upon the ability of family units to oppose their plans for change. Only corporate families, and very extended families to some extent, can seriously obstruct the programs of revolutionary governments and social reformers. In societies in which such families have impeded the establishment of political control and have thwarted the efforts of governments to regulate populations, they have come under serious and persistent attack and have been subject to radical modification.

In a few instances, opposition to family organizations has been so great that their elimination from new social orders has been envisaged—and attempted. These efforts provide a kind of "natural experiment" for social scientists. On the basis of such experiments some students have contended that the family as a clearly differentiated organization is not essential to a complex society. The fact that no such society has existed without them is not a conclusive argument that no such society *can* exist without them. However, other social scientists contend that family organizations are necessary, both for individual human welfare and for the stability and maintenance of societies. In order to reveal the factors that have led to this latter conclusion, experiments in the Soviet Union just after the Revolution and in some of the Israeli *kibbutzim* will be discussed.

THE EXPERIMENT IN THE SOVIET UNION

Summary of Traditional Social Organizations in Russia

Prerevolutionary Russian society was dominated by an elite that was, for the most part, made up of large, bilateral extended families. Patriarchal and authoritarian, they were primarily maintained by their ownership of land and their power over the masses of people who worked it; their authority was perpetuated by intermarriage and family inheritance. These elite families were the mainstay of the autocratic authority of the Czar and of the Eastern Orthodox Church. Together these three elements in Russian society controlled access to the major portion of the national assets of Russia. Political and religious power were united in the person of the Czar and were chiefly administered by members of the aristocratic and upper-class families that surrounded the Royal Court. The powers exercised by the monarchy and its supporters were absolute and ultraconservative. The political revolutions and cultural and technological changes that began in Western European societies in the eighteenth century touched the Russian elite very little.

Basic changes in such a society could only occur by way of revolution; there were no established means for achieving them. Over many years movements were organized, primarily by intellectuals, to overthrow the regime in order to institute reforms that would open up the society to greater civil liberties and industrialization, and thus improve the living conditions of the majority of the population. The failure of these social movements resulted in increasingly repressive measures. Finally, in 1917 the explosion was set off as a result of the devastation and social disorder that followed military defeat in World War I which seriously discredited the monarchy and its ruling elite in the eyes of the masses. Numerous organizations advocating reform and revolution came into being. In the ensuing chaos, the old political regime was overthrown. Today, the nature and consequences of this event have become the almost obsessive concern of many more people than the Russians. For the purposes of this discussion, attention is restricted to the effects of the Revolution on family life in Russia.

Policies of the Revolutionary Leaders

The autocratic monarchy and the Orthodox Church, which had been the chief supporters of the powerful families and the beneficiaries of their support, were anathema to the new regime. Monarchy, Church, and elite families were eliminated, chiefly through death and dispersion. However, there was more to this liquidation than the mere elimination of individuals and families of an elite class. The new leaders had made the abolition of the family institution itself a political principle and goal.

> Madam Kollontay, at one time representative of the Soviet Union in Norway, writer on the family under Communism, and a prominent member of the Old Bolshevik guard, wrote in 1919 that "the family has ceased to be a necessity both for its members and for the State." Likewise, Bukharin . . . characterized the family as "a formidable stronghold of all the turpitudes of the old regime." An anticipation of the disappearance of the family in the Socialist state is evident in the following explanation of the *Soviet Code on Domestic Relations* given in 1927 by Professor Brandenburgsky, the author of standard texts on the subject: "Until Socialism is achieved the individual family is inescapable . . . the

family creating a series of rights and duties between spouses, the parents and children, will certainly disappear in the course of time and will be replaced by governmental organization of public education and social security." [1]

Soviet leaders intended to establish a new society and they believed, in principle, that the kind of people human infants become is entirely determined by the society in which they evolve. The rulers of the old order had just as staunchly upheld the theory that biology determines the personal traits that justify position and privilege. Certainly the personal traits of adult individuals are determined in large measure by the relationships and cultural prescriptions of the social orders in which they live. But the processes involved in this development are more devious and complex than the new Russian leaders thought.

According to the revolutionary theorists, the new society was to result in generations of a new kind of person, and they felt that the training required to achieve this could not be left in the hands of old-fashioned family elders. Only the state was deemed sufficiently trustworthy and competent to undertake the function that is perhaps the most important of family concerns, namely, the socialization of children.

Equality between men and women was another political goal that led to dissolution of family organizations. Many Russian women viewed the abolition of the family as liberation. They vehemently rejected all traditional feminine activities, including childbearing—or, at least, child-rearing, subordination to husbands, housekeeping, and economic dependency. The old dictum that a woman's place was in the home was replaced by the notion that a woman's place was everywhere except the home.

The new leaders in Russia had political and economic reasons for supporting the emancipation of women. They foresaw that the withdrawal of women from their traditional activities would be an effective means of breaking up old family arrangements that

[1] Gsovski, Vladimir: "Family Inheritance in Soviet Law," in Inkeles, Alex, and Geiger, Kent, eds.: *Soviet Society: A Book of Readings* (Boston: Houghton Mifflin Co.; 1961), p. 533.

depended on the virtual seclusion of women in their households. Soviet leaders anticipated that the liberation of women from male domination would make them enthusiastic supporters of the revolutionary government. The new political philosophy stressed productive labor, and economic goals of rapid industrialization required a large labor force. From the point of view of the new government, women would be more profitably employed in factories than in their homes. Finally, the revolutionary Soviet leaders intended that the state, by assuming the care, training, and education of the young, would transfer to itself the strong loyalties and sentiments that in the past were evoked by parents and family members. Women as well as the young, it was thought, would be devoted to the state in recognition of what it was doing for their children and for them in releasing them from the drudgery of child-rearing.

Revolutionary Family Program

All these factors united the government and some of its citizens behind a program to eliminate families from the new social order. Legal requirements for marriage were abolished. Mating was considered to be an entirely personal matter which could be publicly registered or not, according to the desires of the individuals concerned. Their association was to be continued only so long as each was pleased to maintain it. Its dissolution involved no formal procedures. Free choice with regard to parenthood was assured by access to contraceptives and abortion. Since it was assumed that economic dependence of women on men was a chief source of inequality between them, it was decreed that each would be self-supporting when they lived together. When children were born, both parents were expected to contribute to their maintenance. This new program included aids to child care and rearing. Prenatal and maternity clinics, nurseries, free schools, and recreational facilities were all to be supplied by the State.

Extensive participation in this experiment was limited for the most part to the more active supporters of the Party and to people in urban areas. The majority of Russians continued to live in families. But the support and prestige of the political leaders was behind the plan, and consequently the old supports for family life

—church and law and power in community life—were largely withdrawn. The gradual elimination of private ownership of land and industrial resources destroyed the basis for the maintenance of large families. The disestablishment of the Russian Orthodox Church discredited the ethical justifications for the subordination of individuals to family authority and for the submission of women and children to men and elders. The increase in state-provided benefits to children curtailed parental control over them. Women moved out of their households into every phase of Russian economic activity, including heavy manual labor and the professions. Nowhere has equality between men and women with respect to work been so fully achieved as it is in Soviet Russia, unless it is in Communist China.

Pre-revolutionary patterns of family life could not survive these conditions. Great extended families disappeared. The patriarchal family with its large circle of kinship ceased to be the normative ideal. Autonomous nuclear family units, similar in many respects to those of the United States and Scandinavia, became the characteristic type of Russian family. The extensive political regulation of the lives of all Russians as individuals made them equal in their homes. The relationship between husbands and wives and parents and children came to resemble these relationships in American society. In some respects, however, the Russians went much further than Americans in loosening family ties and weakening sentiments of mutual obligation.

The transformation of family life in Soviet Russia did not proceed without strain and disintegration for individuals as well as family units. Revolutions are civil wars, and political conflict was mirrored by conflicts in personal relationships. Family tensions during the years following the establishment of Soviet power were not unlike those engendered in immigrant families in the United States. Young and old, husbands and wives, siblings, and parents and children were divided by mutually incompatible attitudes toward the new order. Russian children were increasingly dependent upon public educational and political organizations for the things they needed for their development. Their parents came to be inadequate, even dangerous, models for adulthood. Emotional attachments became extremely ambivalent at best, a condition which seriously interfered with the socialization of the young. The distress of parents who were unable to evoke respect and affection in their children was matched by that of their children, whose home life had become inconsistent with the demands made upon them by non-family elders in their schools and recreational groups.[2]

Despite the strains it put on family life, the new political policy to eliminate the family from the new order was not realized. Russian families were greatly changed, but they did not disappear. By the 1930's the results of the experiment were disappointing, even to the minority of the population that espoused the new doctrines. It proved impossible to set up enough agencies, or to obtain enough competent personnel for those that were established, to provide adequate care for children. There was widespread neglect of children by parents and irresponsibility by couples to each other. Frequent abortions undermined the health of a good many women. There was an increase in delinquency, while crime, alcoholism, and other manifestations of personal incompetence made many people unfit for work at a time when the working capacity of every citizen was a vital concern to the new regime. Finally, the new arrangements failed to evoke what was most desired, namely, devotion to the State.

General Comments on the Russian Experiment

The Russian failures suggest a number of inferences relevant to this discussion. First, the Russian experiment supports the contention that the transformation of human infants into competent adults and, hence, useful units for collective enterprises, requires long, direct, stable, and intense interpersonal relationships. Second, centralization of the means to food, clothing, shelter, and important personal services for large numbers of people is extremely difficult, if not impossible. Third, acculturation itself is

[2] John Gunther, in his *Inside Russia Today* (New York: Harper & Brothers, Publishers; 1958), p. 67, says: "Still another variety of problem youth has arisen lately, the *Nibonichó*, or 'nonbelievers.' The word derives from the concept that they believe in neither God nor the devil (*ni boga, ni chorta*). These are young men and women so completely disillusioned and inert that they despise all activity; in some respects they resemble strikingly nihilistic youngsters of the lost generation in Paris after World War I—'the youth without youth.' They have been sapped of all convictions, even about patriotism."

not solely a matter of formal training. Much of it is acquired by emulation and requires the regular presence of models. Emulation is the most important means by which folkways and mores are established as personal characteristics, and this achievement is the only sure and stable basis for social control. Fourth, depriving men and women, and parents and children, of familial interdependence places each of them at the mercy of the egocentric whims of the other. This is not only frustrating to individuals in the long run, but gives rise to increasingly large numbers of people who are both incompetent and incapacitated for collective life and who become dependent upon public agencies for support.

In the summer of 1956 a piquant little scandal made news in Moscow. Several young people of the fast set were arrested because they financed their high jinks by pilfering and selling clothes. Two of these youngsters were sons of a cabinet minister, no less, Ivan G. Kabanov, Minister of Foreign Trade. Arrested with them were daughters of prominent Red Army officers and police officials. . . .

On a different level are the *Stilyagi*, young hooligans, zoot-suiters, or juvenile delinquents. The word literally means "style-chaser." These youngsters, who are sometimes called "Teddy boys" or *mitrofanushka*, hang out at restaurants like the Praga, affect long sideburns or other eccentric dress, and dance to boogie-woogie and rock'n'roll. . . .

The Presidium of the RSFSR issued a new decree (December, 1956) to "intensify the struggle against petty hooliganism" and "save Moscow's honor." Henceforth, any Teddy boy or zoot-suiter picked up for minor outrages is subject to fifteen days, without appeal.[3]

In large complex societies families still seem to be the most efficient organizations for acculturating the young, for maintaining individuals and insuring their psychological satisfactions. Many particular families fail in all or some of these respects, but no

[3] *Ibid.*, pp. 66-7.

other social arrangements that have been tried have done as well. The significant unit of family organization in a society may be reduced in size to the autonomous nuclear family, and the degree of regulation over its members and control over the resources for their maintenance may be limited, but nuclear family units are probably a minimum requirement to fulfill basic needs for the populations of modern societies. The failure of the Russian experiment is recorded in the withdrawal of the original plan and reversal of theoretical pronouncements about family relationships by political leaders.[4]

Current Family Policies

Current laws in the Soviet Union require civil marriage and public registration. Marriage is urged for everyone and encouraged by government loans and services. Bachelors are subject to special taxation. Parenthood is expected. It is assisted by government agencies that provide medical care, protect job tenure during pregnancy, set up nurseries, and distribute child allowances. Producing large families is rewarded by prizes, tax exemptions, and public acclaim. It is further encouraged by the outlawing of abortion except on medical grounds. Divorce is required to dissolve marriages and is difficult to obtain.[5]

In recent years, official support for families has gone so far that *Pravda* has published regular articles recommending all the

[4] "On May 28, 1936, *Pravda* commented on the prohibition of abortion and the increase of fees for divorces: 'So-called free love and loose sexual life are altogether bourgeois and have nothing to do in common either with Socialist principles and ethics or with socialist rules of behavior of a Soviet citizen. Marriage is the most serious affair in life. . . . Fatherhood and motherhood become virtues in the Soviet land.'

"Quoting these statements, Boshko, a Soviet professor of law, wrote in the official periodical of the Attorney General: 'Marriage, basically, and in the spirit of Soviet law, is in principle essentially a lifelong union. . . . Moreover, marriage receives its full lifeblood and value for the Soviet State only if there is birth of children, proper upbringing, and if the spouses experience the highest happiness of motherhood and fatherhood.'" (Gsvoski: *op. cit.*, p. 533.)

[5] "As late as 1938 the Soviet jurists insisted that the Soviets 'do not have and could not have what is known in the capitalist countries as divorce proceedings.' Yet, the Soviet divorce proceedings, after 1945, are stricter and offer the parties less privacy and certainty as to the final outcome than those of many capitalist countries." (*Ibid.*, p. 535.)

ceremonies and practices once condemned as manifestations of the irrational sentimentality of the *bourgeoisie* and devices for individual enslavement and exploitation by church and state. Weddings, wedding dresses, honeymoons, celebration of family anniversaries, marital fidelity, feminine concentration on establishing attractive and efficient homes, and masculine acceptance of responsibility for order and discipline in them are more urged and praised than they are in the press of "capitalist" countries.

> Since July 8, 1944, only a marriage registered with the Civil Registry Office has had the legal effect of a marriage and created the rights and duties of husband and wife and fatherhood uniformly in the whole of the Soviet Union. . . .

> It is also significant that a recent law seeks to create an atmosphere of solemnity for the registration of Soviet marriage. Local authorities have been ordered to supply the Civil Registry Offices with well-furnished quarters appropriate for the celebration, with separate waiting room, and to keep them in good order. The date for registration must be arranged in advance; it takes place in the presence of the prospective bride and groom, and, if they wish, of their parents and friends. A certificate is then handed over to the newlyweds in the presence of a representative of the local administration. The managers of the government establishments and the collective farms are advised to furnish newlyweds transportation to the Registry Office and to help them buy furniture, bedding, etc., for cash at fixed government prices.[6]

Russian family life has not returned to what it was before the revolution by any means. The experiment was a failure insofar as the abolition of family organization was intended, but it succeeded in breaking up the old extended, patriarchal type of family arrangement that could threaten political power and monopolize economic resources. Except in rural and remote districts, autonomous nuclear families prevail in Russia today. Not only political policy, but rapidly advancing industrialization, supports this

6 *Ibid.*, p. 534.

change from extended families to autonomous nuclear families.

One of the very great accomplishments of the Soviet regime has been the establishment of a free school system that includes a variety of organizations for specialized and advanced instruction available to all who demonstrate ability to profit from them and who are politically reliable. This is a necessary basis for technological development. But the regime demands that education be put to the service of the State. Occupational requirements have priority over individual and family preference or convenience. Russian citizens are expected to be mobile. Women are expected to work, children to pursue their studies, and men, women, and children to move wherever economic or political requirements of the state make it desirable for them to go. Only nuclear families can hope to maintain their unity under these conditions.

Continued emphasis on the complete subordination of individuals and organizations to political power in Russia, coupled with the educational and occupational demands on family members, makes greater inroads on family life than the typical commitments of Americans and Scandinavians do.

> . . . the Soviets have rediscovered the value of family life and strong family ties for the maintenance of sound public morals and the increase of population of a country which went through the calamity of a devastating war. Soviet marriage has at present the features of a normal marriage. But, on the other hand, recent Soviet legislation, though inconsistent with earlier Soviet laws, shows a consistency of policy of interference of the State with the family life of the citizens. In the early stage, Soviet laws sought to disrupt and weaken family ties. At present the interference goes the other way.[7]

A Soviet journal, *Novyi Mir*, explains what is meant by Stalinist Virtue, which has come into its own since the end of World War II: "A Soviet person cannot 'simply' love someone without criticism, without political and moral watchfulness. Our Soviet citizen can no longer love only because of a natural drive. He wants his be-

[7] *Ibid.*, p. 535.

loved to be worthy of his feeling, to possess the best Soviet qualities." [8]

Both old and young in the Soviet Union are required to participate in political organizations. They cannot absent themselves
from political meetings or youth groups nor fail to attend political
demonstrations. Recreational facilities are to a large extent politically rather than commercially supplied. Coercion by police and
the power of political agents to see that workers are denied jobs
and to exclude the young from schools and occupational training,
are always present. Thus, what families can provide is more limited
than it is in the United States and in Scandinavian countries.
Russian families receive more direct assistance from the State than
American families do. In this respect, they are similar to Scandinavian families. But the nature of political power in the Soviet
Union introduces a kind of threat to individual security that
Americans and Scandinavians are fortunate to escape. Unlike the
heads of Scandinavian political parties, the leaders of Soviet Russia have not discovered that the protection of individual rights is
not necessarily incompatible with Socialist organizations. Insofar
as political threat affects all aspects of life and introduces an ele-
ment of uncertainty in all relationships, it does so in families as
well. American and Scandinavian families do not have to contend
with this type of social pressure. Potentially they can provide
greater psychological satisfaction and security for their members.

It is probable that personal anxiety is mitigated in Russia by
the fact that by this time elders have matured and been educated
in the "new order" and, hence, are "safe" tutors for the young.
This phenomenon must to some extent parallel experience in immigrant families in the United States. It is highly probable that
the rift between parents and children—and between the pre-
revolutionary patterns of the one and the post-revolutionary values
of the other—has become less of a source of individual and collective strain in the case of families that were established after the
new regime became stable. The strain must be greatly diminished
in families in which parents were born after the revolutionary

[8] Durham, Vera S.: "Sex: From Free Love to Puritanism," in Inkeles and Geiger, eds.: op. cit., pp. 541-2.

period and share a common set of experiences with their children. Besides, nuclear families, unlike the old elite families, are not a threat to political agencies in Soviet Russia and so can be supported by them at the present time.

Conclusion

The Russian experiment reveals some of the difficulties attendant upon the extension of political regulation into areas of life that are usually ordered by families. It is true that the transformation of a large, predominantly agrarian society into an industrial one in a short space of time cannot be made by revolutionary political authority so long as "great families" retain disproportionate control of economic and cultural resources. The initiators of the new order in Russia were correct in their conviction that the traditional powers of those families had to go—whatever one may think of their means of destroying them. However, they were wrong in assuming that families can be eliminated altogether from large, heterogeneous, and technologically advanced societies. In Russia, the notion that family institutions and organizations are merely bourgeois arrangements, unnecessary for the maintenance of a Socialist society and its citizens, has been totally discredited if not disproved.

THE EXPERIMENT IN COMMUNAL KIBBUTZIM
IN ISRAEL

Family arrangements in Israel range from the extended, patriarchal, religion-dominated families of the orthodox minority, through a variety of family types chiefly imported from European societies, to the communal *kibbutzim* which attempt to eliminate individual family units. Our principal concern will be with the last-named. The origin and characteristics of Israel's experiments with the family can only be understood in the light of other, and even distant, social conditions.

Summary of Traditional Jewish Social Organizations

A corporate family was the normative ideal among orthodox Jews, and in the past such families were prominent in places with predominantly Jewish populations. They were the chief agencies of social control as well as of cultural transmission among Jews. In societies in which Jews were excluded from political activities and from many occupations, large family organizations were their principal source of protection and opportunity for personal satisfactions and maintenance.

These families were patriarchal and authoritarian. Women and children were dominated by men and elders. The separation between the daily routines of Jewish men and women was almost as complete as it was among Confucian Chinese. Jewish matriarchs could exercise as much power in their own sphere as Chinese matriarchs did. Marriages were arranged by elders in the interest of the families as well as of the individuals concerned. It was as morally essential for Jewish patriarchs as for the heads of traditional Chinese families to provide food, clothing, and shelter for large numbers of relatives, to see that their sons and daughters were properly educated, to establish their sons in suitable occupations, and to arrange desirable marriages for all their children. Respect for age and the privileges of the aged were much the same in both Jewish and Chinese families. Finally, as with the Chinese, it was important to Jews to have grandsons to carry out ceremonies at the time of their death, to perpetuate their memory, and to guarantee family continuity.

Jewish communities were like Moslem communities in that they were theocratic. They were regulated by Sacred Law which defined both personal relationships and the patterns of daily life. The secular laws of the societies in which Jewish communities existed touched them only as unwanted intrusions. The law that was binding and evoked respect was the Sacred Law based on the Old Testament and the Talmud, which was administered by learned and religious Jews in local courts of arbitration. It is still so for many Jews in many places.

In societies in which the economic activities of Jews were restricted and their ownership and cultivation of land often forbidden, the few fully developed corporate families among them usually controlled the largest proportion of wealth available to them. Large Jewish economic enterprises were chiefly limited to finance and trade. Except for a few professional people, Jews were principally small shopkeepers and producers of consumer goods. The accumulation of significant wealth depended upon the establishment of families whose extended units were located in many lands. Dispersion protected Jewish families from the waves of serious discrimination directed against Jews in different places and at different times; one branch of a family could take refuge with another.

The disadvantages that Jews suffered in the past in alien and often hostile societies made their corporate families and family-dominated communities more essential to their survival and maintenance than were the families of the Moslems, Chinese, or the many other peoples for whom the family was the center of individual and collective life. It is surprising, therefore, that any Jews should have considered the elimination of families a desirable social goal when they began to plan a society of their own. A number of factors combined to lead some of them to this decision.

Assimilation of Jews in Western Europe

Most of the Jews who established the communal *kibbutzim* came from the countries of Eastern and Central Europe, but they were not for that reason a homogeneous group. Despite the fact that many of them had lived in isolated Jewish enclaves, they had developed ethnic variations and sectarian differences over the centuries. Some, as a result of their experiences in European societies, had come to question not only points of Jewish doctrine, but membership in the religious community itself. Whenever assimilation into their host societies was open to Jews, many of them moved out of their isolated communities.

For some, the membership requirements of the society which received them came to take precedence over the all-encompassing regulations of Judaism that had prevailed in their old communities. The allegiance of these Jews to the laws of the states whose citizens they were, their participation in the educational, economic, political, and cultural life of their non-Jewish compatriots, and the adaptation of their religious practice to the patterns of life in secular and Christian societies entailed their rejection of religious orthodoxy. In the opinion of many other Jews, these assimilated people ceased to be Jews, whether or not they so considered themselves. A number of Reformed Jewish congregations emerged among Jews who were to varying degrees assimilated into non-Jewish societies. In all of them, secular law was accepted as the basis for order in daily life and clear differentiation was made between religious and nonreligious organizations.

The rejection of the theocratic principles of orthodox Judaism and the acceptance of the responsibilities and opportunities inherent in citizenship in European societies weakened the dependence of these Jews upon their families. Their personal achievements came to depend upon secular education, individual choices in such important matters as occupations and marriages, freedom to move from one place to another, and close ties with non-Jews. The authoritarian control that still characterized these Jewish families led a good many of their sons and daughters to rebel against them and to separate from them.

When this new generation married, its children differed greatly from their parents and grandparents. A good many joined various Christian churches and some abandoned religious practices altogether. Reformed Jews limited their religious activity to weekly observance and the celebration of a few High Holidays. Jewishness for them came to stand for membership in a congregation, not in a community. Except for their religious affiliation and an ever-present, though often suppressed, awareness of degrees of their acceptance and nonacceptance by their non-Jewish countrymen, life in many Jewish families became indistinguishable from that of their non-Jewish neighbors. Distinctly Jewish families are to be found only among orthodox or very conservative Jews.

New Policies in Communal Kibbutzim in Palestine

Before the establishment of the State of Israel, some Jews emigrated to Palestine where they organized communities that were different from any previous Jewish communities. These communities were established on uncultivated land and each strove to be self-sufficient. Although most of the people who founded these communities were members of a political and social movement known as Zionism, their leaders held different religious views and social philosophies and the communities reflected these differences. Some Zionist organizations included a number of people who envisaged the return to Palestine and the establishment of an autonomous homeland for Jews in secular, and chiefly socialistic, terms. Most of these came from the category of Jews who had long since separated from religious orthodoxy and closed Jewish communities. They conceived of their migration to Palestine as a pioneering venture as well as a re-establishment of a Jewish State and a means to escape for all time the hazards for Jews in European countries. Pioneering appeals most to young people, and the original *kibbutzim* were founded for the most part, by adolescents and young adults. The youthful outlook of their populations and the general conditions in which they lived and built their communities shaped many of the conspicuous features of these settlements.

From their beginning, the *kibbutzim* were literally embattled. There was opposition to Jewish communities in Palestine from both British administrators and Arab residents of that country—opposition no less persistent than it had been in many of the places from which the settlers had come. Also, available land was undeveloped and mostly arid. Only the young and vigorous, who were also motivated by a transcendent cause and imbued with hope that it could be realized, were apt to embark upon such a formidable undertaking. As conditions in Europe deteriorated to the point where the lives of Jews were threatened, the desperate were added. For the most part, these people had no choice except to set up small, isolated communities whose survival depended upon the utmost cooperation and on the pooling of all the energy and skills that each had at his command.

These conditions were not entirely different from those that the grandparents of many of these people had also faced. They too had been forced to migrate to inhospitable localities. It is conceivable that without other determining factors the communities in Palestine would have been replicas of the Jewish enclaves in Eastern Europe. They became like them in the intensity of their associations, their isolation, their struggle for self-sufficiency, and the development of strong "in-group" sentiments which is often correlated with a good deal of suspicion of, and downright hostility toward, other communities. Like the old enclaves, the *kibbutzim* ruled themselves.

But unlike the old communities, these communal *kibbutzim* made their own rules which were based, not on the Old Testament and the Talmud, but on various Socialist authorities. Their members were largely followers of people who had been active in Socialist movements in Europe, especially in Germany and Russia. Many of the more adult members had been trained in European labor movements; others were Marxists. There were many young people who sought, or were driven to seek, opportunities for a better life. Many were attracted, as adolescents so easily are, by an ideal and a collective enterprise. Some looked for adventure. But the majority of the leaders who organized the ventures, assigned tasks, formulated goals and promises of reward, and who ultimately dominated the *kibbutzim* has been influenced by Socialists of one kind or another. From the beginning, therefore, these were secular communities with political and economic goals, not religious ones. This alone would eliminate the orthodox Jewish family pattern, but it would not necessarily lead to an abandonment of family organizations altogether. Several factors seem to have contributed to that experiment.

The establishment of communities in a wilderness is the only actual opportunity that people have for initiating a society according to a preconceived plan. Even successful revolutions only modify some aspects of old social arrangements. The realization of "the plan," whatever it is, is often very different from what was originally intended, but pioneers can start with a plan and give some specific direction and form to their new orders. Most of the founders of the communal *kibbutzim* undertook their tasks with a plan in mind. Their communities were socialist and communal from the start. Every member was expected to contribute according to his or her ability. All resources were pooled and each shared according to his or her need. Absolute equality between men and women was a prominent goal. In its pursuit, marriage was abandoned. Mating was deemed an entirely personal affair. Housekeeping was communal; children were raised in nurseries and dormitories. Parents were thus freed for the important work of building and protecting the settlements. They saw their children at their leisure, but the care and education of the young became the specialized task of a few. Children were more the offspring of the community itself than of their biological parents. Whether parents continued their association with each other or not made little or no difference in their children's routines.

There were psychological factors that reinforced intellectual conviction among the members of these *kibbutzim*. In the first place, most of the original settlers were young people. Many were adolescents in terms of personal development, if not of age. Adolescence is the stage of life in which rebellion against elaborate social and family restrictions is most common. An arrangement of male-female relationships that allows easy access to sexual gratification and provision for parenthood and at the same time relieves parents of direct responsibility for the young is probably, to an adolescent, a vision of a brave new world. In the second place, the societies from which most *kibbutzim* people came had been either unrewarding or positively threatening. Neither as nationals or as Jews were they likely to feel inclined to set up a social order modeled after what they had left behind. The founders of the *kibbutzim* did more than dream; they put all their energies into a collective effort to realize their visions.

Finally, the physical conditions of life in pioneer settlements, in Israel or anywhere else, almost compel communal arrangements; limited *ad hoc* divisions of labor; little differentiation between the activities of men and women; the pooling of material, intellectual, manual, and spiritual resources; equality for all; and the development of intense group sentiments. The struggle to satisfy basic needs eliminates a host of elaborations that characterize living and relationships in settled communities.

All of these factors made the *kibbutzim* close-knit, communal, highly self-sufficient units. Their populations were small and were homogeneous in all the things that mattered. The past was not a source of inspiration for their present; it was the future that these populations had in common. So long as the communities were in the making and these conditions prevailed, the early settlers had little cause to question their basic assumptions. Individual impulses were subordinate to the needs of their particular communities, and both were subordinate to the even more compelling goal of establishing an autonomous Jewish State.

This, in brief, is the setting for the experiment with family life in the cooperative *kibbutzim*. Specific arrangements for dealing with the basic needs that are usually the concern of families varied somewhat in different settlements. In some, marriages were continued by those who had previously made them and were contracted by others if they so wished. Marriage was not considered necessary, however. When housing improved so that something other than dormitory living was possible, couples were given quarters of their own whether they were married or not. Sometimes very young children lived with their parents or spent regular hours with them in their own rooms. However, children past infancy and early childhood lived in their own quarters and shared training and recreational facilities in almost all of these *kibbutzim*. They were not reared as members of families, but as members of their communities. In the early years in Israel, these arrangements worked.

General Comments on the Experiment
in Communal Kibbutzim

It is important to note the conditions under which they did work, as well as those which have led to their breakdown. In some respects, these communities in their initial phases were rather like corporate families, although the relationships within them were very different. The customary significance of mothers, fathers, sisters and brothers, uncles and aunts and cousins, was lacking. There were few grandparents present. But the place of children in these communities was very like that of children in the old corporate Chinese families. In the latter, after very early childhood, the young lived in their own courtyards. They were cared for and educated as members of the clan rather than of their nuclear families. Their lives were planned and regulated by councils of family elders, not by their own parents. Nowhere were specific family relationships more elaborated than in Confucian China; yet the vast, extended household was more important than any individual in it and the maintenance of the clan took precedence over any branch of it. The units were communal and each individual was provided both education and maintenance according to his or her need and place in the household.

The conclusion suggested here is that the *kibbutzim, insofar as the care and training of the young is concerned,* provided much the same living conditions that one finds in fully developed corporate families. These conditions have clearly been sufficient for child-rearing under certain general circumstances, some of which influenced life in the *kibbutzim*. There were few other sources of supply in Palestine for the needs of their members. Children were highly valued to insure the continuity of the organization. Their care and cultivation was recognized as a prime responsibility of all the elders. The pioneering character of the settlements gave children even more significance, if possible, than they had for the Chinese, since they were essential for the realization of the dream for the future that motivated so many of the people in the *kibbutzim*. The members of the *kibbutzim* came to think of themselves as "related." In effect, the *kibbutzim* developed into a kind of corporate family.

The universal and basic function of families to regulate sexual relationships between men and women was also transferred to the community in the *kibbutzim*. Traditional or explicit rules were replaced by the informal controls that regulate so much of life in small communities, and by the self-regulation of their members. Pioneering ventures are usually associated with discipline and asceticism. Individual impulse is in general subordinated to the collective good. The *kibbutzim* were no exception to this rule. The absence of formal regulations did not lead to widespread promiscuity in the relations between men and women.

The preparation of the young to live in and preserve their social orders, one of the important functions of family life, was more than adequate in the *kibbutzim* in their early years. For all practical purposes, each community was the society for which the young were trained and there was nothing to interfere with their consistent orientation to it. The socialization of children was insured by the constant presence of others. Their thorough acculturation for membership in their communities could hardly be escaped. They were confronted by no conflicting—indeed, no alternative—patterns for living.

Emphasis in this discussion has been on the early years in the *kibbutzim*. These were the years during which the new arrangements were most satisfactory. Success has changed the *kibbutzim* in Israel. Many of them have outgrown the conditions that supported their original communal arrangements. Community equipment has been built and expanded. Populations have grown and become more differentiated. Parents have become grandparents. The original settlers have aged, and a fully cooperative life is less attractive to the middle-aged and the old. Division of labor between young and old and men and women has increased. Specialization has resulted in clear-cut separation of occupations and offices. Perhaps the greatest change that affects life in the *kibbutzim* has been the establishment of the State of Israel.

No state is likely to tolerate units within it that are self-sufficient and sharply differentiated in important respects from the major patterns of the whole society. The State of Israel is neither socialist nor communal. Its population includes a large number of people who grew up in other lands. Its leaders are predominantly Western European in orientation. Immigration increased greatly after the Jews achieved their political independence and, since the country is small, some newcomers had to be taken into the *kibbutzim*, though most of these close-knit settlements resisted the inclusion of outsiders who had not shared either the original dream or the hardships of the pioneering years. This influx has made the populations of the *kibbutzim* themsleves more heterogeneous.

Furthermore, the establishment of the State of Israel provided the members of the *kibbutzim* with a wider range of personal choices. Absorption in their communities came to seem restrictive to some. Isolation of the young became difficult, and to many of them other pastures looked greener. The change in the attitude of Israelis toward the *kibbutzim* is most important. The prestige of the communities has declined. So long as their people were pioneers, fighters, defenders of a cause, they were heroes. But the state is now concerned with order, the expansion of resources, the molding of a heterogeneous population into a united people, and with national defense. The *kibbutzim* tend to resist assimilation. Since they are certainly not opposed to the state they are not attacked by it. The older national leaders have strong sentimental ties to the settlements. But it is not likely that the *kibbutzim* will be allowed so much autonomy indefinitely. To the extent that they become increasingly subordinate units in the national establishment, they must adapt to its dominant patterns. This adaptation has already happened to some, it is happening to others, and it will probably happen to all if the State of Israel survives.

The *kibbutzim*'s radical experiment with the family has also been changed by the establishment of Israel as a nation. Outside the *kibbutzim*, formal marriage is required by law and there are legal formalities for its dissolution in Israel. If and when individuals leave their communities they must comply with the laws of the state. Families are as much a part of Israeli society as they are of the societies of Europe and the Americas. The rearing of children and the maintenance of adults are not responsibilities of the Israeli government. Family organizations are charged with both, unless individuals choose to live within the confines of the *kibbutzim*, membership in families is important to their welfare.

These factors have introduced tensions and conflicts into the *kibbutzim*. They are not attracting enough young people to meet their needs for manpower or to maintain their populations. If they are to remain self-sufficient, they need new land, which is not available, and more technical equipment than they can afford. Their members, surrounded by the material growth of Israeli society in general, demand a higher standard of living which the communities find difficult to provide. Finally, the desirability of the collective rearing of children has been seriously questioned, not only because women have been demanding a larger part in the lives of their own children, but because the leaders of some of these *kibbutzim* recognize that they cannot supply the kind of education that their children will need in a world that is becoming technologically more and more complex. Besides, many of them are aware that young people in Israel need to be cultivated to be members of their society, not partisans in a small segment of it.

Consequently, arrangements and values that were unquestioned in the early days in the *kibbutzim* are subjects of anxious debate today. The current position of the *kibbutzim* and their members in Israel is well summarized in an article that appeared in the *New York Times*. It reads in part:

The old spirit of the kibbutz movement is fading away in Israel.

The members of these collective settlements have been pulling up their stakes and leaving at a faster rate than new members have been coming in. A few of the settlements have shut down altogether.

Many more of them would have shut down if not for the practice of the more prosperous and populated settlements to "adopt" those with a desperate shortage of hands and lend them members to keep them in business.

To the dismay of the old Zionist pioneers, a growing number of the settlements have found that the happiest solution to their problems was simply to turn away from the concept of a collective, classless society.

Of the 250 kibbutzim in Israel, ninety-eight have turned away to the extent that they have become tiny industrial towns.

It takes only a touch of disillusionment, apparently, to cause a devoted member of a kibbutz to pack his bag and move to Tel Aviv, where there is more scope and freedom. If he is ambitious, he need not feel in the city that he is being held down to the pace of the laziest member of the community.

If he suffered under the Nazis and has come into a lump of money from German reparations, he will not have to give it up so that each can share it "according to his needs," as the ideology of a kibbutz dictates.

The image of the kibbutz women, sunburned and standing guard against infiltrating Arabs, is largely a product of Zionist propagandists. Actually, the women are as housebound as ordinary wives, except that they are confined to the kitchens and laundries of the community, not of their own homes.

It was largely the rebellious women who forced the changes that already have taken hold in the kibbutzim. The mothers are gaining increasing responsibility for the care of their own children. The apartments are being increasingly furnished with radios, paintings, individual wardrobes and electric kettles for brewing tea or coffee at home.[9]

GENERAL CONCLUSIONS ON THE
TWO EXPERIMENTS

The evidence usually presented in support of the belief that family organizations and institutions can be eliminated from societies is drawn largely from experience in communities like the communal *kibbutzim*. The ideal of a completely communal life has appealed to some people throughout the history of mankind. It has been formulated in both religious and secular terms. From time to time, people have endeavored to realize their ideal by setting up communities.

The use of the words "community" and "society" as synonyms has led to untenable conclusions. These experiments in collective living have been restricted to communities that operated as enclaves in societies. None of them expanded into social organizations of the complexity of a society, and most of them have been short-lived. The communal *kibbutzim* have lasted longer than some others, but current evidence does not indicate that they will persist in Israel. Rather, the evidence drawn from the history of these exceptional communities indicates that whenever their isolation breaks down—and it does in time—the organizations of the larger and more complex societies in which they exist prevail.

The elimination of specifically family organizations in communities like the communal *kibbutzim* involves no insurmountable hardship for individuals or for the maintenance of the communities so long as the latter are small, isolated, homogeneous, and self-sufficient. The idea of "family" is not so much abandoned by the people who choose this way of life as it is detached from biological implications and expanded to include all members of the community. The intense and extreme involvement of each individual with all others is similar to that in families. All are "brothers." Children become children of the community, and particular parents are replaced by a kind of collective parenthood. So long as this personal, "primary group" situation continues, specific family organizations are not essential.

[9] Fellows, Lawrence: "Spirit of Kibbutz Fading in Israel," in *The New York Times* (June 18, 1961).

But no society can exist without more complex divisions of labor and differentiation in their populations than this kind of community life can tolerate. The establishment of a society requires an elaborate administrative apparatus, specialized organizations to develop and transmit cultural resources, and complex integrated arrangements for the production and distribution of goods and services. This degree of differentiation always includes family organizations and they are part of the established way of life in Israel. Israel is the society. The *kibbutzim* are merely communities within it.

The goal of Soviet leaders was to transfer the care and training of children to state agencies. Their principal concerns were political, and not for the welfare of either parents or children as such. They viewed the intimate, emotion-charged associations between family members that, for better or worse, are required to satisfy some of the psychological needs of human beings, especially young ones, as threats to the achievement of their ends. Soviet agencies could not, and did not, provide the personal security that the *kibbutzim* do. It was not many years before Soviet leaders conceded that the transformation of children into competent adults in any society requires conditions that are best provided by family units and that the physical maintenance of individuals in large populations is better left to the decentralized and sprawling network of family organizations. In 1960 Chairman Khrushchev used the opening of boarding schools for secondary education as the occasion for the announcement of a plan that envisages state education for all Soviet youth at considerable remove from their families. Despite this intention, even Mr. Khrushchev did not advocate the abolition of families and their nurture of young children.

SUGGESTED READINGS

Russia

Belov, Fedor. *The History of a Soviet Collective Farm.* New York: Praeger, 1955.

Firsthand description by a man who was chairman of the collective from 1947 to 1949.

Fisher, Ralph T., Jr. *Patterns of Soviet Youth.* New York: Columbia University Press, 1959.

The subtitle of this book is "A Study of the Congresses of the Komsomol, 1918-1954." An unusual source for a statement of official Communist Party goals for the education of Russian youth.

Granick, David. *The Red Executive.* Garden City: Doubleday, 1961.

A comparison of Russia's counterpart to the "organization man" in the United States. First-rate study based on personal observation by an economist.

Gunther, John. *Inside Russia Today.* New York: Harper, 1957.

An easy way to acquire a view of life in Soviet Russia today.

Obolensky, Serge. *One Man in His Time.* New York: McDowell-Obolensky, 1958.

The swift course of the fall of the Russian monarchy and aristocracy is vividly portrayed in this autobiography. It provides a description of the life of the court and its great families by one who belonged to one of these families and who has more insight than many into the conditions that led to their destruction.

Turgenev, Ivan. *Fathers and Sons.* New York: Macmillan, 1951.

Portrayal of life in nineteenth-century Russia, especially of family conflicts induced by the beginning of movements for political and economic changes.

WOLFE, BERTRAM. *Three Who Made a Revolution*. New York: Dial Press, 1948.

A history of the establishment of the Soviet state written around the lives and influences of Lenin, Trotsky, and Stalin.

Israel

BARON, SALO W. *A Social and Religious History of the Jews*. New York: Columbia University Press, 1937.

Standard history.

BECKER, HOWARD. *German Youth: Bond or Free*. New York: Oxford University Press, 1946.

A good description and analysis of German youth organizations that influenced some of the early settlers in Palestine.

COHEN, ABRAHAM. *Everyman's Talmud*. New York: Dutton, 1949.

SPIRO, MELFOR E. *Kibbutz: Venture in Utopia*. Cambridge: Harvard University Press, 1956.

An excellent study which describes life in the collective kibbutz in which the author and his wife lived and worked for a year. The analysis of the strains and satisfactions within the community and of its relations to the state of Israel is perceptive and penetrating.

———. *Children of the Kibbutz*. Cambridge: Harvard University Press, 1958.

A description and appraisal of the education and personal development of the first generation born in the kibbutz.

ZBOROWSKI, MARK AND HERZOG, ELIZABETH. *Life Is With People*. New York: International Universities Press, 1952.

A detailed anthropological study of the life in, and the people of, small Jewish communities in Eastern Europe.

PART FOUR

■ ■ ■

Conclusions
and Forecasts

■

XI

THE THREE MAJOR
TYPES OF
FAMILY ORGANIZATION
■
Comparisons and Contrasts

IN THE preceding chapters three major types of family organization have been distinguished and described: *autonomous nuclear, bilateral extended,* and *corporate.* They were differentiated on the basis of degree of autonomy exercised by their nuclear units.

It should be noted again that categorical descriptions are "ideal types." They are conceptual constructs, based upon abstraction from empirical observations and reports, and created to make it possible to analyze and compare phenomena that cannot be compared or sorted directly. Actual families are more or less like the "ideal types" presented here, just as every particular patient's measles or chickenpox is more or less like the "textbook" case. There will always be some particular families that are hard to classify. They may not be fully developed organizations, or they may combine elements of more than one type. The use of "ideal types" makes it possible to distinguish phenomena within a general class. These constructs help to expose small differences that have significant effects. They are the means by which general statements can be made.

THE THREE TYPES OF FAMILY ORGANIZATION IN RELATION TO THEIR SOCIETIES

Types of family organizations tend to be associated with particular combinations of general social and cultural conditions in societies. *Corporate families* are correlated with predominately agrarian societies in which land is the principal source of wealth. They are found in societies in which communications and transportation systems are little developed. Political control is usually authoritarian, but tends to be curtailed at the level of local regulation. Religious organizations are powerful and religious institutions relatively uniform for the population. Cultural levels are often high, but only a small proportion of the populations of these societies have access to the cultural riches available. Those who do are most frequently the people who also control most of the material wealth.

Until modern times, these were the prevailing conditions in most societies. They still characterize societies in the Far and Middle East and Eastern Europe. In societies of this order, where the majority of the population is poor and the development of political, economic, and religious organizations is limited, corporate families fill the gaps in the chain of organizations necessary to maintain a society and provide for its population. Organization on the basis of kinship that guarantees extensive reciprocal aid for members is the only effective means for survival for most of the people, and political and religious formulations justify and reinforce the arrangements and powers of the families. Family authority tends to be dictatorial and absolute. Children are subordinate to parents, and women to men. Relationships both within the family and outside it are strictly hierarchical. The "great families" are important units in all spheres of life.

The extended families that are the chief operational units in corporate family organizations often exercise a great deal of autonomy. Their membership in a larger unity imposes some restrictions upon them, however, and units that are themselves powerful are not apt to contribute to the maintenance of a larger organization unless clear and immediate benefits are forthcoming from it. In societies in which physical survival is not particularly hazardous, means of communication are fairly well developed, and political organizations are capable of protecting the unity of the society from internal strife and external attack, the advantage of the corporate family is diminished. Furthermore, it interferes with the functions of organizations set up to provide for total populations. Under such conditions extended families begin to break away from former corporate organizations, or they do not combine to form them. When extended families do not require monolithic authority for their survival, but are still benefited by extensions of their control over economic resources or positions of power, mergers between the families of both spouses become desirable, and extended families develop into the autonomous bilateral *extended* type.

In the past, *the bilateral extended family* was associated with the ownership of land and with a distribution of power based on privilege established by birth and inheritance. Governments were chiefly monarchial and established churches powerful; however, there was some division between the organizations of church and state and important aspects of life were regulated by secular law. But the bilateral extended family is also found in modern, technologically advanced societies. Control over industrial plants or money replaces or supplements land ownership as the basis for their maintenance and power in their societies. Their nuclear units can enjoy a great deal of autonomy in personal matters and individuals can pursue many of their own interests without disrupting these families. The benefits of the pooling of some resources (principally economic) and the guarantee of access to others (such as education and occupations) are sufficient to keep individual members and nuclear families attached to extended families even in industrial and urban social settings. In modern societies some bilateral extended families are survivals from the past, but others are the result of special achievements by some of their members. The latter are found most frequently in the upper-middle and upper classes.

The emergence of the *autonomous nuclear family* as a fully developed family organization—not to be confused with small independent households among the poor and dispossessed that have always been numerous—is a relatively modern phenomenon. Autonomous nuclear families can be viewed as specialized family organizations in societies in which specialization is highly developed in all spheres of life. They are associated with clear divisions between political and religious organizations; the dominance of secular law; secular education; advanced technology; the mechanization of agriculture, means of production, and even of housekeeping; the extensive development of lines of communication and transportation; and extensive urbanization. Since autonomous nuclear families have little control over the social and material resources necessary to their maintenance, their efficiency in the performance of family functions is far more dependent upon assistance from non-family sources than is that of corporate or extended families. Autonomous nuclear families are not important units in non-family organizations and have little power to command their support. This degree of dependence on the other organizations in their societies is one of the important sources of their relative instability.

ADVANTAGES AND DISADVANTAGES IN THREE TYPES OF FAMILIES

There are inherent assets and liabilities in the different forms of family organization that are relatively independent of the settings in which they operate. Autonomous nuclear families provide greater freedom for extensive and varied personal development, social relationships, activities, and physical mobility. But often they fail to provide security. Further, they demand great individual personal resources and effort on the part of the people who maintain them. In corporate families the assets and liabilities are reversed. They provide more security and less freedom. For the majority of family members, the range of personal cultivation is much curtailed. To a great extent the lives of women and young people are regulated by men and elders. The few heads of households frequently wield excessive power and monopolize a dispro-, portionate share of the available benefits. On the other hand, these families control most of the social and material resources that they need and they are very efficient security systems for large numbers of people. Like large economic corporations in industrial societies today, they offer many "fringe" benefits to their members as the reward for loyal service. The special asset of the bilateral extended type of family organization is its ability to provide its member with a good deal of individual freedom along with a fairly dependable base for security. Extended families do not usually sacrifice one to the other.

These three basic forms of family organization also differ in their potential efficiency for meeting the needs of their members at different periods of their lives. The authoritarian nature of corporate families favors the aging and the old who are usually the administrators and executives of households and family enterprises. Children benefit from their collective significance as the guarantors of family continuity. They are welcome and, generally, well nurtured and cultivated. On the other hand, the need for many children to insure the survival of the clan tends to place emphasis on the child-bearing and child-rearing functions of women at the expense of their other potentialities. The lives of most women are highly restricted in corporate families. Finally, since age-grading is an important part of the exercise of authority in these families, young adults have to await the passage of years for opportunity to develop their own abilities. During this time, their personal lives are usually still supervised by their elders. Thus, what they gain in security is often achieved at the expense of their individual development and achievement.

Autonomous nuclear families tend to favor children and youths. Since children are generally viewed as sources of personal satisfaction and are often conceived as the result of a deliberate decision by their parents, the latter tend to feel deeply obligated to supply them with every possible material asset and personal opportunity. Autonomous nuclear families are frequently child-centered and their children are often greatly indulged. These families impose few specific restrictions on young adults and the middle-aged. The paths to personal cultivation and achievement are theoretically open, but they are often blocked by the heavy responsibilities of family life, which must be shouldered by only two people as a rule. Autonomous nuclear families are not felicitous for the aging, the old, the sick, or people handicapped in any way. They are too small and the resources they command are usually too limited for them to absorb inactive members without overburdening their own organization.

In general, the dependence of autonomous nuclear families on non-family organizations tends to weaken family ties. The members of these families scatter daily in pursuit of economic, educational, religious, and educational services. Non-family relationships compete with family relationships for the affection and loyalty of individuals. The limitation of the range of services that parents *can* provide their children in these families diminishes their authority over their young and seems to have all but eliminated filial responsibilities other than physical maintenance in cases of want. Siblings go their own ways and continuing reciprocities between them are voluntary. Since parents cease to be oriented toward their own parents, ties between grandparents and grandchildren lose institutional significance.

Consequently, autonomous nuclear families are often unreliable sources of personal help in the periods of strain or crisis that are almost inevitable in the life course of everyone. Young children may suffer from the dissolution of marital ties, adolescents may find themselves estranged from family support before they are able to establish the stable associations they need for their own maintenance, the middle-aged may be bereft of affection and respect from their children, and the aging and aged may be isolated and even exiled from family participation. The case histories behind mounting rates of delinquency, addiction, crime, neurotic disabilities, mental illness, and senility in societies in which autonomous nuclear families prevail suggest that frequent failure to develop enduring family ties is a serious inadequacy for both individuals and societies.

With respect to meeting the needs of different age levels, the bilateral extended family again seems to serve its members better.

It accords neither children, nor young adults, nor the middle-aged, nor the old the degree of privilege that is awarded one or another of these categories by the corporate or the autonomous nuclear family. Each category has rights and obligations associated with its stage of life. The young are welcome, cared for, and cultivated, but they are taught concern for family welfare and are prepared to contribute to it. Adults are assisted to marriages and occupations and given help in times of need, but they are expected to maintain and augment family enterprises and give heed to the council of their elders. The aging and the old are usually guaranteed respect and care when they need it, but they are expected to direct their skill and wisdom to the enrichment of their family circles, to refrain from wasting family resources by drawing upon them needlessly, and to distribute their property fairly and efficiently among family members when they die. Bilateral extended families can and do take care of their dependent and handicapped members, but they demand active participation in their organizations by every member who is capable of it.

COMMON CHARACTERISTICS OF THE
THREE FAMILY TYPES

Although the types of family organization vary in the important respects discussed above, they are all directed toward the same basic functions. Sexual satisfaction, procreation, the care and socialization of children, psychological and physical security for all, the introduction of the young into organization that are necessary for the attainment of their individual satisfactions, and the protection and provisioning of adults while they work in other spheres are services rendered by all types of families. The needs for which families chiefly provide are so closely related to human biological growth and maintenance that biological uniformities give rise to regularities in family arrangements. All organizations have some basic requirements for their own maintenance, so all types of families have some similar provisions for insuring their survival. Finally, all families serve the societies in which they live by contributing to their populations, transmitting folkways and mores, transforming their young into dependable social units, distributing goods and services, and regulating the relations between young and old and men and women in important respects. To these ends family organizations are all interconnected with non-family associations. For all these reasons, there are some characteristics that all family types manifest in some degree.

Prerequisites for Membership

One thing that all types of families have in common is their prerequisites for membership. Family membership is chiefly based on biological relationship. The vital exception to this is, of course, the husband-wife relationship. In most societies, marriage between close blood relatives has been forbidden. Whether or not this ancient "incest taboo" was based on empirical observation that prolonged inbreeding results in defects in organisms or on such social considerations as the need to expand membership or control property, marriage with someone outside one's own biological circle has in any case been the general rule. Exceptions to it have been made where the positions of great power have been connected with birth or when consolidation of lands and herds depended largely on family ties. In such circumstances, royal Egyptian brothers and sisters married each other, and first-cousin, or uncle-and-niece marriages are deemed desirable among Moslems and a good many royal families in European states. One other common exception to the general principle that family membership is based on biological relationship is the provision in almost all family organizations for the adoption of children to guarantee family perpetuation in the event of biological failures. It is mainly the marriage of two people of different blood strains, however, that extends family membership to include relations-in-law.

Hierarchy of Relationships

Both in different types of families and in different times and places, cultural prescriptions have produced variation in the nature of the relationships among relatives. Family relationships are arranged in a hierarchy of authority and are attached to a stable program of specific rights and obligations which are defined by custom, religious doctrines, and secular laws. But since these definitions are largely explicit formulations of fundamental family experience, family relationships have many similar characteristics despite differences in their over-all organization.

Relationships beyond the nuclear unit of husband, wife, and children are never without importance; the overlap of generations makes this inevitable. Marriage and the establishment of a new nuclear unit does not end attachments to the families in which spouses were raised. The parents of the newly married pair become the grandparents of their children; the siblings of a couple become their children's uncles and aunts and their children are first cousins. The important family reciprocities that were the means of support and cultivation in the past persist in some measure for all people. In autonomous nuclear families, members of the larger circle of relatives usually perform few, if any, obligatory functions for each other, but almost always some of them are closely integrated with the nuclear family. The formal and occasional gathering of relatives for weddings and funerals continues and is witness to the past functional significance of distant relatives and, possibly, to the maintenance of a reserve of potential help in the event of future need.

Relationships that unite three generations and siblings are the "nearest of kin" in all types of family organization. The extent of their mutual obligations is usually reflected by the number of kin that typically or often constitutes a single household. However, they are recognized as "relatives" even by autonomous nuclear families, and the hierarchy of significance attached to particular family relationships is similar in all forms of family organization despite the fact that the general importance of family membership is much greater in corporate and extended families than it is in autonomous nuclear ones.

Parent-child relationships are the most developed. This is one indication of the central significance of parenthood as the basis of family organization. Husband-wife relationships are next in importance. In all family organizations it is marriage that promises new family units and legitimizes children. Reciprocities between siblings are the next most significant family relationships; then come those between uncles, aunts, nephews, and nieces, those between cousins, and, finally, in very extensive corporate families, between all people of the same name. All family organizations include a specific series of relatives-in-law that—with the possible exception of the parents-in-law of women in corporate families, who are cut off from regular association with their own parents and siblings—are usually experienced by individuals as of secondary importance to their biologically connected relatives. "Blood is thicker than water" is a sentiment found in almost all societies. The great exception to this is the marital relationship, which is usually based on law. Otherwise, the hierarchy of relatives-in-law more or less parallels that of blood relationships. These relationships, in various combinations, constitute clearly defined kinship circles in all societies, whether they are regularly united in close family organization as corporate or extended families or merely augment nuclear families. The essential mutual services that they provide are universal.

Provisions for Maintenance and Survival

All family forms have some similar arrangements for preserving their organizations. Since family unity depends upon stable relations between men and women, all family organizations regulate them in specific ways. Marriage is always the most important formal means for bringing new couples into families and for directing male-female associations into well-defined channels. Multiple marriages, concurrent or sequential, may or may not be permitted, but all marriages are generally expected to endure until the death of one of the partners. Corporate families include other sexual unions within the family organization itself, chiefly regulated as concubinage or limited contractual marriage. The number of sexual relationships countenanced by family organizations seems to be related to the number of members they need to guarantee their survival and the performance of their functions. Monogamy in families is associated with the restriction of family services to essential family functions.

Like all organizations, families have to establish standards for the competent fulfillment of the obligations of membership and provisions for the exclusion of defaulting members. All kinds of families have formal rules for the divorce or separation of spouses and specify the inadequacies that are grounds for them. Provisions for the expulsion of children from households and for their disinheritance are found in all families, although they are rarely used. Abandonment of parents is not condoned, even in autonomous nuclear families, except under very unusual circumstances. In corporate families, the exclusion of other relatives from the family organization must be justified by established rules; in extended families such a step requires the consensus of the kinship circle. In general, disruption of relationships between relatives who are not active members of family organizations is usually left to personal and individual inclination. The maintenance of family organizations requires these arrangements. Serious incompatibility between family members, or grave incompetence in their performance of basic functions, is too threatening to a family's integration and support not to evoke regular means for remedy.

The continuity of family organizations depends chiefly on children. Since most of them become family members by birth, all family organizations have rules that define the kind of parentage that confers legitimacy on a child. Family regulations concerning the chastity of women are principally directed toward ascertaining the identity of the fathers of their children. Considering the very great importance given the authenticity of parentage in determining family membership, it is somewhat surprising that the overwhelmingly common practice for tracing descent has been relationship in the male line. But so it is, and legitimate family membership by birth is usually defined by the nature of the relation of the mother to the father. When births fail to fill the family ranks, adoption is practiced in all types of families. The nature of the contracts that bring a child into a family by this means varies, and the family rights of adopted children are not always equal to those of biological children. However, in all cases membership in a family is established by adoption and the children of adopted sons and daughters are usually included in the lines of descent.

In its importance for the survival of family organizations, the perpetuation of economic resources is second only to the replacement and addition of family members. Consequently, all families have specific arrangements for the orderly transfer of rights, obligations, and property in the event that a member becomes incompetent, leaves the organization, or dies. Incompetence, if it does not lead to expulsion, is usually handled by informal redistribution of the duties and property of the incompetent one within the family circle. The voluntary departure of family members does not usually separate them from their family rights and obligations. However, when property is involved and the departure is expected to be permanent, as in the case of emigration, for example, a redistribution of rights and functions may be required.

Family inheritance often regulates positions and rights in non-family organizations. In monarchies, succession in political offices is determined by family inheritance, positions of authority and wealth are inherited by members of aristocratic families. Membership in parliaments and religious organizations is often perpetuated by family inheritance, as is the right to practice particular professions or crafts in guilds or unions. The administration of large industrial enterprises is often passed from father to son, or to brother, uncle, or nephew. These family-provided benefits are as much a basis for the maintenance of family organizations as the possession of real property, and all families have rules, defined by custom and law, for the transfer of assets upon the death of their members.

Management

Finally, all family organizations include systematic arrangements for their management. Some of these rules stem from non-family sources, such as religious or political organizations, or they may be part of the folkways and mores of the societies in which families live. Some grow up within particular families and are outcomes of improvisation. In any case, inescapable conditions of life evoke divisions of authority between young and old and divisions of labor between men and women. Individual differences in talent and skills and the different clusters of needs associated with the stages of growth, development, and decline of family members require orderly management of family resources and, hence, an established authority to assign tasks and distribute goods and services.

The elaboration and rigidity of rules regulating the distribution of authority vary in different kinds of family organization. The size and complexity of corporate families make necessary sharply differentiated executive and administrative hierarchies with fixed lines of command. In extended families, nuclear units have some autonomy and individual members have some freedom from regulation over their personal affairs. Therefore, authority in these families falls to members who are characterized by special combinations of age, achievement, talent, and wealth. Positions of authority in these families are subject to some manipulation by members within defined limits. In autonomous nuclear families, authority depends more on the "consent of the governed," but even they are not peer groups in which authority can rest on rotating leadership determined by the choice of their membership. Age, the power of the purse, and control over access to goods and services determine authority in autonomous nuclear families as they do in others. Even in American nuclear families, with their great emphasis on equality between husbands and wives and parents and children, husbands are generally "more equal" than wives, and fathers and mothers exercise considerable authority over their children until they have reached the legal age of majority and move out of parental households.

The very great significance of all family organizations, whatever form they take, flows from the fact that they are for the overwhelming majority of people the most encompassing and frequently the all-providing social organizations. (Exceptions, such as religious orders, are themselves patterned on family organizations; their members are "brothers" and "sisters" and superiors are "mothers" and "fathers.") For most people, their families, small or large, are their most stable centers of personal associations and private life. Family members meet each other oftener than the members of any other group. It is in families that the distribution of services and goods and the exchange of messages pertaining to the most vital concerns of individuals occurs. It is from their family base that most people move into other organizations and it is their families that chiefly prepare them to do so.

SUGGESTED READINGS

DeMille, Agnes. *Dance to the Piper*. New York: Atlantic Monthly Press, 1958.

The scattering of American families is well revealed in this autobiography of a distinguished American dancer.

Hoyt, Edwin. *The Vanderbilts and Their Fortunes*. Garden City: Doubleday, 1962.

The rise and fall of an extended American family.

Marquand, John P. *The Late George Apley*. Boston: Little, Brown, 1937.

Portrait of an upper-class family in Boston.

Michener, James A. *Hawaii*. New York: Random House, 1959.

Good descriptions of Chinese, Japanese, and American corporate families.

Morton, Frederic. *The Rothschilds: A Family Portrait*. New York: Atheneum, 1962.

An absorbing history of one of the foremost Jewish families which is, at the same time, an excellent description of the rise and maintenance of a corporate family based on financial and industrial rather than agricultural wealth.

Wake, Joan. *Brudenells of Deene*. London: Cassell, 1953.

This history of one of the distinguished families of England gives an excellent description of the dynamic aspects of an extended family over many generations.

Waln, Nora. *The House of Exile*. Boston: Little, Brown, 1946.
Excellent picture of a traditional Confucian corporate family and household.

· XII ·

GENERAL EFFECTS OF
SOCIAL CHANGES ON
FAMILY ORGANIZATION
AND FAMILY LIFE

■

THE INTERCONNECTIONS between organizations and institutions in societies make it inevitable that they influence each other. However, in modern, technologically advanced societies family life is more determined than determining. The effects of families on non-family activities—political, economic, religious, and educational—are not insignificant, but they are chiefly disseminated by individual members. The family exerts its influence on the abilities of its members to cooperate with their fellows; on their evaluations of the ethnic, religious, and racial traits of the people they meet; on their political preferences; and on their tastes and goals. However, family organizations as such do not directly determine the political or economic policies of modern societies in any marked degree. They do not initiate drastic social changes. On the contrary, in modern industrial societies family organizations are called upon to adjust their routines to educational and occupational programs and to fulfill their functions by means that are largely controlled by non-family organizations.

This was not always the case and is not true in technologically backward societies today. As earlier chapters have indicated, in ancient societies political leadership, economic enterprise, protection from invaders, and the codification and transmission of knowledge and skills were chiefly provided by family organizations. This was largely true in China until the present century. In some of the kingdoms of the Middle and Far East it is true today. Contemporary societies are not all modern by any means, nor are technologically advanced societies evenly developed. Government by royal and aristocratic families prevailed in Western Europe until the eighteenth century and continues into the twentieth.

The enormous influence of family organizations on life in ancient societies is reflected in the almost universal terminology that is used by their people when they refer to their society. Societies are still called "Fatherlands" and "Motherlands." The languages that are spoken by most of their citizens are called "mother tongues." Harmony between peoples is "brotherhood." Even the all-powerful heads of current radical Utopias are addressed as "Big Brothers." Despite this conventional imagery, modern societies are not like families. Their political leaders are not "fathers" and citizens are not "brothers." Populations are no longer folk, "a kindred people" bound to each other by common traditions and sentiments and attached to "motherlands." The greater complexity of modern social organizations, the heterogeneity of populations, the intricacy of the techniques by which they are maintained, and the accumulation of knowledge on which all these social phenomena are based, have modified traditional associations among members of modern societies. Family relationships have changed, and are changing, with the rest.

The number and size of political and economic organizations have increased greatly. Religious and family organizations are subordinate to them. In some societies the fusion of political and economic organizations seems to be replacing the union of church and state that characterized theocratic societies in the past. Science has made change itself a conspicuous and routine aspect of modern life. The cultural accumulation is so vast and increases so rapidly that educational organizations proliferate and specialize. Most of them are sharply separated from religious organizations and religious doctrines.

Wherever modern industry and technology have developed, or have been imported or imposed, the social relationships of people have increased in number and variety. The citizens of modern societies have to move out of their small circles of relatives and friends in pursuit of education, means of support, religious services, advice and council, food and clothing, marital partners, and recreation. Public living has greatly expanded, and in large measure it has done so at the expense of private associations. Membership in a variety of organizations produces highly individuated people and sharp differentiations among the members of families. Social and physical mobility dulls the edges of social strata. Divisions between estates and classes, between ethnic and religious categories, between political parties, between people who are highly educated and those who are not, must be bridged in order for the daily life of modern societies to proceed. Personal ties based on homogeneity of belief, sentiment, experience, and family relationship diminish in number for most individuals in modern populations. People suppress their private allegiances that would be barriers to relationships and form impersonal associations.

Family life, on the other hand, is always personal and its efficiency depends largely on the degree to which true intimacy is developed among family members. When families control economic resources and positions in all spheres of life, social relationships radiate out from family circles. This cannot be the case for the majority of the populations of modern societies. And so, for many reasons, forms of family organization that prevailed in the past disappear or are profoundly modified; there emerges a new type of family that is better adapted to modern conditions of life.

Corporate families tend to disintegrate in modern societies. They require such extensive control of political and economic resources that they interfere with the development and operations of political and economic organizations. They are entirely incompatible with socialist governmental and economic arrangements. The effects of political and economic change upon corporate families is apparent today in China and some Moslem societies. There, family monopolies over positions of power, based on inheritance or control of the means to achieve the requisites of office, have been dissolved. Family control of material wealth is either greatly restricted by taxes, death duties, and laws that enforce redistribution of property, or is eliminated by confiscation. The first alternative is employed in every modern society; the second characterizes revolutionary states.

Corporate family organization depends upon the power of family executives and administrators to regulate every aspect of the lives of family members. Individual interests must be subordinate to family interests and family members must be oriented toward their families and clans from birth to death. But this kind of family authority rests upon the power of family elders to meet the needs of their members. Nurture, support, education, jobs, marriages, friendships, and a host of other services are the return for submission to family regulation. In modern societies few families can adequately provide all these services except for the very young. Nowadays the maintenance of family organizations themselves depends upon the individual endeavors of family members in fields outside the family. Besides, the complex unity of modern societies requires the participation of individuals in many organizations and the subordination of allegiance to any one organization—including the family—to allegiance to the society itself.

Corporate family organization has depended upon moral justifications supplied by religious and ethical doctrines. This is revealed by the fact that corporate families can be classified by religions—Confucian, Moslem, Catholic, or Jewish, for example. The attenuation of orthodoxy in religious organizations themselves, their separation from political power, and the replacement of sacred law by secular law for the regulation of daily life undermine the family organizations that most fully embodied religious doctrines and beliefs. Stages of this aspect of the dissolution of corporate families are found in various Moslem societies in which secularization of government and the routines of life has been accomplished in varying degrees.[1]

Corporate family organization depends upon the domination of women by men and of the young by their elders. The doctrine of social equality between the sexes in all spheres of activity and before the law changes the life of a society almost as much as does the introduction of modern technology. Division of authority between men and women in the family modifies the relation of husband and wife, and of parents and children. It puts an end to the practice of separating women from their own parents and siblings and subordinating them to their husbands' families. This alters relationships at the level of the grandparents. Division of authority also changes property rights of husbands and wives, as well as the distribution of their material benefits. The introduction of the right of women to move out of their households into a variety of occupations and to establish personal relationships with both sexes outside their family circles shatters the foundation of corporate family organizations. The recognition of the right of young men and women to pursue their own careers without regard to family

[1] "TUNIS, March 5—President Habib Bourguiba of Tunisia sipped fruit juice in his office at noon today.

'I can be more useful to my country if I am not sitting in a corner yawning and hungry because of Ramadan,' he said.

The gesture was significant because strict Islamic observance requires abstention from all food and drink and even from cigarettes from dawn to sundown during the holy month of Ramadan.

The President had just received from Ahmed Ben Salah, Secretary of State for Finance and Planning, a three-year plan for investing 265,000,000 dinars ($636,000,000) in Tunisian development.

Mr. Bourguiba was enthusiastic about the plan, which the United States has agreed in principle to help finance. However, he said: 'It can only succeed if the women of Tunisia stop producing children faster than we can provide for them. . . . The people must become aware of the problem. For that I am counting on a nation-wide campaign by the National Union of Tunisian Women in the cities and in the countryside. We must cut down the birth rate.'

Mr. Bourguiba's mood was dynamic as he voiced his faith in liberal modernism. . . . 'Eventually I hope to make Ramadan the most productive month of the year. For those who want to deny themselves, I suggest an extra hour of work rather than fasting. That will help our economic struggle.' " (*The New York Times*, March 6, 1962, p. 8.)

interests breaks the bonds that guaranteed continuity for these families.

These general conditions increasingly characterize modern societies and are uncongenial to the development or maintenance of corporate families. In Western European societies in which private economic enterprise and private property are associated with advanced technology, it is still possible for established corporate families to survive. A few royal families are supported by dynastic political organizations. Great financial and industrial wealth and the powers associated with them are sufficient to perpetuate families like the Duponts and the Rothschilds. Corporate families frequently reinforce each other by intermarriages and economic collaboration. Their capital accumulations from the past coupled with financial and industrial acumen in the present keep a few corporate families united and powerful.

But current political and economic trends oppose them. Every step in political control over national resources, or regulation of economic activities, or limitation on inheritance, or taxation of income, threatens their survival. It is unlikely that new corporate families can arise in "capitalist" societies, and certainly corporate families have no place in "socialist" ones. One of the most disruptive aspects of the struggle for modern governments and economies in the new African nations is its destruction of tribal family organizations, which are still the basis for most of the political, economic, religious, and personal relationships of these people. It seems probable that the spread of modern social techniques, such as representational government, economic transactions based primarily on money, deliberately enacted laws and planning for social welfare, and modern technology will continue and that tribal life is doomed, but it is certain that the transformations that accompany current changes in these societies will continue during the lifetime of several generations and will cause a good deal of distress for these African populations.

Membership in greatly modified corporate family organizations may persist in modern societies as a symbol of prestige and a source of personal relationships and private satisfactions. This is evident in the clans of Ireland and Scotland. The members of these families are not organized into an operational corporation.

Most of them are not routinely tied to each other either by mutual obligations or by bonds of affection. But recognition of the relationship between them, especially by outsiders, provides them all with a modicum of social distinction. To this end, the achievements of many people over several generations are symbolically represented by a nominal family corporation, as it were, to provide a status dividend for each of them.

Bilateral extended families do not necessarily interfere with political and economic arrangements in societies or with the participation of individual family members in non-family organizations. So long as they do not, bilateral extended families seem to be compatible with modern societies of all kinds. The benefits that extended families provide derive from mutual personal help, pooled information, and occupational opportunities rather than from monopoly over societal resources or positions of power. The members of extended families may have an advantage in competition for educational opportunities, jobs, or political offices, but they do not escape outside competition.

For these reasons, established families of the extended type persist. New ones arise chiefly as the result of exceptional individual achievement. The Ford and Kennedy families illustrate this development in the United States and so do the families of successful bureaucrats in Communist countries. People who attain high positions in political or economic fields can make it easier for their children and other relatives to succeed. The consolidation of family talents and resources augments the welfare of individual members, and so their loyalty to an extended family organization is evoked and sustained.

The autonomous nuclear family is fostered by the conditions of life that prevail in modern societies. Households consisting of only husband, wife, and their children are not new. They have existed in large numbers in all societies. But they were, for the most part, fragments scattered by the disruption of extended or corporate families. A union of nuclear families into corporate or extended families has been the "normal" form of family life in the past, supported by tradition and religious and ethical precepts. Isolated nuclear families were autonomous by default and their members usually suffered serious disadvantages in their societies.

The autonomous nuclear family that has become a normative ideal in modern societies is a fully developed type of organization. These families are content to dissolve their organizations and disperse their assets when a new generation reaches maturity. Their children scatter to establish autonomous families of their own. Family authority and regulation by elders is assumed to be limited from the start. Continuity for the family organization itself is not important. The perpetuation of some family relationships during the lifetime of particular individuals is valued and sought, but the number of relatives with whom such personal bonds are established, or even desired, is small. Even ties between siblings may be broken once they have moved out of their parents' households. No one planned such family arrangements. They emerged as part of the differentiation, specialization, and secularization that characterize modern societies. In essence, autonomous nuclear families are organizations that specialize in providing the stable relationships and reciprocal services necessary for the satisfaction of the basic psychobiological needs of their members.

In modern societies the same degree of specialization characterizes non-family organizations. Economic organizations are overwhelmingly concerned with production and distribution of goods and services impersonally supplied for money; their members are transformed from "persons" into "personnel" in the interest of impersonal efficiency. Educational organizations specialize in the formal transmission of knowledge and skills. Close personal associations between teachers and students and among students are found chiefly at the primary levels, if there, and in small private schools. Increase in numbers, size of classes, and the introduction of technical aids such as movies, television, and teaching machines are increasingly depersonalizing school life. Political organizations have become so large and require so much expert knowledge that their direct impact on the majority of individuals is extremely limited. The requirements for the administration of modern societies are beyond the ken of most of their citizens.

Families as such have no place in these extra-familial organizations, whose purposes demand individuals with special skills and knowledge who are free to join them and to move wherever a job or service is available. Recognition by individuals that their own satisfactions and achievement depend upon non-family organizations is essential for the recruitment of their staffs and for the performance of their functions. But these do not include the essential family functions.

The minimum organization capable of meeting the highly personal needs of human beings appears to be the autonomous nuclear family. Potentially, it can provide the all-encompassing personal matrix necessary for the healthy development of the human young. It can provide what is so important for the personal integration of adults—regular access to other people in relatively anxiety-free relationships. It can regulate access to sexual satisfaction and prepare, distribute, and care for the things that adult human beings need for their physical maintenance. It can train children to move into non-family organizations and adult participation in their societies. It can still be an important center for private life, an incubator and protector of intimacy among friends as well as family members.

Autonomous nuclear families are correctly described as "autonomous" only insofar as their freedom from fixed obligations to any but nuclear family members is concerned. The great problem for these families in modern societies is establishing control over the material and social resources that they need to perform their highly specialized functions. In doing so, autonomous nuclear families suffer from three important inherent weaknesses. The performance of their functions demands the cultivation of intensive relationships between husbands and wives and parents and children, yet there are many inescapable interferences with them. Secondly, the maintenance of these families depends upon non-family organizations. Thirdly, autonomous nuclear families are largely the responsibility of only two people. The demands that this responsibility makes upon them as individuals are often heavier than their personal resources can support. Consequently, a great many autonomous nuclear families fall short of achieving their goals.

For some of the same and also for different reasons, family organizations in the United States and Scandinavia as well as in Russia and China have been viewed as "social problems." Psychological studies have revealed the connection between child-rearing in families and the performance of adults as social units in their societies. Family failures are associated with destructive incompetency, such as crime and mental illness, in adult populations. To a considerable extent it has been these problems that have turned the attention of social leaders to the family and stimulated the spread of political and economic arrangements to provide regular assistance to families. It has become clear that regular support is necessary for the majority of nuclear families if the needs of large populations in modern societies are to be met. It is highly probable that the kind of social legislation that serves nuclear families in Scandinavian countries will be enacted in all modern societies. Modern states must supply the margin of security that was provided nuclear units by corporate and extended family organizations in the past, if they are to benefit from the freedom that autonomous nuclear families can allow their members in fulfilling their obligations as citizens.

The notion is widespread that the trend in family arrangements throughout the world toward increasing isolation of nuclear units from extended kinship organization is a direct imitation of developments in Western European societies. No doubt there has been some aping of Western ways in this respect. But the bulk of the evidence suggests that what has been directly borrowed is Western science, technology, and political and economic formulations—not Western European family patterns. It seems that the gradual but persistent breakdown of corporate and very extended families around the world is an outcome of the changes that secularization, industrialization, mechanization, and urbanization are effecting. To the extent that these impose upon societies similar restrictions on family life and similar demands upon individuals, the family arrangements in these societies will become similar. Autonomous nuclear families, supported by political and economic organizations, will probably dominate the family life of the societies that are undergoing radical change today if, or when, they succeed in establishing modern social orders.

Change in prevailing family organizations and in the relative position of families with respect to non-family organizations inevitably modifies the nature of relationships within the family itself. Not only is the number of relatives who are obligated to exchange reciprocal services diminished, but relations between parents and children, husbands and wives, siblings, and grandparents and grandchildren cannot follow traditional patterns. Many religious and ethical formulations of the obligations, many traditional expectations and sentiments about them, become inappropriate.

The idea of equality between men and women is a very modern notion and it is one of the most important issues in all contemporary revolutions. It is associated with the progressive secularization of daily life. The sacred documents that were the ideological basis for social order in most societies until recent time assume that women are inferior to men and that male domination over them is not only natural, but has been ordained by supernatural powers. So it is in the Bible and the Koran, and in Confucian doctrine.

This assumption has been central to family organization almost everywhere. Respect for women has been related principally to the performance of their biological functions as sexual partners and mothers and their skills for the tasks that stem from these functions. Such powers as women have had to influence decisions in their homes and beyond them, and to exercise some autonomy over their own lives, have for the most part been the result of their indirect manipulation of men and children and have depended upon individual wit and ability, not on institutional guarantees. With few exceptions the power of women has been exercised within limits imposed by men, and women have had little opportunity to participate directly in activities outside the sphere of family life.

In modern societies, whether or not women take advantage of their rights and opportunities for participation in political and economic spheres, the fact that these rights exist has changed the lives of all wives and mothers and, therefore, their relations to husbands and children. Their right to choose their mates, to divorce them, to share their wealth, to regulate the lives of their children as well as to care for them—even their right not to marry or have children and to live in ways and by means that were strictly masculine prerogatives in the past—have greatly changed the experience and significance of being a wife and mother. The activities that absorb the time and energies of most women are much the same as they were in the past, although many of their techniques are new, but the values and sentiments attached to these endeavors are not.

The ideal of partnership and companionship between husbands and wives that is associated with autonomous nuclear families has added a new dimension to marriage for many men and women in societies like the American, Scandinavian, and British. It probably foreshadows the prevailing pattern of husband-wife relationships in most societies in the future. But at the present time it tends to downgrade the activities, domestic and maternal, that in the past dominated the lives of most women and were the basis of their respect. Consequently, women in modern societies seek esteem and satisfactions outside their homes in increasing numbers. The actual interdependence between mothers and children and between husbands and wives is decreased. The bonds between them depend upon many new and highly individual factors. Institutional directives and guarantees to reinforce the personal associations in modern families are probably in the making, but they are not yet firmly and widely established, even in the most technologically advanced societies. Until they are, a good deal of family instability is to be expected.

Men still dominate non-family organizations in modern societies. Equal opportunity for women in these spheres has not yet been realized. However, men can no longer exercise absolute authority over women and children. The "Patriarch" has vanished from modern social scenes. The significance of men as husbands and fathers in modern families is slight compared with their power in corporate and extended families in the past, and their ties to their families are fewer. For many men today, achievement in occupational spheres is their main goal, and they have become increasingly absorbed in their work. In modern families, men may or may not evoke strong affection and respect from wives and children, and their institutional importance to their families has been narrowed to their procreative, sexual, and "breadwinning" functions.

The traditional collective significance of children as perpetuators of family organizations and sources of support for parents all but disappears in modern families. Their birth is increasingly subject to parental choice and their importance is measured in personal and individual terms. Somewhat paradoxically, these changes have tended to place children in the very center of family life. The sacred injunctions to honor fathers and mothers are giving way to an expanding list of legally defined and protected rights for children, while little more is required of them on behalf of their parents than physical care in case of need. The aging, therefore, are increasingly the responsibility of non-family agencies.

When the goal of child-rearing is the achievement of equality with parents, extensive supervision and regulation of children's lives is restricted to their early years; parental authority is progressively limited as children approach maturity. Because their socialization and acculturation is, to an important degree, left to strangers, the adult models and prescriptions for children's behavior are various, often mutually exclusive. The personal integration of children is made difficult by inconsistencies in their upbringing, by a widening range of choices open to them, and by the expanding scope of knowledge and experience required for competent adult life in modern societies. Social maturity takes longer to achieve and the ways to it are more hazardous for children in modern populations.

These revolutionary changes are just beginning in many countries and adaptations to them are not stable in any. Traditional sentiments and expectations are still conspicuously mixed with new demands in the United States and Scandinavia as well as in Turkey and China. Ambivalence and conflict have to some degree been introduced into all forms of family life. Some facts are plain enough to warrant a few general conclusions about the nature of family organizations in the relatively near future.

First, *family organizations will persist as distinct and specialized arrangements best suited to meet some of the basic needs of mankind.* Communal organizations may attempt to eliminate family units, as they have in Israel and China, but it is very doubtful that they can survive as part of the regular establishment of modern societies.

Second, *corporate families will disappear as operational organizations* in societies that become industrialized, secularized, and highly differentiated.

Third, *bilateral extended families will persist in all types of societies.*

Fourth, *autonomous nuclear families will become both the normative ideal and the most numerous in fully developed, technologically advanced societies.*

Finally, *regular assistance from political and economic organizations will augment the resources of autonomous nuclear families in all modern states.*

There are few societies today, and there will be progressively fewer, in which families can be the center of life for their members, except for the very young. At most, they can be the principal source of personal satisfactions in the realm of private life. Families in modern societies are specialized organizations for specific purposes. If they seem less important than they once were, it is not because the functions that remain theirs are any less vital to their members, but because families no longer provide non-family services. Political, economic, educational, and religious organizations are also highly specialized in industrial societies, and individuals are dependent upon all of them for a comfortable and richly developed life. Nevertheless, no other organizations are so closely tied to the psychobiological satisfactions of human beings throughout their lives as is the family organization. Everywhere, except under the most extraordinary circumstances, " 'Home is the place where, when you have to go there,/They have to take you in.' " [1] No other social organization in any society guarantees so much.

[1] From "The Death of the Hired Man" from COMPLETE POEMS OF ROBERT FROST. Copyright 1930, 1939 by Holt, Rinehart and Winston, Inc. Reprinted by permission of Holt, Rinehart and Winston, Inc.

SUGGESTED READINGS

ARON, RAYMOND. *The Century of Total War*. New York: Doubleday, 1954.

A comprehensive analysis and interpretation of world movements and events that have transformed various aspects of life in every country. The author is one of the most distinguished French intellectuals, a writer, teacher, and sociologist.

BERLE, ADOLPH A., JR. *Power Without Property*. New York: Harcourt, Brace, 1959.

A recent statement of changes in American economic practices related to the growth of the number and size of economic corporations.

CAMERON, JAMES. *Mandarin Red*. New York: Rinehart, 1955.

A personal account of contemporary China by a first-rate journalist, based on travel through China in 1954.

CARLSON, EVANS FIRDYCE. *Twin Stars of China*. New York: Dodd, Mead, 1940.

An account of the early period of revolutionary struggle in China written by a participant observer. It covers the movements led by Sun Yat-Sen, Chiang Kai-shek, and Mao Tse-tung.

CARR, E. H. *The Bolshevik Revolution*. Vols. I-IV. London: Macmillan, 1954.

Probably the most comprehensive history of the Soviet period of Russian history. Especially valuable because of Carr's analysis of Russian organizations and institutions, past and present.

MATHEWS, HERBERT L. *The Yoke and the Arrows*. New York: George Braziller, 1957.

A reassessment of the Spanish Civil War and an account of changes in Spain under the Franco regime by a *New York Times* correspondent.

REED, JOHN. *Ten Days That Shook the World*. New York: Random House, Modern Library, 1935.

An eye-witness account of the first days of the Russian revolution by an American journalist who was sympathetic to the side of the revolutionists.

SMEDLEY, AGNES. *Battle Hymn of China*. New York: Knopf, 1943.

Personal, firsthand report of the Chinese Civil War, chiefly from the side of the Communist armies.

VIDICH, ARTHUR AND BENSMAN, JOSEPH. *Small Town in Mass Society*. Princeton: Princeton University Press, 1958.

The impact of increased industrialization and urbanization on a United States town that once had an agrarian base.

WEBB, SIDNEY AND BEATRICE. *Soviet Communism: A New Civilization*. New York: Scribner's, 1936.

An early, exhaustive, and over-optimistic account of the Communist social system. Full of information, but a reader must be cautious of the Webbs' interpretations.

WHEELOCK, KEITH. *Nasser's New Egypt*. New York: Praeger, 1960.

A firsthand account of the significant political and economic events in Egypt since the fall of King Farouk.

WILBER, DONALD. *Iran: Past and Present*. Princeton: Princeton University Press, 1955.

Scholarly study of social change in Iran.

YALMAN, AHMED EMIN. *Turkey in My Time*. Norman, Okla.: University of Oklahoma Press, 1956.

A personal and partisan account of political life in Turkey since World War I by a Turkish newsman and editor who was closely associated with many of the men who brought about revolutionary changes in Turkey.

· BIBLIOGRAPHY ·

Social histories, professional books and studies, periodicals (professional and otherwise), newspapers, novels, biographies, and autobiographies constitute a vast and cumulative source of materials for studies of this kind. The following bibliography consists of an assortment, limited to books, that has contributed more and less directly to this book.

AMERICAN

BARZUN, JACQUES. *Teacher in America*. Garden City: Doubleday, 1954.

———. *The House of Intellect*. New York: Harper, 1959.

BECK, DOROTHY F. *Patterns in Use of Family Agency Service*. New York: Family Service Association of America, 1962.

BERGER, PETER L. *The Noise of Solemn Assemblies*. Garden City: Doubleday, 1961.

BERLE, ADOLPH A., JR. *The 20th Century Capitalist Revolution*. New York: Harcourt, Brace, 1954.

———. *Power Without Property*. New York: Harcourt, Brace, 1959.

——— AND C. C. MEANS. *The Modern Corporation and Private Property*. New York: Macmillan, 1951.

BLACK, HILLEL. *Buy Now, Pay Later*. New York: William Morrow, 1961.

CALHOUN, ARTHUR W. *A Social History of the American Family*. 3 vols. New York: Barnes & Noble, 1917-1919.

CASH, W. J. *The Mind of the South*. Garden City: Doubleday, 1954.

CATHER, WILLA. *My Antonia*. Boston: Houghton, Mifflin, 1961.

COMMAGER, HENRY S. *The American Mind.* New Haven: Yale University Press, 1950.

DEMILLE, AGNES. *Dance to The Piper.* Boston: Atlantic Monthly Press, 1958.

FRAZIER, E. FRANKLIN. *The Negro in the United States.* Chicago: University of Chicago Press, 1939.

GALBRAITH, J. K. *American Capitalism.* Boston: Houghton, Mifflin, 1952.

————. *The Affluent Society.* Boston: Houghton, Mifflin, 1958.

GLAZER, NATHAN. *American Judaism.* Chicago: University of Chicago Press, 1957.

GOODE, WILLIAM J. *After Divorce.* Glencoe, Ill.: The Free Press, 1956.

HAGEDORN, HERMAN. *The Hyphenated Family.* New York: Macmillan, 1960.

HERBERG, WILL. *Protestant, Catholic, Jew.* New York: Doubleday, 1953.

HOLLINGSHEAD, AUGUST B. *Elmtown's Youth.* New York: Wiley, 1949.

HOYT, EDWIN. *The Vanderbilts and Their Fortunes.* Garden City: Doubleday, 1962.

LERNER, MAX. *America as a Civilization.* 2 vols. New York: Simon and Schuster, 1957.

LYND, ROBERT S. AND MERRELL, HELEN. *Middletown.* New York: Harcourt, Brace, 1929.

————. *Middletown in Transition.* New York: Harcourt, Brace, 1937.

MAYER, MARTIN. *Madison Avenue, U.S.A.* New York: Harper, 1958.

MILLS, C. WRIGHT. *White Collar: The American Middle Classes.* New York: Galaxy Books, 1957.

————. *The Power Elite.* New York: Oxford University Press, 1956.

MYRDAL, GUNNAR. *An American Dilemma.* 2 vols. New York: Harper, 1944.

PACKARD, VANCE. *The Hidden Persuaders.* New York: David McKay, 1957.

REDDING, SAUNDERS. *No Day of Triumph.* New York: Harper, 1942.

SIRJAMAKI, JOHN. *The American Family in the Twentieth Century.* Cambridge: Harvard University Press, 1953.

STEFFENS, LINCOLN. *Autobiography.* New York: Harcourt, Brace, 1931.

TOCQUEVILLE, ALEXIS DE. *Democracy in America.* 2 vols. New York: Vintage Books, 1954.

VIDICH, ARTHUR AND BENSMAN, JOSEPH. *Small Town in Mass Society.* Princeton: Princeton University Press, 1958.

WARNER, W. LLOYD AND SROLE, LEO. *The Social Systems of American Ethnic Groups*. New Haven: Yale University Press, 1945.

———— AND LOW, J. O. *The Social System of the Modern Factory*. New Haven: Yale University Press, 1947.

WESTOFF, CHARLES, POTTER, ROBERT, JR., SAGI, PHILIP, AND MISHLER, ELLIOT. *Family Growth in Metropolitan America*. Princeton: Princeton University Press, 1961.

WHYTE, WILLIAM H., JR. *The Organization Man*. Garden City: Doubleday, 1956.

CHINESE

BUCK, PEARL S. *The Good Earth*. New York: Random House, 1931.

————. *The Pavilion of Women*. New York: Pocket Books, 1949.

CAMERON, JAMES. *Mandarin Red*. New York: Rinehart, 1955.

CARLSON, EVANS F. *Twin Stars of China*. New York: Dodd, Mead, 1940.

CREEL, H. G. *The Birth of China*. New York: Reynal and Hitchcock, 1937.

————. *Confucianism and the Chinese Way*. New York: Harper Torchbook, 1960.

CUSAK, DYMPHNA. *Chinese Women Speak*. London: Angus and Robertson, 1959.

FAIRBANK, JOHN K. *The United States and China*. Cambridge: Harvard University Press, 1948.

FORMAN, HARRISON. *Report From Red China*. New York: Henry Holt, 1945.

HERSEY, JOHN. *A Single Pebble*. New York: Knopf, 1956.

HOGG, GEORGE. *I See A New China*. Boston: Little, Brown, 1944.

HUGGINS, ALICE. *The Red Chair Awaits*. Philadelphia: Westminster Press, 1948.

KATES, GEORGE. *The Years That Were Fat*. New York: Harper, 1952.

LANG, OLGA. *Chinese Family and Society*. New Haven: Yale University Press, 1946.

LATAURETTE, KENNETH SCOTT. *The Chinese: Their History and Culture*. New York: Macmillan, 1951.

LEVY, MARION. *The Family Revolution in Modern China*. Cambridge: Harvard University Press, 1949.

LIN YUTANG. *My Country and My People*. New York: John Day, 1935.

————. *Moment in Peking*. New York: John Day, 1939.

MACE, DAVID AND VERA. *Marriage East and West*. Garden City: Doubleday, 1959.

MAURER, HERRYMON. *The Old Fellow*. New York: John Day, 1943.

MICHENER, JAMES. *Hawaii*. New York: Random House, 1959.

PAYNE, ROBERT. *Forever China*. New York: Dodd, Mead, 1945.

————. *China Awake*. New York: Dodd, Mead, 1947.

————. *Portrait of a Revolutionary: Mao Tse-tung*. New York: Abelard-Schuman, 1961.

PECK, GRAHAM. *Two Kinds of Time*. Boston: Houghton, Mifflin, 1950.

SIAO-YU. *Mao Tse-tung and I Were Beggars*. Syracuse: Syracuse University Press, 1959.

Taoist Teachings. Translated by Lionel Giles. London: John Murray, 1939.

TSAO, HSUEH-CHIN. *Dream of the Red Chamber*. Translated by Chi-Chen Wang. New York: Twayne, 1958.

WALES, NYM. *The Chinese Labor Movement*. New York: John Day, 1945.

WALEY, ARTHUR. *Three Ways of Thought in Ancient China*. Garden City: Doubleday, 1956.

WALN, NORA. *The House of Exile*. Boston: Little, Brown, 1946.

Wisdom of Confucius. Translated by Lin Yutang. New York: Random House, The Modern Library, 1938.

WONG, SU LING. *Daughter of Confucius*. New York: Farrar, Straus, and Young, 1952.

YANG, C. K. *The Chinese Family in the Communist Revolution*. Cambridge: Technological Press, 1959.

————. *A Chinese Village in Early Communist Transition*. Cambridge: Technological Press, 1959.

YUNG, MARTIN C. *A Chinese Village*. New York: Columbia University Press, 1945.

ISRAEL

BARON, SALO. *A Social and Religious History of the Jews*. New York: Columbia University Press, 1937.

BECKER, HOWARD. *German Youth: Bond or Free*. New York: Oxford University Press, 1946.

COHEN, ABRAHAM. *Everyman's Talmud*. New York: Dutton, 1949.

EPSTEIN, LOUIS M. *Sex Laws and Customs in Judaism*. New York: Bloch, 1948.

GANZFRIED, SALOMON. *Code of Jewish Law*. New York: Hebrew Publishing Co., 1927.

GOLDIN, HYMAN E. *The Jewish Woman in Her Home*. New York: Jewish Culture Publishing Co., 1941.

INFIELD, HENRIK. *Cooperative Living in Palestine*. New York: Dryden, 1944.

KURLAND, SAMUEL. *Cooperative Palestine*. New York: Sharon, 1947.

LEVENSOHN, LOTTA. *Outline of Zionist History*. New York: Scopus, 1941.

MORTON, FREDERIC. *The Rothschilds: A Family Portrait*. New York: Atheneum, 1962.

ROTH, CECIL. *The Magnificent Rothschilds*. London: Robert Hale, 1939.

SPIRO, MELFORD. *Kibbutz: Venture in Utopia*. Cambridge: Harvard University Press, 1956.

————. *Children of the Kibbutz*. Cambridge: Harvard University Press, 1958.

WEINGARTEN, MURRAY. *Life in a Kibbutz*. New York: Reconstructionist Press, 1955.

WIRTH, LOUIS. *The Ghetto*. Chicago: University of Chicago Press, 1928.

ZBOROWSKI, MARK AND HERZOG, ELIZABETH. *Life Is With People*. New York: International Universities Press, 1952.

LATIN-CATHOLIC

ARON, RAYMOND. *The Century of Total War*. New York: Doubleday, 1954.

BEAUVOIR, SIMONE DE. *Memoirs of a Dutiful Daughter*. New York: The World Publishing Co., 1959.

BENSUSAN, SAMUEL LEVY. *Homelife in Spain*. London: Methuen, 1910.

BOWERS, CLAUDE. *My Mission to Spain*. New York: Simon and Schuster, 1954.

CACHARD, HENRY (ed.). *The French Civil Code*. London: The Lecram Press, 1930.

ESPINAS, JOSEPH M. *By Nature Equal*. Translated by Anthony Bonner. New York: Pantheon, 1961.

GIRONELLA, JOSE MARIA. *The Cypresses Believe in God*. New York: Knopf, 1955.

KENNY, MICHAEL. *A Spanish Tapestry: Town and Country Life in Castille*. Bloomington: Indiana University Press, 1962.

KNOX, RONALD. *The Beliefs of Catholics.* Garden City: Doubleday, 1958.

LAMPEDUSA, GUISEPPE DI. *The Leopard.* New York: Pantheon, 1960.

LEVI, CARLO. *Christ Stopped at Eboli.* New York: Farrar, Straus and Young, 1947.

MADARIAGA, SALVADOR DE. *Spain, a Modern History.* New York: Praeger, 1958.

MATHEWS, HERBERT. *The Yoke and the Arrows.* New York: George Braziller, 1957.

METRAUX, RHODA AND MEAD, MARGARET. *Themes in French Culture.* Stanford: Stanford University Press, 1954.

PADOVER, SAUL. *French Institutions, Values and Politics.* Stanford: Stanford University Press, 1954.

PITTS, JESSE. *The French Bourgeois Family and Economic Retardation.* Ph.D. thesis. Cambridge: Harvard University, 1957.

SCHOENBRUN, DAVID. *As France Goes.* New York: Harper, 1957.

SFORZA, CARLO. *Italy and the Italians.* New York: Dutton, 1949.

SMITH, DENIS MACK. *Italy.* Ann Arbor: University of Michigan Press, 1959.

THOMAS, HUGH. *The Spanish Civil War.* New York: Harper, 1961.

WRIGHT, GORDON. *France in Modern Times.* Chicago: Rand McNally, 1960.

WYLIE, LAURENCE. *Village in the Vaucluse.* Cambridge: Harvard University Press, 1957.

MOSLEM

ASAD, MUHAMMED. *The Road to Mecca.* New York: Simon and Schuster, 1954.

BISBEE, ELEANOR. *The New Turks.* Philadelphia: University of Pennsylvania Press, 1951.

DOUGLAS, WILLIAM O. *Strange Lands and Friendly People.* New York: Harper, 1952.

FISHER, SYDNEY. *The Middle East.* New York: Knopf, 1959.

GUILLAUME, ALFRED. *Islam.* London: Penguin Books, 1956.

HAMAD, AMER. *Growing Up in an Egyptian Village.* London, 1954.

ISHAQ, IBN. *Life of Mohammed.* Translated by Alfred Guillaume. London: Oxford University Press, 1955.

LAMMENS, H. *Islam: Beliefs and Institutions.* Translated by Sir E. Denison Ross. New York: Dutton, 1929.

LENGGRIL, EMIL. *Turkey.* New York: Random House, 1941.

LUKE, SIR HARRY. *The Old Turkey and the New*. London: Geoffrey Bles, 1955.

Meaning of the Glorious Koran. Translated by Marmaduke Pickthall. New York: Mentor Books, 1954.

MEHDEVI, ANNE SINCLAIR. *Persian Adventure*. New York: Knopf, 1953.

NAJAFI, NAJMEH. *Persia Is My Heart*. New York: Harper, 1953.

ORGA, IRFAN. *Portrait of a Turkish Family*. New York: Macmillan, 1950.

PATAI, RAPHAEL. *Sex and the Family in the Bible and the Middle East*. Garden City: Doubleday, 1959.

PAYNE, ROBERT. *The Holy Sword*. New York: Harper, 1959.

————. *The Splendor of Persia*. New York: Knopf, 1957.

STEINER, M. J. *Inside Pan-Arabia*. Chicago: Packard, 1947.

VAN ESS, DOROTHY. *Fatima and Her Sisters*. New York: John Day, 1961.

WHEELOCK, KEITH. *Nasser's New Egypt*. New York: Praeger, 1960.

WILBER, DONALD. *Iran: Past and Present*. Princeton: Princeton University Press, 1955.

YALMAN, AHMED EMIN. *Turkey in My Time*. Norman, Okla.: University of Oklahoma Press, 1956.

RELIGION

THE BIBLE

BERGER, PETER. *The Noise of Solemn Assemblies*. Garden City: Doubleday, 1961.

BROWNE, LEWIS. *The World's Great Scriptures*. New York: Macmillan, 1961.

COHEN, ABRAHAM. *Everyman's Talmud*. New York: Dutton, 1949.

CREEL, H. G. *Confucianism and the Chinese Way*. New York: Harper, 1960.

GANZFRIED, SALOMON. *Code of Jewish Law*. New York: Hebrew Publishing Co., 1927.

GUILLAUME, ALFRED. *Islam*. London: Penguin Books, 1956.

HERBERG, WILL. *Protestant, Catholic, Jew*. Garden City: Doubleday, 1953.

KNOX, RONALD. *The Belief of Catholics*. Garden City: Doubleday, 1958.

LAMMEN, H. *Islam: Belief and Institutions*. Translated by Sir E. Denison Ross, New York: Dutton, 1929.

Meaning of the Glorious Koran. Translated by Marmaduke Pickthall. New York: Mentor Books, 1954.

Taoist Teachings. Translated by Lionel Giles. London: John Murray, 1939.

WALEY, ARTHUR. *Three Ways of Thought in Ancient China.* Garden City: Doubleday, 1956.

Wisdom of Confucius. Translated by Lin Yutang. New York: Random House, 1938.

RUSSIA

ANDERSON, PAUL B. *People, Church and State in Modern Russia.* London: Student Christian Movement Press, 1944.

BELOV, FEDOR. *The History of a Soviet Collective Farm.* New York: Praeger, 1955.

CARR, E. H. *The Bolshevik Revolution.* Vols. I-IV. London: Macmillan, 1954.

DALLIN, D. J. *The Real Soviet Power.* New Haven: Yale University Press, 1950.

———. *The Changing World of Soviet Russia.* New Haven: Yale University Press, 1956.

DEUTSCHER, ISAAC. *Stalin.* New York: Oxford University Press, 1949.

DUDINTSEV, VLADIMIR. *Not By Bread Alone.* New York: Dutton, 1957.

FISHER, RALPH T., JR. *Patterns of Soviet Youth.* New York: Columbia University Press, 1959.

GRANICK, DAVID. *Red Executive.* Garden City: Doubleday, 1961.

GUNTHER, JOHN. *Inside Russia Today.* New York: Harper, 1957.

KENNAN, GEORGE F. *Russia and the West Under Lenin and Stalin.* Boston: Little, Brown, 1960.

KSCHESSINSKA, MATHILDE. *Dancing in Petersburg.* Garden City: Doubleday, 1960.

OBOLENSKY, SERGE. *One Man in His Time.* New York: McDowell-Obolensky, 1958.

OGNYOV, N. *The Diary of a Communist Schoolboy.* Translated by Alexander Wirth. New York: Payson and Clarke, 1929.

PAYNE, ROBERT. *The Terrorists.* New York: Funk and Wagnalls, 1957.

REED, JOHN. *Ten Days That Shook the World.* New York: Random House, The Modern Library, 1935.

SCHLESINGER, RUDOLPH (ed.). *The Family in the U.S.S.R.* London: Routledge and Kegan Paul, 1949.

STEVENS, LESLIE C. *Russian Assignment.* Boston: Little, Brown, 1953.

TROTSKY, LEON. *The Russian Revolution.* Garden City: Doubleday, 1959.

TURGENEV, IVAN. *Fathers and Sons.* New York: Macmillan, 1951.

WEBB, SIDNEY AND BEATRICE. *Soviet Communism: A New Civilization.* New York: Scribner's, 1936.

WOLFE, BERTRAM. *Three Who Made a Revolution.* New York: Dial Press, 1948.

YOUSSOUPOFF, PRINCE FELIX. *Lost Splendor.* New York: Putnam, 1954.

SCANDINAVIA

ANDERSSON, INGVAR, *et al. Introduction to Sweden.* Stockholm: Swedish Institute, 1951.

ARNESON, BEN A. *The Democratic Monarchies of Scandinavia.* New York: Van Nostrand, 1949.

BUDD, LILLIAN. *April Snow.* Philadelphia: Lippincott, 1951.

DANSTRUP, JOHN. *A History of Denmark.* Copenhagen: Wivels Forlag, 1949.

DUNN, OLAV. *The Big Wedding.* Translated by Arthur Chater. New York: Knopf, 1932.

ELIOT, THOMAS D., HILLMAN, ARTHUR, *et al. Norway's Families.* Philadelphia: University of Pennsylvania Press, 1960.

GALENSON, WALTER. *The Scandinavian Labor Movement.* Berkeley: University of California Press, 1952.

———. *The Danish System of Labor Relations.* Cambridge: Harvard University Press, 1952.

———. *Labor in Norway.* Cambridge: Harvard University Press, 1949.

HAMSUM, KNUT. *Growth of the Soil.* New York: Knopf, 1921.

HOJER, KARL. *Social Welfare in Sweden.* Stockholm: Ahlen and Akerlands, 1949.

LARSEN, KAREN. *A History of Norway.* Princeton: Princeton University Press, 1948.

MOBERG, VILHEIM. *The Emigrants.* New York: Simon and Schuster, 1951.

MYRDAL, ALVA. *Nation and Family.* New York: Harper, 1941.

NELSON, GEORGE (ed.). *Freedom and Welfare-Social Patterns in the Northern Communities of Europe.* Ministries of Social Affairs of Denmark, Finland, Iceland, Norway, Sweden, 1953.

SCOTT, FRANKLIN D. *The United States and Scandinavia.* Cambridge: Harvard University Press, 1950.

SHIRER, WILLIAM. *The Challenge of Scandinavia*. Boston: Little, Brown, 1955.

STRODE, HUDSON. *Sweden: Model for a World*. New York: Harcourt, Brace, 1949.

THEORETICAL WORKS

ANSHEN, RUTH (ed.). *The Family: Its Function and Destiny*. New York: Harper, 1959.

BENDIX, REINHARD. *Max Weber: An Intellectual Portrait*. Garden City: Doubleday, 1960.

COOLEY, CHARLES H. *Human Nature and the Social Order*. New York: Scribner's, 1902.

———. *Social Organization*. New York: Scribner's, 1909.

DURKHEIM, EMILE. *Division of Labor in Society*. Translated by George Simpson. Glencoe, Ill.: The Free Press, 1949.

———. *Suicide*. Translated by John Spaulding and George Simpson. Glencoe, Ill.: The Free Press, 1951.

FREUD, SIGMUND. *Collected Papers*. London: Hogarth Press, 1950.

MANDELBAUM, DAVID (ed.). *Selected Writings of Edward Sapir*. Berkeley: University of California Press, 1949.

MEAD, GEORGE H. *Mind, Self, and Society*. Chicago: University of Chicago Press, 1946.

MEYER, ADOLPH. *The Commonsense Psychiatry of Adolf Meyer*. Ed. by Alfred Lief. New York: McGraw-Hill, 1948.

PARSONS, TALCOTT AND BALES, ROBERT F. *Family, Socialization and Interaction Process*. Glencoe, Ill.: The Free Press, 1955.

PIAGET, JEAN. *The Moral Judgment of the Child*. Glencoe, Ill.: The Free Press, 1932.

———. *The Language and Thought of the Child*. New York: Humanities Press, 1952.

SIMMEL, GEORG. *The Sociology of Georg Simmel*. Translated by Kurt Wolff. Glencoe, Ill.: The Free Press, 1950.

SPYKMAN, NICHOLAS. *The Social Theory of Georg Simmel*. Chicago: University of Chicago Press, 1925.

SULLIVAN, HARRY STACK. *Conceptions of Modern Psychiatry*. Reprinted from *Psychiatry*, Vol. 3, No. 1 (February 1940) and Vol. 8, No. 2 (May 1945).

———. *The Interpersonal Theory of Psychiatry*. New York: Norton, 1953.

SUMNER, WILLIAM GRAHAM. *Folkways*. New York: Ginn, 1906.

THOMPSON, CLARA. *Psychoanalysis: Evolution and Development.* New York: Hermitage Press, 1950.

WALLER, WILLIAM AND HILL, REUBEN. *The Family: A Dynamic Interpretation.* New York: Dryden Press, 1951.

WEBER, MAX. *The Theory of Social and Economic Organization.* Translated by A. M. Henderson and Talcott Parsons. New York: Oxford University Press, 1947.

————. *The Protestant Ethic and the Spirit of Capitalism.* Translated by Talcott Parsons. New York: Scribner's, 1952.

· INDEX ·

ABOUT THE AUTHOR

DOROTHY R. BLITSTEN is currently Associate Professor of Sociology at Hunter College. She received her Ph.B. from the University of Chicago and her Ph.D. from Columbia University. In addition to extensive training in psychiatry, her background includes pre-medical work and two years of medicine. She is the author of *Psychoanalysis Explained,* a book for the lay reader, and *Social Theories of Harry Stack Sullivan.*

A NOTE ON THE TYPE

This book is set in Electra, a Linotype face designed by W. A. Dwiggins. This face cannot be classified as either modern or old-style. It is not based on any historical model, nor does it echo any particular period or style. It avoids the extreme contrasts between thick and thin elements that mark most modern faces, and attempts to give a feeling of fluidity, power, and speed.